"A startling book"

"The selection and training of the crew, the frictions that developed between man and man, between the 509th and the other units on Tinian, the almost minute-by-minute story of the operation itself is unrivaled in World War II accounts."

"Not only a readable narrative but a contribution to the raw material of history . . . a minute-by-minute account . . . a strong sense of proximity to the great events, personalities made real."

"A large cast of characters . . . reads like an exciting novel."

"EXTRAORDINARY, ENGROSSING"

"Never wavers in its drama"

The authors of **Enola Gay,** Gordon Thomas and Max Morgan Witts, met at the BBC where they both worked as writers and producers. Their investigative books include **The Day the World Ended, The San Francisco Earthquake, Shipwreck, Voyage of the Damned,** and **Guernica.** None of the significant revelations in any of the Thomas-Witts collaborations has ever been disproved. Their books have sold over 20 million copies worldwide.

Enola Gay, an international bestseller, has been translated into French, German, Dutch, Spanish, Norwegian, Japanese, and other languages throughout the world.

ENOLA GAY

BY GORDON THOMAS
AND MAX MORGAN WITTS

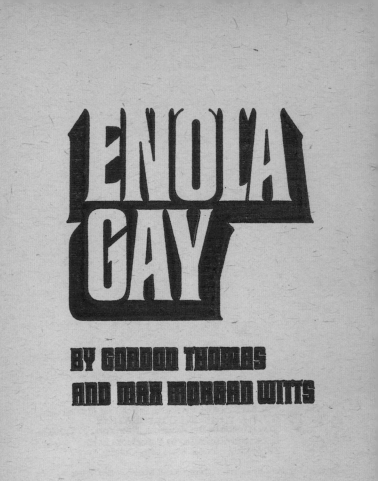

A KANGAROO BOOK
PUBLISHED BY POCKET BOOKS NEW YORK

Distributed in Canada by PaperJacks Ltd., a Licensee
of the trademarks of Simon & Schuster, a division of
Gulf+Western Corporation.

POCKET BOOKS, a Simon & Schuster division of
GULF & WESTERN CORPORATION
1230 Avenue of the Americas, New York, N.Y. 10020
In Canada distributed by PaperJacks Ltd.,
330 Steelcase Road, Markham, Ontario.

Published by arrangement with Stein and Day Publishers
Library of Congress Catalog Card Number: 76-44343

ISBN: 0-671-81499-0

First Pocket Books printing June, 1978

Trademarks registered in the United States and other countries.

Printed in Canada

Contents

Prologue

On August 2, 1939, a month before World War II began in Europe, Albert Einstein signed a letter addressed to President Franklin Delano Roosevelt. Couched in careful terms, the letter stated that recent nuclear research indicated "extremely powerful bombs of a new type," based on uranium, might soon be possible. Einstein warned that secret work with uranium was going on in Nazi Germany. He urged that similar American research be accelerated.

Alexander Sachs, economist, financier, and friend of Roosevelt, agreed to deliver the letter to the president. Before he could do so, war in Europe broke out, and Roosevelt was unable to see him until mid-October. Then, after much persuasion by Sachs, Roosevelt marked Einstein's letter for action.

The first result of the president's decision was the expenditure of just six thousand dollars. It bought graphite, essential for one of the early experiments that would, in time, lead to the atomic bomb. Substantial funds for the specific purpose of producing such a bomb were first authorized by Roosevelt on December 6, 1941.

Next day came Pearl Harbor. Roosevelt vowed vengeance. "Remember Pearl Harbor" became the rallying cry.

By the summer of 1942, it was clear that enormous amounts of money and effort would be required to build an atomic bomb. Huge manufacturing and processing plants had to be erected in remote areas to produce the sometimes dangerous materials required;

research work in widely scattered university and commercial laboratories had to be initiated and put on a wartime footing; new laboratories needed to be created. And all in the utmost secrecy.

A cover name was invented for the project: the Manhattan Engineer District, later simplified to the Manhattan Project.

In October 1942, Site Y, Los Alamos, in the New Mexico desert, was chosen by physicist J. Robert Oppenheimer, a former pupil at the Los Alamos Ranch School for Boys, for his key research laboratory. His old classrooms would come to be used by eminent scientists, among them Enrico Fermi, Edward Teller, and that other giant of European physics, Niels Bohr.

It was Fermi who masterminded the crucial experiment on December 2, 1942, that produced the chain reaction needed to make an atomic bomb. He conducted his experiment on a bitterly cold day in an unused squash court at the University of Chicago. There were fears that the city itself might be endangered by the nuclear energy released. But the reaction was controlled, and scientists had demonstrated that when a uranium atom splits, it releases neutrons which can themselves then split more uranium atoms, creating the chain reaction. They formally christened this process "The K Factor"; among themselves they called it "The Great God K."

In secret war plants during the following months a sense of urgency hovered over the complex processes for producing the relatively small amounts of uranium 235 needed to make atomic bombs. Plutonium, also suitable for atomic weapons, was being produced as well.

Roosevelt backed the project without the knowledge of Congress or the electorate. Funds for the venture were disguised in the federal budget. Eventually, two billion dollars would be spent in financing the work.

By 1944, a deep division was brewing among the scientists. Those now opposed to the military use of their research included Niels Bohr, who, in late August

1944, asked Roosevelt to authorize the sharing of U.S. atomic secrets with the world's scientific community. He believed science belonged to the world.

At about the same time during the summer of 1944, uranium 235 was beginning to be produced in the quantities required for a weapon. Success seemed in sight. The problem of how to enclose "The Great God K" in a bomb casing was being dealt with. If, despite the qualms of some of the scientists, work was to go forward, the time had come to choose the man to train and lead the men who would drop the bomb.

ACTIVATION

SEPTEMBER 1, 1944,
TO JUNE 27, 1945

The commanding general of the Second Air Force, Uzal G. Ent, looked up as Colonel John Lansdale of U.S. Army Intelligence led Paul Tibbets into his office.

He glanced inquiringly at the intelligence officer.

Lansdale nodded.

General Ent then introduced the two men seated beside his desk. One was U.S. Navy Captain William "Deak" Parsons, whom he described as an "explosives expert" but who was, in fact, one of the most influential men in the Manhattan Project; the other was a civilian, Professor Norman Ramsey, a twenty-nine-year-old Harvard physicist.

Lieutenant Colonel Paul Tibbets was struck by Ramsey's comparative youth; he had always associated scientists with gray hair and stooped shoulders. To Tibbets, the two men looked fit enough to fly combat, even if Parsons's baldness made him appear older than his forty-four years. And it seemed strange that this naval captain should be involved in what appeared to be an Army Air Force meeting.

"Have you ever heard of atomic energy?" Ramsey had the firm, incisive voice of a natural tutor.

"Yes," said Tibbets.

"How?"

"I majored in physics, so I know the atomic scale."

There was an expectant pause.

"What do you know of the present situation in the field?" asked Parsons.

Tibbets looked at General Ent. There was no encouragement there. A few days earlier, when Ent first became aware of the Manhattan Project, he himself had been warned he would be court-martialed if any leak of information were traced to him. Tibbets looked to Lansdale, who gave a barely perceptible nod.

As confidently as he could, Tibbets began to speak. He understood there had been some experimenting by the Germans to try to make heavy water so that they could split the atom.

"Good." Ramsey's gentle praise was more suited to the campus than the bleak office of a fighting general. He paused, weighing his words, a mannerism Tibbets would come to recognize.

Ramsey continued. "The United States has now split an atom. We are making a bomb based on that. The bomb will be so powerful that it will explode with the force of twenty thousand tons of conventional high explosive."

General Ent then told Tibbets he had been chosen to drop that bomb.

It was September 1, 1944. The place was U.S. Army Second Air Force Headquarters, Colorado Springs.

Only moments before this conversation, Lansdale had led Tibbets into the cloakroom adjoining General Ent's office. There, Lansdale had asked Tibbets a highly personal question.

Tibbets had given no visible reaction. Nevertheless, he was stunned. How did this stranger know of that private event of ten—or was it twelve—years ago; an experience of such a passing nature that he himself could not now exactly remember its date? Why had Lansdale been probing something that had happened all those years back?

Tibbets recognized that this assault upon his privacy, his sense of self-respect, was calculated. But how should he cope with it?

He knew that Lansdale's question had nothing directly to do with military intelligence. Therefore, he would be perfectly justified in not answering. Then he could walk out, unchallenged, through one of the two doors in the cloakroom. *That* door would return him to the conventional military world where nobody would dare ask such an intimate question of a much-decorated war hero.

Tibbets decided to tell the truth. "Yes. I was once arrested by the police in North Miami Beach."

"What for?"

"The chief of police at Surfside caught me in the back of an automobile . . . with a girl," confessed Tibbets.

The rest took little telling—his arrest, a spell in the cells, the intervention of a judge who was a family friend, the indiscretion hushed up.

By admitting the truth about the backseat dalliance with a girl whose name he now had difficulty recalling, Paul Tibbets had assured himself of a place in history. Within a year his name would become forever linked with the destruction of Hiroshima, a Japanese city he was yet to hear of.

Until three days earlier, on Tuesday, August 29, 1944, Tibbets had not been considered for the task. Then, late in the afternoon, General Barney Giles, assistant chief of air staff, decided to replace an earlier nominee with Tibbets. Lansdale, one of the less than one hundred men who knew what the Manhattan Project was meant to do, immediately supervised the most thorough investigation of Tibbets, staging the cloakroom meeting as the climax.

Lansdale's question about a teenage sexual peccadillo was intended as the final test of Tibbets's character. If he told the truth, he was in. Lansdale was satisfied.

In General Ent's office, Ramsey and Parsons gave Tibbets a thorough briefing on the history and problems associated with building America's first atomic bomb. Then Lansdale took over.

"Colonel, I want you to understand one thing. Security is first, last, and always. You will commit as little as possible to paper. You will tell only those who need to know what they must know to do their jobs properly. Understood?"

"Perfectly understood, Colonel."

General Ent concluded the meeting by formally assigning the 393rd Heavy Bombardment Squadron, based in Nebraska, to Tibbets. Its fifteen bomber crews would provide the world's first atomic strike force, capable of delivering nuclear bombs on Germany and Japan. Their training base would be at Wendover, Utah. The code name for the air force's part of the project would be "Silverplate."

Tibbets briefly wondered who had chosen such a homely name for a weapon "clearly designed to revolutionize war." Even so, he still could not accept that *one* bomb dropped from a single aircraft could equal the force of twenty thousand tons of high explosive. Ordinarily, some two thousand bombers would be required to deliver such a payload.

But he had more pressing problems to deal with. He must gather together some of the trusted men who had served with him before; he must inspect Wendover; he must devise a training program; finally, he must be prepared to work alongside "a bunch of civilians who would give me a glimpse of Pandora's box."

As Tibbets was leaving the office, General Ent stopped him.

"Colonel, if this is successful, you'll be a hero. But if it fails, you'll be the biggest scapegoat ever. You may even go to prison."

• 2 •

Tibbets was a stocky, medium-sized man with a crisp, detached manner. It would have been hard to guess that he was one of America's most successful bomber pilots; a combat veteran who had flown the first B-17 across the English Channel on a bombing mission in World War II; who had piloted General Dwight D. Eisenhower and General Mark Clark to Gibraltar to plan the Allied invasion of North Africa; who had taken Clark on to Algiers, landing on a field being bombed and strafed. Tibbets later led the first American raid on North Africa. Returning to the United States, he took charge of flight-testing the new B-29 Superfortress at a time when the bomber was thought too dangerous to fly; it had killed its first test pilot. Tibbets was courageous, used to command, able to give and execute orders with speed and efficiency.

Some people, though, found him difficult to work with. He did not suffer fools, and, by his own standards, there were many fools. Restrained and reticent, Tibbets appeared the paragon of service correctness. Few knew he concealed his sensitivity by steely control, that behind his outward appearance was a shy man who had suffered acutely the loss of any of his fliers in action. All that invariably showed on his face was a pleasant, noncommittal intelligence.

Tibbets was born in Quincy, Illinois, in 1915. His father, a wholesale confectioner, was a strict disciplinarian who severely punished the slightest infringement of the many rules which hedged in his son's formative years. Paul's mother, Enola Gay, was as gentle as her unusual forenames. She adored her only son and strongly opposed her husband's decision to send Paul, at the age of thirteen, to the Western Military Academy at Alton, Illinois. Afterward, it was his mother who first encouraged him to be a doctor, and later, against strong family opposition, to join the U.S. Army Air Corps; she quietly accepted Paul's wish to abandon medicine in favor of flying. But in those difficult post-Depression days a military career was not viewed with great favor in the middle-class community of which Paul Tibbets's father was a pillar. When his son enlisted in 1937, his father's last words on the subject were, "You're on your own." His mother had said, "Son, one day we're going to be real proud of you." She reminded him always to "dress neatly," never to promise more than he could do, and always to tell the truth.

It was because Tibbets had followed her advice that he was able, in such unlikely surroundings, to answer truthfully Lansdale's intimate question.

· 3 ·

When Brigadier General Leslie Groves took command of the Manhattan Project, he was answerable only to Secretary of War Henry Stimson and, through him, to President Roosevelt.

Both knew more about this man with old-fashioned manners than they did about any other serving officer. An FBI check—the only occasion the bureau became involved in the atomic project—turned up Groves's passion for candy, his concern about middle-age spread, his mean tennis playing, his ability to solve complicated mathematical problems while eating. The probe revealed Groves was known as "Greasy" at West Point, that he had few interests outside his work, that he was stable and happily married.

Stimson also knew his professional background: an outstanding West Point engineering graduate who had helped build the Pentagon; a man reputed to be the "best barrack-builder in the Army."

His service record showed Groves to be a cornercutter, a dime-saver, tough, tireless, and resilient. He was used to working to time and budget. He got things done. Although he tended both to ruffle the tempers of his equals and inspire fear in his subordinates, Groves seemed to Stimson and Roosevelt the best possible choice to run the world's biggest-ever military project.

From the outset, Groves worked a fifteen-hour day, seven days a week. He gave up tennis and put on weight, sustaining himself with pounds of chocolates which he kept locked in the safe where he also stored the project's most important secrets.

But Groves was not just a builder going from site to site with a bag of candy in his pocket. Even his friends in the project—and they numbered few—believed, in the words of one, that Groves "not only behaves as if he can walk on water, but as if he actually invented the substance." Another, less cruel, claimed "he has the most impressive ego since Napoleon."

Forty-eight years old, with a vocabulary capable of blistering a construction worker—though many found more unnerving his deep sigh at a piece of misfortune—Groves came from the same mold as MacArthur and Patton.

Ultimately, nobody could withstand his barrage of orders and demands. Opposition was crushed and arguments he regarded as pointless ended with a crisp "Enough." He drafted industrial tycoons as if they were buck privates, and drove his work force to exhaustion as he built and ran his empire.

Bullying, cajoling, bruising, buffeting, occasionally praising, and rarely apologizing, Groves had achieved a feat he himself had once thought impossible. In two years he had brought the atomic bomb from the blueprint stage to the point where it would soon be ready for testing.

Groves would allow no one to stop that momentum.

He had approved the choice of Tibbets as the commander of the special atomic strike force because he had all the professional qualities Groves believed were needed to get the job done.

Working from a temporary office in the Pentagon, Tibbets was coming to realize, a week after the meeting in Colorado Springs, just how vast his powers were as commander. He could demand anything he wanted, merely by mentioning the code name Silverplate. Using that prefix, he had instituted a search for some of the men who had served with him in Europe, North Africa, and on the B-29 testing and training program. Some had already been traced and were on their way to Wendover in Utah; others were having their orders cut.

Here, at the Pentagon, General Henry Arnold, chief of the Army Air Force, had said, "Colonel, if you get any trouble from anybody, you can call on me."

Arnold had designated two senior officers to serve as liaison with Tibbets when he got to Wendover. Arnold's order to them was simple. "Just give him anything he wants without delay."

Tibbets had stopped at Wendover on his way from Colorado Springs to Washington. He found it "the end of the world, perfect." It was close enough to Los Alamos by air, an important consideration, for Ramsey had warned him that "the scientists will be bugging you day and night." It was only some five hundred miles by air from the Salton Sea area in Southern California, an ideal bombing range. The location of Wendover would simplify security. The existing facilities on the base were suitable for immediate occupancy.

He knew his men would hate the place.

But he planned to work them so hard that they would not have time to dwell on their surroundings.

By now, Tibbets had surmised there were only two possible targets for him to bomb: Berlin or Tokyo. He thought the Japanese capital more likely; the war in Europe was already approaching a decisive stage.

If it was to be Japan, then he would need a base within striking distance of the Japanese home islands.

He recalled reading that the U.S. Marines had recently captured the Mariana Islands in the Pacific. The newspapers had dubbed one island "the place where the Seabees are going to build the largest aircraft carrier in the world." It was just thirteen hundred miles from Japan. Its name was Tinian.

Tibbets filed it in his memory.

• 4 •

The fall of Tinian in late July had totally failed to shake Second Lieutenant Tatsuo Yokoyama's belief in the invincibility of the Imperial Japanese Army.

This September evening, as usual before gunnery practice, the forty men at the antiaircraft gun post on Mount Futaba, in the northeastern outskirts of Hiroshima, were lectured by their young commander on the need to keep faith with the high command's belief in ultimate victory.

In appearance, Yokoyama at first glance seemed the classic caricature in countless American cartoons: buck teeth, slanted eyes, sloping forehead; a wiry figure in baggy blouse, with sloppy leggings encasing bandy legs.

But his image was deceptive. He was a crack rifle shot at seven hundred yards. He was capable of carrying four hundred rounds of ammunition—double that carried by an American infantryman—and trained to exist on a bowl of rice and fish a day. He regarded surrender as the greatest shame he could inflict upon his family and country. Deeply religious and hyperpatriotic, he devoutly believed in the divinity of the emperor and the sacred duty of the army to protect his majesty. He would not spare his family, his soldiers, or himself to serve the emperor.

Yokoyama had three heroes: first, Minoru Genda, the young officer who had convinced the high command that an unexpected, carrier-based air attack on Pearl Harbor was feasible and militarily desirable; second, Captain Mitsuo Fuchida, Genda's close friend, who had led the 354 planes to Hawaii. Both had connections with the city where Yokoyama was now based. Genda had relatives in Hiroshima; Fuchida sometimes visited friends there. Yokoyama's third hero was General Hideki Tojo, "The Razor," Japan's architect of war.

Yokoyama told his men that they should look upon the "withdrawal" from the islands of Saipan, Tinian, and Guam in the Marianas as a predetermined action, part of a carefully prepared plan to draw the enemy closer to Japan.

There, as they all knew, a vast army was waiting, and eager, to deal America and her Allies a blow which would send them reeling. The Americans could win a battle, he reminded his men, but Japan had never lost a war since 1598. He told them that the Japanese "departure" from the Marianas meant the day must be approaching when enemy bombers launched from there against Japan would at long last come within range of their guns.

In anticipation of that moment, he drove his bored gun crews hard. The men knew he would punish them severely at the first sign of slackness. Under his commands the guns moved smoothly on their greased bearings, their slim barrels traversing the air over Hiroshima.

Yokoyama passed among the gunners, urging them to imagine they were in action. Suddenly, one of the guns jammed. Yokoyama saw that a piece of waste cotton had been left in the mechanism. He halted the practice and furiously ordered the crews to strip, clean, and reassemble the guns. He then returned to his quarters to write up the incident in the daily report book and to think of a suitable punishment for the errant crew. He decided on two extra drills.

But first he would enjoy a ritual he performed every evening. At the window of his billet, he surveyed the city through binoculars. He knew there would have been little change during the last twenty-four hours, but the panorama always soothed him.

When he had first surveyed the city from his vantage point close to the crest of Mount Futaba a year before, Yokoyama had been struck by an oddity: Hiroshima resembled a human hand. By holding out his right hand, palm down, fingers spread, he reproduced a rough outline of the city. The port was at his fingertips in the south; beyond lay the depths of Hiroshima Bay and the

Hiroshima, 1945

Inland Sea. His wrist corresponded to that area where the Ota River ended its uninterrupted flow from the hills in the north and entered a broad, fan-shaped delta. There it broke into six main channels, which divided the city into islands. These were linked by eighty-one bridges. Directly under his palm was Hiroshima Castle, the center of a huge military operation.

Yokoyama amused himself by identifying various installations and placing them in the corresponding positions on the back of his hand. At the tip of his index finger was Hiroshima Airport, with its military aircraft. On his thumb he located Toyo Industries—the company made rifles and gun platforms for warships. At the end of his little finger was the Mitsubishi works, with its dockyards and cranes.

The factories, together with the dozens of smaller plants in the city, maintained round-the-clock shifts. A recent edict had inducted schoolchildren into working eight hours a day making weapons. Almost every man, woman, and child in the city was actively engaged in the war effort.

Now, in September 1944, most factories in Hiroshima faced a shortage of materials. The patrol boats used for coastal duty were immobilized for lack of fuel, and training flights from the city's airfield were curtailed.

Yet this evening the war seemed as remote as ever to Yokoyama. The city below him was peaceful, a vast cluster of black-tiled roofs encased in a natural bowl of reclaimed delta surrounded by green hills and peaks.

But in Yokoyama's opinion Hiroshima was highly vulnerable to air attack. All a bomber need do was drop its load within the bowl to be almost certain of causing damage. Apart from a single kidney-shaped hill in the eastern sector of the city, about half a mile long and two hundred feet high, Hiroshima was uniformly exposed to the spreading energy that big bombs generate.

Structurally—like San Francisco in the earthquake and fire of 1906—Hiroshima was built to burn. Ninety percent of its houses were made of wood. Large groups of dwellings were clustered together. And, unlike San Francisco in 1906, Hiroshima in 1944 had antiquated firefighting equipment and poorly trained personnel.

From where he stood, Yokoyama could clearly see the city boundaries. Only thirteen of Hiroshima's twenty-seven square miles were built up, and only seven of these densely, but in that area some thirty-five thousand people were crammed into every square mile. His battery on Mount Futaba was there to protect them.

He saw that the gun crews were ready. Another practice began. Yokoyama watched them. The men were stripped to the waist, sweating in the warm evening air. Load, aim, unload. A new traverse. Load, aim, unload. A swift, stylistic ritual of crisp commands and grunts.

He was pleased with them now, the way they responded promptly to his orders. They were the same commands he had given them for every drill since the battery was commissioned as part of the Hiroshima antiaircraft defense system in May 1943. Twenty-one guns of various calibers now defended the city. They had yet to be fired in anger in the third year of the war.

The practice over, the crews were about to relax when Yokoyama ordered the first punishment drill. As soon as that ended, he began the second one, watchful for any signs of slackness. That would earn the crews further punishment.

Satisfied, he relieved the gunners and led them to their quarters. There, as usual, he listened solicitously to their small talk. It was part of his duty to listen, just as he was expected to eat, drink, and sing with his men, to lend them money from his pocket, to invite them to visit his parents' home in Tokyo. This was traditional behavior for a Japanese officer—the fostering of a comradely feeling, the encouraging of a relationship in which he was both father figure and close friend. It was what had helped to make the Imperial Japanese Army so formidable.

This evening his crews asked him a familiar question: when would they see action?

He understood their desire to fight. It was part of the samurai tradition, of the two-thousand-year history of Japan. The wish for battle was coupled with an absence of fear. Japan, more than any other nation, had excised fear from its warriors; death for them was part of living.

Yokoyama told his men to be patient. But he worried whether they would ever have the chance to shoot, to taste that special excitement. He wondered whether the story he had heard was true. A man who worked in local government had mentioned it to him. Yokoyama had at first dismissed it. But his friend had been so insistent, so specific, claiming "inside sources" for his information. Could there be any substance to the tale that many people in Hiroshima had relatives in San Francisco and Los Angeles who had petitioned Roosevelt to spare Hiroshima from attack and that he had agreed to do so as "a gesture of goodwill"?

Yokoyama knew that if this were true, then the enemy bombers would never come to Hiroshima, and all his practices would have been in vain.

• 5 •

Tibbets arrived at Wendover three days before the 393rd Heavy Bombardment Squadron. His prediction proved to be right. The officers and men hated Wendover, the bleaching heat, the inhospitable desert, the primitive accommodations, the dust, the rank drinking water, the termites, the rats and mice, the sheer remoteness of their position.

They hated not knowing why they were there.

On September 12, their second morning at the base, they awakened to find further cause for hatred. A formidable wire fence now penned them in. Inside its perimeter were warning signs. The largest, beside the base exit gate, read:

> WHAT YOU HEAR HERE
> WHAT YOU SEE HERE
> WHEN YOU LEAVE HERE
> LET IT STAY HERE

Sentries stopped anybody leaving.

Thickly coiled barbed wire barred the entrance to a number of hangars and workshops. Freshly painted notices announced that behind the wire lay the ordnance, armament, engineering, and radar shops. Each notice carried the legend:

> RESTRICTED AREA

The wire was thickest around hangar No. 6. There, a notice announced:

> TECH AREA "C"
> MOST RESTRICTED

What was a Tech Area? Why "C"? Where were "A" and "B"? Nobody knew.

Those who tried to talk their way past the military policemen guarding the Tech Area were curtly told they faced arrest if they persisted.

A week ago, at the end of their training in Nebraska, the men of the 393rd had been proud that their squadron's record was way above average. They had expected to go overseas soon. Some of the more enterprising had purchased quantities of silk stockings, soap, and perfumes to tempt the English and French girls they had heard so much about. One enlisted man had packed his record collection of jitterbug 78s, planning to sell them on London's black market.

Instead, the 393rd had been shuffled off to Wendover.

There were no bombers at Wendover. Just a few rundown transport planes. Rumor said they had come to Wendover to pick up factory-fresh B-29s. But where were they? And why here?

Nobody knew.

The brief optimism withered. Other rumors rose, welled, and faded. Officers, like their men, had no idea of what was happening. Their commanding officer, Lieutenant Colonel Thomas Classen, had gone into the base headquarters on arrival and had hardly been seen since. And when he did appear, he deflected all questions.

By breakfast time, MPs were everywhere, their motorcycles and jeeps sending scuds of dust into the air. The 393rd had never tasted such sand. It permeated their clothes, skin, and food. The flavor to their cereals, eggs, and hash-browns this morning came from the great salt flats around the airfield.

After the meal, the squadron listened in stunned disbelief as their intelligence officer, Captain Joseph Buscher, tried to make light of their situation. He reminded them that he was a lawyer, used to pleading—and he said he was pleading with them now to "give the place a chance."

Buscher admitted that he could not tell them why they were at Wendover, but he could tell them that the base was "only 125 miles from Salt Lake City, Utah. Elko in Nevada was "as close." Buscher hoped they would find Wendover itself "fascinating." The town, with a population of 103, was split down the middle by the Utah–Nevada state line. Half of Wendover ran their lives according to Utah's Mormon Church. On the other side of town, there were bars, eateries, and slot machines.

"What about broads?"

The questioner was Captain Claude Eatherly, a tall, wickedly handsome pilot with a way with girls, cards, and a bottle of bourbon. With his small-boy grin, Texas drawl, and fund of jokes, Eatherly was the squadron playboy.

Buscher ignored Eatherly's question and launched into a solemn recital of how the flats had been formed,

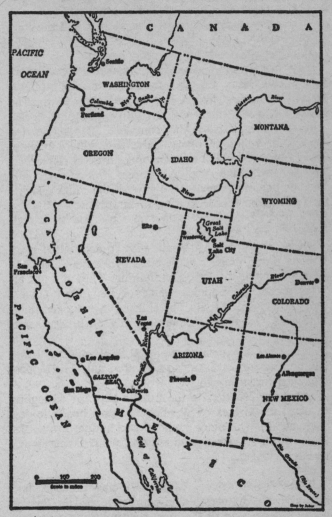

The Western United States

how the pioneer wagons of 1846 had foundered in the salt. For those who liked exploring, enthused Buscher, the tracks of some of the wagons were still embedded in the flats.

"So will our bones be if we stay here!"

The words were spoken by a frustrated first lieutenant, Jacob Beser, the squadron's radar officer. Beser longed for action. When Britain had gone to war, he had tried to join the Royal Air Force. His parents had stopped him, insisting he complete his engineering studies at Johns Hopkins University. The day after Pearl Harbor, Beser had overcome parental opposition and enlisted in the Army Air Force. He had eventually become one of the service's highest-rated radar officers. Radar was new and growing in importance. That did not impress Beser—not unless he could use his knowledge "to kill a few Nazis."

Beser was a Jew. A small, wiry, quick-witted man, fiercely proud of his middle-class background, he held strong opinions on almost everything. They did not always make him popular. Some of his fellow officers thought him an oddball. The enlisted men looked upon him as a "longhair" because of his university background.

When the squadron was posted to Wendover, Beser had applied for a transfer to a combat unit. His request had been turned down.

But now, listening to the urbane Buscher struggling to extol the virtues of Wendover, Beser began to feel excitement. "The place sounded so goddam awful that there just had to be a good reason for my being there," he later recalled.

Tibbets's old friend, Major Thomas Ferebee, had also arrived. His formidable combat record in Europe made Ferebee one of the most seasoned and respected bombardiers in the air force. He was the perfect choice to train the 393rd's bombardiers in the precision-bombing techniques that Professor Ramsey had told Tibbets were going to be essential for dropping an atomic bomb.

Although he was glad to see Ferebee, unexpected problems stopped Tibbets from sitting down with him for a relaxed talk.

For a start, there was the delicate position of Classen. The 393rd's CO was a Pacific veteran with a distinguished combat record. His leadership qualities had made the squadron a cohesive unit. To move him at this stage would be unthinkable. Tibbets had discussed the situation with Classen, explaining that in effect the squadron would have two commanders: Classen would be responsible for its day-to-day running; Tibbets would make all the important policy decisions. He had told Classen he trusted this somewhat unusual arrangement would work. Classen had shown no real reaction.

Tibbets had tried to sweeten matters by giving Classen a briefing on their unique mission. He hoped that would instill a mood of equally divided responsibility "in all but a few areas." But after Classen had gone, Tibbets wondered whether dual command was really possible.

Other matters soon pushed such thoughts from his mind.

Since breakfast, two men had been closeted with him. He knew the older man well. Lieutenant Colonel Hazen Payette had served with him in England and North Africa as intelligence officer. A shrewd and penetrating questioner, Payette was at Wendover to supervise security at Tibbets's request.

Major William L. "Bud" Uanna had arrived unannounced. He politely explained that Colonel Lansdale had sent him, plus some thirty agents detached from the main Manhattan Project, to help "police" the 393rd.

Tibbets liked Uanna's style. He was coolly pleasant and uninterested in anything but his work.

Uanna had arrived with a bulky briefcase. The files it contained were a further reminder to Tibbets of the vast intelligence-gathering resources of the Manhattan Project.

There was a detailed dossier on each member of the 393rd. The information had been gathered from their families, friends, school reports, employment records, and medical files.

Many thousands of man-hours and dollars had been spent on tapping telephones, secretly opening letters, collecting details of extramarital affairs, homosexual tendencies, and political affiliations. The dossiers represented the most thorough secret investigation until then carried out in the name of the U.S. government.

Uanna produced the file on Eatherly. It showed the pilot was an obsessional gambler, with an "emotional problem."

Tibbets studied Eatherly's service record. He had logged 107 flying hours as a pilot ferrying Lockheed Hudsons to Canada; 103 hours flying LB-30s; a spell on antisubmarine patrol in the Panama Canal Zone; regular transfers from one squadron to another. A normal enough flying record. Eatherly's fitness reports spoke of his "flamboyance" and of his being "an extrovert." Tibbets knew the type. He had flown with "wild Texans" like Eatherly in Europe. They frequently got into trouble on the ground. But they were good pilots. Tibbets decided he would let Eatherly remain in the 393rd.

By late morning, the jokers in the 393rd were running out of steam. One of them had been sharply reprimanded by an MP for trying to post a slogan:

WELCOME TO ALCATRAZ

The first letters were being written to loved ones. A number contained the inevitable phrase: Wendover is a good place to be—from.

Uanna's agents had infiltrated the squadron, carrying forged papers which allowed them to pose as clerks, cooks, even a garbage detail. They were not always successful. Captain James Strudwick found a man checking the wiring in his quarters who "didn't know one end of a socket from another." Mess officer Charles Perry discovered two men in the mess hall "who had trouble distinguishing a soup ladle from a carving knife." Executive officer John King was astonished to see "a man dressed in a line chief's overalls whose hands had never come near a wrench."

But not all the newcomers were security men.

Technical Sergeant George Caron arrived dusty and thirsty from a trans-American journey, with his collar unbuttoned and wearing a flying jacket, a double breach of military regulations.

The MPs at the gate pounced on the diminutive air gunner. They marched him to the orderly room in the headquarters building. There, a policeman began to berate Caron.

Suddenly, from an adjoining office, Caron heard a familiar voice. "Is that you, Bob?"

"Sure is, Colonel."

Tibbets was one of the few officers who called Caron by his nickname, "Bob."

"Come on in."

Smiling impishly at the stunned policemen, Caron strolled from the orderly room in to see Tibbets. They greeted each other like the old buddies they were.

Caron had been gunnery instructor on Tibbets's B-29 training program. Feet up on his desk, Tibbets now explained to the gunner why he had sent for him. "Bob, I need a man who knows what he's doing—and can teach others to do a similar job. And keep their mouths shut."

"Colonel, I won't even mention I'm here," said Caron.

Tibbets smiled, reestablishing the easy contact which had marked their previous working relationship. He did not find it unusual to be imparting information to a noncom while senior officers in the 393rd still had no idea of what was happening. It was the way Tibbets preferred to do things, dealing first with the men who had already proved themselves to him. Tibbets believed that the privileges of rank were limited; men had to earn the right to his confidence.

On the B-29 program, onlookers had spoken scathingly of "Tibbets's private air force." He had shrugged such criticism aside. He meant to adopt the same policy at Wendover, sometimes confiding to enlisted men information he would not entrust to an officer.

The first time he saw his new outfit assembled, he was not overly impressed. They were trying too hard to look nonchalant, "the way they had seen Alan Ladd do it in the movies." Tibbets thought they looked decidedly inexperienced. He guessed most of the officers were in their early twenties. The enlisted men seemed even younger. Ferebee and Caron know what it's all about, thought Tibbets, the others are trying to pretend they do.

The smartly dressed officer standing ramrod stiff, cap squared off—that must be the executive officer, King. Tibbets had heard about him from Classen. King was a peacetime professional, Regular Army. Tough but fair, Classen had said. The unit needed such a man, judging by what Tibbets had read in Uanna's dossiers.

The 393rd later agreed that, standing there, Tibbets looked tough, mean, and moody. One officer put it, "He looked as if one mistake from us, and he would happily fry us for breakfast and use our remains to stoke his lunchtime stove."

Beser thought: This is the man I want to go to war with. Feeling Tibbets's stare fall upon him, the radar officer visibly straightened; he wished now that he hadn't worn his cap at such a rakish angle.

Command had taught Tibbets a trick: surprise people, shake them by the unexpected. "I've looked at you. You have looked at me. I'm not going to be stuck with all of you. But those of you who remain are going to be stuck with me."

This was a new Tibbets to Caron. He shared in the ripple of expectancy around him.

Tibbets continued. "You have been brought here to

work on a very special mission. Those of you who stay will be going overseas."

A muted cheer came from the rear ranks. Tibbets froze it with one look. "This is not a football game. You are here to take part in an effort that could end the war."

This time he allowed the murmur to rise and fall of its own accord. He had them now. "Don't ask what the job is. That is a surefire way to be transferred out. Don't ask any questions. Don't answer any questions from anybody not directly involved in what we will be doing. Do exactly what you are told, when you are told, and you will get along fine.

"I know some of you are curious about all the security. Stop being curious. This is part of the preparation for what is to come. Nobody will be allowed into a fenced-off area without a pass. Lose that pass, and you face court-martial.

"Never mention this base to anybody. That means your wives, girls, sisters, family."

There was dead silence when he paused. Years ago, when he first became an officer, his mother had given him a piece of advice: sometimes he would have to be tough, but he should always try to temper it by showing the other side of his character, gentleness.

"It's not going to be easy for any of us. But we will succeed by working together. However, all work and no play is no fun. So, as of now, you can all go on two weeks' furlough. Enjoy yourselves."

Classen was about to dismiss the squadron when Tibbets spoke again. "If any of you wish to transfer out, that's fine. Just say the word."

He waited.

Nobody moved.

"I'm glad," Tibbets said, "really glad."

By midafternoon, the men were already leaving the base. Many had begun to wonder why, if their assignment was so important in ending the war, they had been given two weeks' leave. Some believed Tibbets had tried too hard to impress them.

Second Lieutenant Eugene Grennan, the engineer on Eatherly's crew, decided after strolling down the flight line that the talk about security was "hogwash." A hangar door had been open. He peered inside, "and there was this German V-1 rocket."

A triumphant Grennan decided that the squadron was going to Europe "to knock down Nazi rockets."

The rocket was a plywood mockup, and the hangar door had been deliberately left ajar—a trap devised by Uanna. Within minutes, an agent reported that Grennan had swallowed the bait. But Uanna was in no hurry to catch the engineer. He had other snares to set.

Navigator Russell Gackenbach reached Salt Lake City and was stopped by an NCO asking if Wendover was the "headquarters of the Silverplate outfit." Gackenbach had never heard of Silverplate, but he suspected a trap and sternly warned his questioner that "darn-fool questions could get us both in the pen."

Gackenbach had survived Uanna's obstacle course. Others found themselves enmeshed.

Two NCOs were accosted by an officer in a Salt Lake City hotel. He said he was joining the 393rd. What sort of outfit was it? The men obligingly told him. The officer thanked them. Two hours later, as the talkative NCOs boarded a train for home, MPs stopped them and drove them back to base. In Tibbets's office they were confronted by the officer. He was a Manhattan Project agent. Within an hour both noncoms were on the way to Alaska.

Grennan reached Union Square, Chicago, before his trap sprung. There he ran into a friend from college days. Grennan told him about "the crazy setup at Wendover." His friend listened attentively. They parted company. Grennan arrived home to find a telegram ordering his immediate return to Wendover. There, Uanna keelhauled the young flier for talking. His friend was a project agent. All that saved the crestfallen Grennan from transfer was his fine flying record. From then on, he became one of the most security-conscious men in the squadron.

Five more members of the 393rd were netted by Uanna's agents. They were also swiftly shipped to Alaska. Their records were not good enough to save them.

In the late afternoon, Groves telephoned Tibbets, wanting to know why the squadron had gone on furlough. He was told about the security operation now in progress.

The two men had met briefly in Washington. Then, Tibbets had been uncomfortably aware of the immense pressures the project chief was under. Now, Groves appeared to have ample time to talk. He promised new B-29s would be available soon, and reminded Tibbets that "the world is yours."

This was Groves at his most cajoling. Now he switched moods. He talked about the scientists who would soon be descending on Wendover. They were "brilliant men," but they had little understanding of "the military side of things." Therefore, it would be best if Tibbets did not "inform them unduly" about the training program.

Groves wanted to restrict news of the Army Air Force's involvement to a few scientists—and then only to those he knew supported his view that the bomb must be produced as soon as possible. He saw those who questioned the validity of what they were doing as befuddled meddlers who were straying out of the scientific and into the political arena. He sensed that if these "longhairs" were aware that a strike force now existed to drop the bomb, their protests would become shriller.

He put it differently to Tibbets.

"Colonel, what people don't know about they can't talk about. And that is good for security."

Beser was ordered to remain on base. Tibbets had told him to expect important visitors soon.

When the radar officer attempted to question Tibbets,

he "received the coldest stare any man could give. I just shut up, went to my quarters, and waited."

Tibbets was being hard-nosed "because I wanted to impress on Beser, and everybody else in the outfit, that I didn't fool around."

Now, late in the evening of September 12, Tibbets and Ferebee finally settled down for their eagerly awaited reunion.

Ferebee was taller than Tibbets, and rakishly elegant. He could have played the hero in a war movie. He sported a neat RAF-style moustache which made him look older than his twenty-four years.

He had survived sixty-three combat missions, twenty more than Tibbets. They shared the same philosophy about war: it was a rotten business, but it was either kill or be killed.

They had flown together in Europe, been shot up, known the meaning of fear, and become firm friends. It was almost a year since they had last met, but Tibbets was pleased to see the old bonds were still there.

They rambled through the past, remembering English airfields they had flown from, German-occupied French towns they had attacked. They talked excitedly about that summer's day in 1942 when they had tangled with Göring's personal squadron of yellow-nosed Messerschmitts. On that occasion one of the gunners on their bomber had had his foot shot off, the copilot had lost a hand, and Tibbets himself had been wounded in the arm. But Ferebee had successfully bombed the Germans' Abbeville air base, and in daylight. That evening the BBC had mentioned the raid on its nine-o'clock news. They remembered other fliers, men who had died, men who had vanished into German prison camps, men whose fate was uncertain.

Finally Tibbets turned to the present. "Tom, we are going to need good men for this job. If it works, we'll flatten everything within eight miles of the aiming point."

Ferebee considered what he should say. "That's quite a bang, Paul."

The bombardier made no other comment. Restraint was one of Ferebee's qualities. He was always prepared to wait and to listen. His friends said the only time he really asserted himself was in combat, at the poker table, or when a pretty girl passed.

Tibbets asked him if he could recommend anybody they should bring in for "the job."

"What about 'Dutch'?"

Theodore "Dutch" van Kirk had been their navigator in Europe. Quietly professional in the air, he and Ferebee had caroused and gambled off-duty. Occasionally Tibbets had joined them in their whoopee making, smiling indulgently as his younger companions staged their own blitzkrieg on London's nightlife. Ferebee explained that van Kirk was back in America, had married, and was now based in Louisiana. Tibbets said he would have the navigator transferred to Wendover. Van Kirk could raise the standards of the 393rd's navigators to that required for an atomic strike mission.

"Tom, I want every one of these crews to be lead crews, capable of finding their way to a target without having pathfinders up front leading the way and dropping marker bombs."

Ferebee had two further suggestions for men who could meet Tibbets's requirements. One was a bombardier, Kermit Beahan; the other was a navigator, James van Pelt. Both had previously impressed Ferebee.

Tibbets said they would be recruited. He announced his own choices. They were all men who had served with him on the B-29 testing program. Three of them were pilots: Robert Lewis, Charles Sweeney, and Don Albury.

Lewis, Tibbets explained, was a little wild, but a natural pilot; Sweeney was Boston Irish "and would fly a B-29 through the Grand Canyon if you asked him"; Albury "was about the most competent twenty-five-year-old I have ever known."

He had one other selection, Staff Sergeant Wyatt Duzenbury, his former flight engineer. "Tom, Dooz can coax magic out of airplane engines, and he's a helluva guy when you're in a corner. Give him an engine fire and he becomes steady as a rock. Give him two and he becomes even steadier."

By the end of the evening, Tibbets and Ferebee had virtually decided on the men who would fly the first atomic strike.

• 6 •

Lieutenant Commander Mochitsura Hashimoto of the Imperial Japanese Navy had ordered a trim dive for 1700 hours on September 17. Submarine *I.58* was to dive three hundred feet below the waves of Hiroshima Bay to test the watertightness of all hull valves and openings.

I.58 had been commissioned at Kure four days earlier; this was the first time she would be submerged. From the day he had first seen her, back in May, Hashimoto had been impressed by the boat; she was one of the *I*-class submarines, larger and faster and better equipped than almost any boat of a comparable class anywhere in the world. Two diesel engines gave *I.58* a cruising speed of 14 knots; submerged, her motors drove the submarine at 7 knots. With a range of 15,000 miles, she could remain at sea for three months. For her six torpedo tubes, all forward, she carried nineteen torpedoes, the most advanced in the world. Oxygen-fueled, leaving no wake, they had a speed of 58 knots and a range of 5,500 meters. Each 2-foot-diameter torpedo carried a 1,210-pound explosive charge.

Today, for the hull tests, the torpedo room was empty, except for the rats that infested the submarine. Every effort to exterminate the rodents had been unsuccessful. But they were the only problem that Lieutenant Commander Hashimoto had failed to overcome. His endless battles with the Kure Naval Dockyard, the Naval Technical Department, and the Naval Research

Bureau had paid off. *I.58* was equipped exactly the way he wished.

Standing on the boat's bridge, as it moved through the water a little over a mile south of Hiroshima, Hashimoto looked through his binoculars at the naval academy on the island of Etajima. Nothing seemed to have changed since he had been a cadet there from 1927 to 1931. Three years later, in 1934, he had been assigned to submarines; he had loved the life. But a spell of duty in destroyers and subchasers, operating in the waters off China, had intervened. It was not until 1938 that he was selected to be a full-time member of the submarine service. By then he was married, and in 1940 his wife gave birth to their first child, a son.

Professionally, Hashimoto had found himself caught up in events which stirred him deeply. He was assigned to the naval task force supporting the air attack on Pearl Harbor, a torpedo officer on one of the five submarines which had each launched a two-man midget submarine against the American fleet. The midget subs had failed in their mission; all were sunk. But Hashimoto's own craft had made good its escape. Since then, he had enjoyed an unspectacular war.

He liked it that way. The first time he had assembled the crew of *I.58,* he told them he was expecting competence, not "senseless heroics."

Hashimoto had personally selected many of his 105 officers and men. Some of them had been with him on his previous submarine. They thought their thirty-five-year-old captain firm but fair. He was widely experienced and had a reputation for surviving.

A few of the newcomers were young; Hashimoto looked upon this as another sign that the war was demanding a supreme effort. But, like the others, his youngsters were eager and shaping up well.

I.58 reached its diving station.

Hashimoto climbed down from the bridge to the control room. He watched and listened to the final preparations for diving; the air was filled with quiet orders, reports, the sounds of bell signals.

The main engines were clutched out; the electric motors began to run at full whine. The outboard exhaust and air-induction valves were closed off.

The engine room informed the control room that it was ready to dive. The lookouts came below. The officer of the watch spun the handwheel which clamped the flanged lid leading to the conning tower against its seating. The seamen at the ballast-tank vent levers reported that all the main vents were clear. The chief turned to Hashimoto and reported that the boat was ready to dive.

Hashimoto gave the order. "Dive! Dive! Dive! Thirty feet."

He watched as the sailors opened the main vent levers. A roar of air escaped from the main ballast tanks. *I.58* was no longer buoyant. The depth gauge began to move, slowly at first, then with gathering speed. Outside, the sea could be heard slapping against the conning tower. Then the sound died. The bridge was beneath the waves. The electric motors took over.

The chief reported that the boat was properly trimmed.

Hashimoto ordered the main vents shut. *I.58* continued to drop through the water. Suddenly, a vibration ran through the boat. The chief ordered the submarine to be retrimmed. At one hundred feet, *I.58* was suspended on an even keel, held in place by the careful balance of water in the compensating and trimming tanks.

Leakage points and discharge-pump capacities were once more tested. There were no defects.

Hashimoto ordered *I.58* to be taken deeper. The trouble came suddenly, and with a gush of water at two hundred feet.

A leak had developed in the torpedo room. The area was at once sealed off.

Hashimoto gave his orders quickly, with no sign of concern, aware now of the anxious faces around him.

I.58 steadied and then began to climb rapidly toward the surface. There, the diesel motors took over.

Hashimoto quietly cursed the dockyard fitters whose carelessness had nearly caused a disaster. Hiroshima Bay was deep; there was little chance grappling crews could have recovered the submarine. The fear that was always at the back of his mind—the dread of being entombed forever on the seabed—made Hashimoto almost physically sick. If he had to die, he wanted the end to come in battle. All but five of his classmates from the naval academy were dead, victims of American destroyers. Nowadays the life expectancy of a submarine crew was measured in weeks, not months, without the slipshod Kure dockyard workers shortening the odds still further.

Hashimoto was not a superstitious man. But he liked to believe that "anything which begins so badly must only improve."

It was a comforting and very necessary philosophy for a commander who knew that every day the odds of his surviving were lessening. His great hope was that before he succumbed, he would have a chance to sink an enemy ship.

• 7 •

The drab, olive-green sedan stopped on the outskirts of Santa Fe, New Mexico. Lansdale told Tibbets and Beser to remove their air force insignia. He handed them corps of engineers' emblems. In explanation, although it was hardly necessary, he said, "Security."

The security chief was glad to be dealing with Tibbets and Beser. They were used to military discipline—not like the scientists who tormented his agents with their childish games. Lansdale was still smarting from the latest prank. A physicist had somehow opened the secret steel safe in the Los Alamos records office and placed a piece of paper on top of the priceless atomic secrets it contained. Printed on the paper were the words "Guess who?"

Beser was too overwhelmed by events to play any games. Yesterday he had been called to Tibbets's office. The radar officer had immediately recognized by name the "important visitors"; Norman Ramsey and Robert Brode were physicists whose papers he had read as a student. They had questioned him for an hour on his academic background and radar qualifications. Finally Brode had told Beser he could do the job—on the understanding that his life was expendable.

Nobody had yet told Beser what the job was, but Beser knew better than to ask.

Early this morning, September 19, he and Tibbets had flown south from Wendover to Albuquerque, New Mexico. Lansdale was driving them on to Santa Fe. He cautioned them again. "You have nothing to do with the air force. You have never heard of Wendover. Don't volunteer anything you know."

They drove into town, stopping before a wrought-iron gate, centuries old, through which they entered a small, Spanish-style courtyard.

For two years this patio had been the receiving point for some of the world's most distinguished scientists. Here, those men and women were given coffee, doughnuts, and comforting words from motherly Dorothy McKibben, who acted as "front-office receptionist" for the Manhattan Project's most secret center—Site Y, Los Alamos.

Norman Ramsey was waiting on the patio to escort Tibbets and Beser there. He enjoined them never to address anybody they would meet as "doctor" or "professor."

"Security," Beser said solemnly.

Two considerations had influenced the choice of Los Alamos as an atomic laboratory. It was remote enough for security purposes; if one of the experiments conducted there resulted in a premature explosion, there was no sizable civilian population nearby to be imperiled by the release of radioactivity.

Tibbets's first impression was disappointing. He felt

"the birthplace of the actual bomb should look more factorylike."

What he saw were clusters of buildings set out on a flat tableland, part of the plateau of the Jemez Mountains. Six thousand scientists, technicians, their wives and children now lived within the high wire fences. Beser thought the place looked like a concentration camp. Inside, this unhappy image persisted. Many of the buildings were of rough construction: speed, not comfort, had been the rule. As at Wendover, there were areas marked RESTRICTED and MOST RESTRICTED.

Waiting for Tibbets and Beser in his office was J. Robert Oppenheimer, the shy, frail theoretical physicist who was the scientific director of the Manhattan Project. He greeted them warmly but was less effusive toward Lansdale.

For months now, the security chief had been playing cat-and-mouse with Oppenheimer because of the scientist's former association with various Communist organizations, his financial contributions to left-wing groups, his friendship with "fellow travelers." He had been under surveillance since March 15, 1943. He was followed, his mail opened, his telephone tapped, and, in Lansdale's later admission, "All sorts of nasty things were done to keep a watch on him."

Groves himself had questioned Oppenheimer and was satisfied that his "closest, most indispensable collaborator" had severed all connections with his offending past. He had ordered the watch lifted on his scientific director.

Lansdale had ignored the order. His agents continued to harass Oppenheimer.

They were watching the wrong man.

This morning, after Beser and Lansdale had left for Ramsey's laboratory, Oppenheimer said to Tibbets, "You had better know everything."

Pandora's box was finally opening for the flier.

Here at Los Alamos, Oppenheimer began, men were

delving into the unknown world, asking such questions as "What is matter?" and "How short can a 'short time' be?" Here they spoke of thousands of tons of energy as if energy could be weighed. They talked of a thousandth and then a millionth of a second as they devised ways to reduce time itself almost to nothing. They argued over the relative merits of the gaseous-diffusion and electromagnetic processes for separating uranium 235 from uranium 238; the uranium 235 produced could be measured in thimblefuls.

These men were also discovering the special nature of a chain reaction and studying the unique problem of critical mass: how to bring together two lumps of uranium 235 of the right potency to cause an atomic explosion at the right time.

Oppenheimer reduced the problem to a few words. "Time. That's the problem, Colonel. Getting the timing right. If we are successful in solving that, then your problems will begin."

The scientist looked benignly at Tibbets. "There will probably be problems right up until the moment when the bomb explodes."

Oppenheimer explained how they intended to build the uranium bomb. A suitable mechanism had to be devised to bring two hemispheres of uranium 235 into contact quickly so that their combined mass reached the critical point and detonated. The amount of uranium 235 to be used, the size of the two spheres, the speed with which they must collide, the scattering angle, the range of the neutrons projected by the chain reaction —those, Oppenheimer said, were just some of the questions to be answered.

He rose to his feet and told Tibbets to follow him. They went into a nearby building, unmarked except for a sign:

POSITIVELY
NO
ADMITTANCE

This was where Captain Parsons and his team were dealing with how to ensure that the bomb would explode at a predetermined height above the target.

Oppenheimer said that Parsons would probably be going along on the first mission.

"Good. Then if anything goes wrong, Captain, I can blame you," Tibbets said.

"If anything goes wrong, Colonel, neither of us will be around to be blamed," Parsons replied.

He described to Tibbets one of the experimental machines they had built to test the theory of critical mass. It had been nicknamed "The Guillotine." A piece of doughnut-shaped uranium was placed in the machine. Then another piece of uranium was dropped through the hole in the doughnut. For a split second, the extra uranium plunging through the gap brought both pieces close to critical mass. It was a dangerous game to play. They called it "twisting the dragon's tail."

Parsons explained more about the bomb's mechanism to Tibbets. "It is designed to ensure that the bringing together of the two 'subcritical' pieces occurs for the first time at the moment of planned detonation over the target. The pieces will then combine in a critical mass, causing the chain-reaction explosion. That's the theory. Until that moment, we cannot know for sure whether the bomb will work."

Parsons described how the heart of the bomb was really just "a good old gun, a five-inch cannon with a six-foot-long barrel. After the bomb has left the plane and is on its way, a piece of uranium two-three-five about the size of a soup can will be fired down the barrel into a second piece of uranium fixed to the muzzle."

"And if it doesn't work?" persisted Tibbets.

"We will just make a nice big dent in the target area and go back to the drawing board," said Parsons.

To avoid that dismal prospect, explained Oppenheimer, in the coming months Tibbets's unit would drop test bombs. These would help the scientists develop the final shape of the atomic-bomb casing as well as prove the proximity fuzes, which governed the height at which the bomb would explode.

So far, the proximity fuzes were proving troublesome.

Tibbets continued to be astonished by Oppenheimer during his conducted tour of Los Alamos. Late in the afternoon, they were walking down another corridor, past identical rooms whose inner walls were lined with blackboards covered with formulas and whose occupants pored over slide rules and logarithm tables.

Suddenly, Oppenheimer halted in midstride. His head was cocked like a dog scenting game. He turned and stalked back to an office.

Inside, a man sat slumped on a straight-backed wooden chair, staring fixedly at a blackboard. He was unshaven and disheveled.

Tibbets wondered if he "might be the building janitor taking an unauthorized rest after a night out."

Oppenheimer stood silently behind the man. Together they stared at the blackboard with its jumble of equations.

Oppenheimer moved to the blackboard and rubbed out part of an equation. Still, the man on the chair did not move.

Oppenheimer quickly wrote a new set of symbols in the space he had erased.

The man remained transfixed.

Oppenheimer added a final symbol.

The man rose from his chair, galvanized, shouting, "I've been looking for that mistake for two days!"

Oppenheimer smiled and walked out of Enrico Fermi's office, leaving one of the founders and greatest geniuses of nuclear physics happily restarting work.

Beser was enjoying "the most fantastic day in my life." He had met and talked to a dozen renowned scientists who were his teenage heroes.

Hans Bethe and Ernest O. Lawrence were among those who gave Beser a glimpse of their work. The scientists told him about the strange kinds of guns they had devised that used atomic bullets. When fired at each other, on impact the bullets devoured one another. They described how they hoped this phenomenon would be used to produce an atomic explosion. They spoke of temperatures they hoped to create which would make a light "brighter than a thousand suns."

Ramsey outlined the role the radar officer would play on the mission. Beser would be taught how to monitor enemy radar to see if it was trying to jam or detonate the intricate mechanism of the bomb. To understand how this could happen, Beser must learn what few of the scientists involved knew—the minute details of the bomb's firing mechanism, including its built-in mini-radar system.

On this first day, nobody seemed concerned about how much they should tell Beser. They poured information over him, "leaving me sinking in a scientific whirlpool."

Late in the evening, Beser was introduced to a dour young technician, David Greenglass. Nobody yet suspected Greenglass had just stolen the first of many blueprints. His haul would eventually include schematic drawings of a special lens crucial to detonating the plutonium bomb which was being developed in parallel with the uranium bomb. The drawings would be spirited to Russia through the highly professional espionage ring the Soviets had been able to set up from inside Los Alamos. Greenglass would receive a few hundred dollars for his treachery.

Later, Beser would believe that, on this very evening, he had interrupted Greenglass in his espionage activities.

When the radar officer left Greenglass, it was dark. With difficulty, he reached the small guesthouse assigned to visitors. He opened the front door and stopped dead in his tracks. Sprawled on a couch, sipping a drink, was an attractive brunette, stark naked. She carefully lowered her glass and rose to her feet.

"Can I help you?" The voice had just a trace of a German accent.

It was Katherine Oppenheimer, wife of the scientific

director. She had left Germany when fourteen; her relatives included Nazi Field Marshal Wilhelm Keitel.

"Ma'am, I'm sorry. . . ."

Blushing furiously, Beser stammered into silence. He had never seen a naked woman before.

"Are you looking for someone?"

"Yes, ma'am . . . No, ma'am . . . My . . . bed . . . I mean, the guest quarters, ma'am."

"They are in the back of the house. You have come in the wrong door, but you can go through here." Mrs. Oppenheimer sat down and resumed sipping her cocktail.

Averting his eyes, the bashful Beser stumbled past the languid first lady of Los Alamos.

Her husband was startling Paul Tibbets. The two men were alone in Oppenheimer's office, reviewing what Tibbets had been shown. The flier felt that in a few hours he had received "a better scientific education than all my years in school."

Now Oppenheimer began to question him. Apart from enemy interference, the scientist wanted to know what other risks were involved in a bombing mission. Tibbets explained there was always the chance of bombs jamming in their bays, or a faulty mechanism detonating them prematurely. Oppenheimer was confident such risks could be eliminated in the atomic bomb.

Then he stared intently at Tibbets. "Colonel, your biggest problem may be after the bomb has left your aircraft. The shock waves from the detonation could crush your plane. I am afraid that I can give you no guarantee that you will survive."

• 8 •

The scraping against the stone floor of his *geta,* the Japanese wooden clogs he favored, was the only sound in the Osaka University laboratory of Dr. Tsunesaburo

Asada, possibly Japan's most imaginative scientist. His staff had come to recognize that this habit of shuffling his feet was a signal that Asada was content.

Putting his weight first on one foot, and then on the other, the white-coated scientist studied his latest creation, a proximity fuze. It was similar in design and purpose to those being perfected at Los Alamos.

Months of work had gone into the fuze's development in Asada's well-equipped laboratory. He rarely left the campus now, working well into the night, catnapping on a couch in a corner of the laboratory, impatient of any interruptions.

He was still, as he had been when the war began, chairman of the physics department. But since late 1941, he had done no teaching. His brilliance made him one of the scientists crucial to Japan's war effort.

Since 1937, Asada had regularly lectured at the Naval Technical Research Institute in Tokyo and at the Naval Aeronautical Research Institute in Yokosuka. Besides lecturing, Asada had worked closely with the military authorities before Japan entered the war. And on December 17, 1941, he was one of the scientists selected to work on Project A.

This was the code name for Japan's atomic research. Eleven days after President Roosevelt had authorized the go-ahead for the Manhattan Project, the Japanese had entered the field, determined to develop an atomic bomb.

Asada would always remember the mood of blind patriotism which had gripped the first meeting after Pearl Harbor at the Naval Club in Tokyo. There had been promises of generous funding for the atomic research. His caution about the vast technical problems to be overcome had been brushed aside. Those were the days when the Japanese appeared invincible. A naval officer had said that perhaps their new allies, the Germans, could help. Asada had pointed out that many of Germany's leading atomic scientists were Jewish, and if they had not been expelled from the country, they were probably dead. Some, he added, might be in the

United States. He had expressed the opinion that it was likely America had the potential to develop atomic weapons.

The naval officer had reprimanded him. "America—and Japan."

For a year he and the other scientists involved had studied the question. In December 1942, they had presented their conclusions. It would take them ten years to produce "some atomic weapons." Even that was optimistic, as Japan did not have the essential raw uranium.

Project A was quietly shelved by the navy, although development work by the army on Japan's atomic bomb would continue in a desultory fashion until well into 1945.

Project B was then initiated by the navy. Asada immediately recognized its potential. It was concerned with developing radar, navigation techniques, and the proximity fuze.

In the past eighteen months, astonishing progress had been made on all three. Two famous British warships—the *Prince of Wales* and the *Repulse*—had been of great help in the development of Japan's radar. The ships had been sunk off Singapore in the high days of 1941. Japanese divers had located them on the seabed and performed the herculean feat of dismantling the radar apparatus from both ships. It had been shipped to Japan, reassembled, and provided invaluable information to research workers.

Asada himself had developed the proximity fuze. Soon it would go into full-scale production. His contribution on that aspect of Project B completed, he had joined a small and select band of scientists working on the most staggering of all weapons.

They were building a death ray.

It was a machine from the pages of science fiction. It was designed to project an invisible beam that would pluck an aircraft out of the sky either by shattering its propellers or killing its crew.

With such a weapon, Asada knew that Japan could snatch a stunning victory. No plane would be safe against the deadly ray. Carefully placed batteries of death rays could guarantee all Japanese cities immunity from air attack. Other batteries could be deployed against hostile craft approaching by sea. Later, the navy could have death rays mounted on its ships to destroy the enemy far away from the home islands.

The potential was heady and limitless. So far, a prototype had killed a laboratory rat. This modest success gave Asada hope. The next step Asada planned was to direct the death ray at a larger mammal.

• 9 •

Surprising the enemy was the abiding concern of Major General Seizo Arisue. Surprises were his business. He created them, spread them, anticipated them, and defused them.

He was head of Imperial Army Intelligence, Japan's acknowledged spy master.

This bantam-sized man with a formidable intellect and a fearful temper to match his harsh, rasping voice kept a file on every important Japanese politician and officer. He knew more secrets than any man in the army, and often used them to maintain his own position.

In turn, the file on Arisue kept by his rivals in naval intelligence described him as "arrogant, supremely confident in his own abilities, and dangerously ambitious."

The relationship between the two intelligence branches was icy. They were locked in a power struggle over which could provide the most valuable information.

Arisue was coming to believe that at last he might have the opportunity to resolve that issue with a striking espionage coup. He had been in his cramped office in a wing of the monolithic General Army Headquarters in Tokyo since early morning, trying to verify an intriguing report sent by his contact in Lisbon. Ordinarily, the report would not have reached Arisue personally. But he had given an explicit order that he must see "everything relating to America."

Some of it came from the Abwehr in Berlin; there were outdated snippets from Madrid and Mexico City. The weekly summaries of the American press were more helpful. Army intelligence subscribed to 140 American newspapers and magazines. Very often *The New York Times,* the *Saturday Evening Post, Collier's, Time,* and *Newsweek* contained clues of troop movements and battle casualties that helped Arisue piece together a surprisingly accurate mosaic of the United States at war. At first he had been suspicious of the material gleaned from the American press. He thought it might be a trap laid by enemy intelligence. But repeatedly he had been able to confirm independently the newspaper reports. He grew astonished at the American censors for allowing such important material to be published.

Now, as he studied the Lisbon report, he wondered what the Portuguese censors had made of it. No doubt they had passed copies on to British and American intelligence; in the past six months he had suspected this was happening regularly.

Arisue's man in Lisbon had picked up a whisper that the United States had embarked on a huge new war project.

After hours of pondering, Arisue knew there was only one way to verify the truth of this claim. He must slip an agent into the United States.

That would be the most difficult operation he had yet mounted. No native Japanese could hope to remain undetected for long in North America. Arisue could call upon the flourishing German spy network in South America to provide an operative, but it might take months to clear matters through Berlin, especially as the tide was turning against Hitler. The Italians were already in disarray.

Arisue ruled out any help from the Axis.

He considered his own resources. His Lisbon contact was not qualified for such a dangerous mission. His men in Madrid and Mexico City were local recruits, capable of little more than acting as intelligence "post boxes."

Brazil—he put a question mark next to the name of his agent there. He was a good man. But where would he begin?

The message from Lisbon had given no clue as to where the new American war project was being carried out, or what it was.

The problems were immense. But if he could discover what this new American project was, it might be enough to stiffen the government's resolve to fight on to the end.

Arisue sent for Lieutenant Colonel Kakuzo Oya, chief of the American Intelligence Section at Arisue's headquarters. The two officers spent the rest of the afternoon discussing the prospects of infiltrating a spy into the United States.

• 10 •

Orders crackled over the B-29's intercom. "We'll do it by the book. They're all gonna be watching. Nobody's gonna screw it up. Right?"

The crew of the huge bomber didn't respond to the pilot, Captain Robert Lewis. For the past hour they had been "doing it by the book," strictly following the procedures laid down in the buff-colored manual. They had checked the outside of the bomber, clambered aboard, stowed their parachutes, and begun the preflight countdown.

Duzenbury, the engineer, and Caron, the tail gunner, who had flown with Lewis many times before, were surprised at how serious he was this crisp fall morning at Wendover. They knew Lewis as a joking twenty-six-year-old who wore a battered peaked cap and a stained flying jacket. He looked like a combat veteran, even though he had never seen action.

Lewis was treating this flight, in the words of Caron, "as if he had on board the president and the Cabinet."

Squashed in the tiny tail turret, the gunner was tempted to snap on the intercom and tell the pilot to relax.

The impulse passed. The checking continued.

"Equipment secure, Navigator?" The intercom emphasized Lewis's Brooklyn accent.

"Secure."

Captain Theodore "Dutch" van Kirk, the navigator, settled himself more comfortably in the padded seat with its fitted armrests. He wondered who Lewis was trying to impress. In the week he had been at Wendover, van Kirk had noticed that Lewis enjoyed an audience.

Tibbets had tried to reassure the navigator. He told van Kirk that Lewis was "just letting off tension. In the air, he's a natural." Van Kirk had his own ideas about "naturals." Too often he had found them "daredevils trying to prove things to other people." He hoped Lewis was not like that.

Lewis had always thought all navigators a strange breed, with their blind belief that any pilot could steer a course to an absolute degree. Today, though, the pilot intended to follow explicitly any course change van Kirk indicated. In that way, Lewis could not be blamed for any foul-up.

Seated in the cockpit watching the winking lights on the instrument panel, Lewis experienced a familiar feeling of well-being; he had come a long way.

In his boyhood days on the streets of Brooklyn, a swift pair of fists had been better than a classy accent; in flying school, he knew, his abrasive manner had worked against him. But in the end, even his most demanding instructor had conceded that Lewis was a highly gifted pilot. He'd never forgotten the pride his mom and pop had shown when they first saw him in an officer's uniform, and his own satisfaction while walking through his Brooklyn neighborhood and being "greeted as somebody." Then there had been the day he had taken the legendary Charles Lindbergh up in a B-29. After the flight, Lindbergh had said he would have been happy to have had Lewis fly with him on his epoch-making flights.

It was Tibbets who had developed Lewis into one of the most experienced B-29 pilots in the air force. The summons to Wendover had not surprised Lewis. He had written to his father: "Paul needs me because I am so good at my job."

Modesty, as Lewis would admit, was not one of his endearing qualities. But he had others: generosity and a fierce loyalty to his crew, especially the enlisted men. Down on the flight line, mechanics hero-worshiped Lewis because he bent regulations to get them better working conditions.

He had joined his flight crew a few days earlier when the B-29 arrived, the first one to be delivered to Wendover. There had been keen competition among the pilots to fly it, and Lewis had been almost schoolboyishly excited when he was chosen to do so. He immediately began to talk of "my crew" and "my ship."

But for this flight van Kirk and Ferebee had taken the places of his usual navigator and bombardier. Tibbets explained to Lewis that van Kirk and Ferebee would take turns flying with all the crews. Tibbets added a promise. "It will be just like the old days, Bob."

That cheered Lewis. The "old days" were when he had "a one-to-one relationship with Paul without other people getting in the way."

In his ten days at Wendover, it had not been like that. Lewis felt that Tibbets never had time to sit down with him and reminisce about those old days. Worse, "He didn't laugh at my jokes, he wasn't so tolerant if I made a small mistake. I put it down to nerves over a new command."

The last flight checks were ending. Lewis asked van Kirk the estimated flying time to the initial point, or IP, the map reference from which the bomber would commence its bombing run. From the IP to the AP, the aiming point, would be a matter of a few miles. Over that distance, Lewis would work with the bombardier, Ferebee. He had disliked Ferebee from the day they met. He thought the bombardier acted "superior," talked like "a playboy in the movies."

One night, Lewis and Ferebee had played poker. Lewis had lost half his month's salary. He could ill afford to do so; a broken marriage had left him short of cash. Half-jokingly, Tibbets had told Lewis to stay in his "own league."

Tibbets knew Ferebee was one of the best poker players in uniform. He also felt Lewis was a "poor loser"—an accusation the pilot would always hotly deny—and Tibbets did not "want card games creating unnecessary problems."

In his mind, Lewis ran through the main points of the briefing Tibbets had given. He was to climb to thirty thousand feet and fly south to the bombing range, the man-made lake, Salton Sea, in Southern California. There, Ferebee would try to drop a single blockbuster, filled with ballast, into a seven-hundred-foot circle on the northern edge of the lake. Tibbets had told Lewis that once the bomb was dropped he was to execute a 155-degree diving turn, which would take him back in the direction from which he had just come. Tibbets had emphasized, "Keep your nose down, and get the hell out of the area as fast as you can."

Tibbets hoped the maneuver would provide the answer to how an aircrew could survive the expected shock wave from an atomic bomb. He had calculated that Lewis should be some seven miles away when the test blockbuster hit the ground. He did not explain to Lewis the reason for this action, "because that would have meant telling him too much too soon."

Shortly before boarding the B-29, Lewis had received another surprise. Beser had arrived on the apron saying he was bringing along on the trip some three hundred pounds of special equipment.

"Can't tell you why," said Beser cheerfully. "It's a matter of security."

That didn't endear Beser to Lewis. Waiting for take-off, the radar officer was squatting on the floor of the B-29, aft of the toilet in the rear section of the plane, with his spectrum analyzers, direction finder, search receivers, and antennas.

Beser was about to make the first flight in which he would practice coping with enemy attempts to interfere electronically with an atomic bomb. Some of his instruments had been specially modified at Los Alamos. During the flight, they would receive signals from the ground simulating enemy radar beams. It would be Beser's task to recognize, anticipate, and deflect the beams.

"Ready to start engines?"

Duzenbury studied the engineer's panel before answering Lewis. He was, at thirty-one, the oldest man in the crew. Duzenbury hadn't questioned why Tibbets had brought him to Wendover. It was enough for him "to work for the finest gentleman in the air force."

He also liked Lewis; next to the colonel, Lewis was the best pilot Duzenbury knew.

"Start engines, Captain."

One by one, each of the four Wright turbo-supercharged engines roared into life, and the tower cleared Lewis for takeoff. At the end of the runway he boosted the engines to 2,300 rpm while Duzenbury checked the magnetos and generators. Then, Lewis advanced the throttles to their full power position and slowly released the brakes. At 95 mph, just as the manual said, Lewis lifted the largest bomber in the world into the air.

Exactly on time, he reached the IP. Minutes later, Ferebee announced he had the AP in his Norden bombsight. "Bombs away. Correction. Bomb away."

Lewis banked the bomber violently to the right, dropping its nose to give him more speed. A surprised Caron far back in the tail shouted into the intercom. "Cap'n, it's like a roller coaster back here!"

Lewis shouted back. "I'll charge you for the ride when we get home."

Beser was too involved to notice the maneuver; two of his instruments had lost power, and he had no idea how effective his electronic countermeasures had been against the invisible beams. Disgusted, he gave up monitoring.

The blockbuster fell within the circle. Cameramen from the Manhattan Project reported they had managed to record its fall. Their films were flown to Los Alamos, where they were studied by scientists still trying to determine the best final shape for the atomic bomb.

Measuring instruments around the AP calculated that Lewis was over seven miles away when the bomb hit.

Tibbets was relieved. The maneuver meant that an aircraft should be able to avoid the atomic bomb's shock wave. He expressed his relief to one of the scientists who was with him on the bombing range.

The man gave Tibbets a chilling response. "Seven miles, twenty miles, fifty miles. There is no way of telling what the safe distance is until we drop a real atomic bomb."

It was evening when Tibbets returned to Wendover. In his office he continued to review the tactical requirements for delivering an atomic bomb.

Though by October 21 he knew a great deal more than he had a month earlier, he was far from reassured. The uncertain nature of the explosion—nobody could be positive how big it would be—and the predicted shock wave—another imponderable—had helped to rule out the use of a fighter escort. To be sure of surviving the shock wave, fighters would have to be so far away from the explosion just when the bomber was at its most vulnerable that it was unlikely they could provide proper protection. Further, a fighter escort might succeed only in drawing attention to the bomber. Tibbets made up his mind.

The bomber would go in alone.

That, too, raised problems: flak and enemy fighters. It was likely that the final approach would be made over enemy-held territory, at least part of which would undoubtedly have fighter protection. The more Tibbets thought about it, the less the chance of success seemed. The bomber could be destroyed long before it reached its objective.

Then Tibbets recalled his experience in New Mexico.

Months before, he had been there carrying out tests to assess a B-29's susceptibility to fighter attack. He had been irritated to find that his usual B-29, the one he used for all his tests, was out of commission. He was offered another one—stripped of its guns.

He decided to fly it to give the fighter pilots a chance to practice. Tibbets quickly discovered the stripped B-29 could operate some four thousand feet higher than his usual bomber. It was faster and more maneuverable. He was able to outpace the P-47 fighters making mock attacks on him. Finally, at thirty-four thousand feet, the fighters had to give up; the strain on their engines was too great.

As he recalled the experience, Tibbets began to feel excited. Flak was largely ineffective at over thirty-two thousand feet, and Tibbets knew that a P-47 fighter was similar in performance to a Japanese Zero.

With Japan likely to provide a target city, Tibbets reasoned his best possible chance of survival would be to use a stripped-down B-29 for the mission. He would take out all the armor plating and all the guns, apart from the two in the tail.

He telephoned the flight line and told the ground crews to begin work at once on stripping down the two bombers already at Wendover.

"Tonight?" asked an incredulous line chief.

"Now," said Tibbets firmly.

The mechanics thought the idea "plumb crazy." Later, they would christen the emasculated bombers *Sitting Target One* and *Sitting Target Two.*

• 11 •

In tight formation, five aircraft flew east over the Pacific. All their pilots hoped to die soon.

The fliers wore white scarfs loosely knotted around their necks. Under their leather flying helmets, concealed by their goggles, each man also wore a *hachi-maki,* a replica of the headband that samurai warriors had traditionally worn in battle in ancient Japan. This morning the band was the symbol of the Special Attack Corps of suicide pilots, the *shimpu,* or "divine wind." Later these pilots, and many others like them, would be called *kamikazes,* a Western transliteration of the characters that in Sino-Japanese are pronounced *shimpu.* The first *shimpu* were the momentous typhoons of 1241 and 1281 which, according to legend, rescued Japan from the fury of the Mongols.

The men chosen to launch this new *shimpu* had been told just before taking off a few hours earlier that they were "gods without earthly desires." Their Zeros contained 250-kilogram bombs. The pilots planned to crash-dive onto the ships of the American fleet now just beyond the horizon.

This plan had been devised only six days previously by Vice-Admiral Takijiro Onishi. To all the adjectives applied to the moonfaced commander—arrogant, brilliant, condescending, and uncompromising—another could be added in these last days of October: desperate.

Onishi was no longer the confident leader who had helped devise the attack on Pearl Harbor; who had launched the crippling assault on Clark Field, Manila, which had wiped out America's air force in the Far East; who had sent his pilots marauding through the Pacific.

Those days were over. Retaliation was on the way. A huge American fleet had been spotted heading toward the Philippines. If those islands fell, Japan's supply lines would be fatally ruptured. Onishi was given command of the First Air Fleet, operating from Manila. This once-impressive force consisted now of less than a hundred aircraft. But they were enough for Onishi. On October 19, he had presented his plan for *shimpu.*

There had been an enthusiastic response from his pilots. The men now over the Pacific were about to deliver the first blow.

They had, of course, written their final letters and farewell poems. Some had left brief wills. Each, in accord with the tradition of samurai leaving for their final battle, had enclosed locks of hair and nail parings, all that was to remain of their bodies on earth.

Before takeoff, Onishi himself had poured every man a ceremonial cup of sake and offered him a dish of dried cuttlefish. As each pilot took his cup, he had bowed and lifted the sake in both hands to his lips. Onishi had then handed every pilot a small lunch box, *bento,* to provide them with the comfort of a last-minute snack.

At 10:45 A.M., the suicide squadron sighted their enemy, an American carrier force with destroyer escorts.

The pilots bored in, scattering tinfoil to jam the American radar. Each pilot pulled a toggle which prepared the bomb in his plane for detonation.

At 10:53 A.M., the first Zero crash-dived onto the flight deck of the aircraft carrier *St. Lo.* Plane and the pilot disintegrated in a huge explosion. This was the "splendid death," *rippa na saigo,* which Onishi had promised.

The *St. Lo* began to sink.

By 10:59 A.M., October 25, 1944, all five planes had hit their targets. The mission had been a total success.

More would follow.

• 12 •

The 393rd received its fifteenth stripped-down B-29 on November 24. The squadron was now at full strength. The removal of armor plating and all guns except those in the tail turrets no longer caused comment. Pilots found it gave them extra height and speed, although they were not totally convinced by Tibbets's contention that in combat they would be out of range of flak and enemy fighters.

"Today," Lewis wrote to his parents, "was typical for its routine. Morning briefing followed by bombing practice; back for lunch (good), then more practice. I don't ask why. Nobody does."

The letter would be read by Manhattan Project agents attached to the base post office. They would decide it did not contravene security and allow it to be mailed. The many letters that failed to pass ended up on Uanna's desk. The watchful major made sure the writers were sufficiently scared by the time they left his office to be more careful in the future about what they wrote home.

Three hundred blockbuster casings were available for the crews to use on their practice mission to the Salton Sea. Cameramen continued to film the bombs dropping and the aircraft making their jolting 155-degree turns.

The maneuver, practiced both left and right, was the subject of much speculation. Pilots soon discovered that failing to execute a proper turn meant being temporarily grounded. Such punishments were an integral part of Tibbets's method. He also encouraged excellence by example. He himself had flown several runs, with Lewis as his copilot, and performed the turn perfectly.

The bombing circle was being steadily reduced. Now it was no more than four hundred feet in diameter.

Ferebee had demonstrated it possible to drop a casing into the circle from thirty thousand feet. Van Kirk proved that on long training flights, and over water, it was feasible to navigate the distance with no more of an error than half a mile. The workshops remained open twenty-four hours. The flight line worked around the clock keeping the bombers aloft.

Mess officer Charles Perry was told by Tibbets that if he had any problems, "just use the word *Silverplate*." Perry was skeptical. But one day, tired of arguing with a food-supply depot, he had used the code word. His goods had arrived within hours. Every air force depot in America had special orders to give priority to Silverplate.

The 393rd became the best-fed unit in the service. Tibbets had been known to send a transport plane a thousand miles to collect a cargo of tropical fruit. Fresh fish from New Orleans, Miami, and San Francisco were regular items on Perry's menus. On one occasion, Tibbets himself flew an eighteen-hundred-mile round trip to Portland, Oregon, to pick up a load of coffee cups.

He took care of his men in other ways. When they tangled with police in Salt Lake City over traffic violations or rowdy behavior, or got involved with the local married women, he intervened—if a man's work record justified it.

Executive officer John King struggled to maintain the standards of discipline he thought essential. But Tibbets made it clear he was not overly concerned with smart salutes, knife-edged creases in khakis, or gleaming toecaps. All that concerned him was a man's capacity to work well. Gradually, the 393rd became one of the most casually attired units in the air force. Earlier in November Tibbets had introduced a new pilot with the most unusual appearance of all: bobbed hair, rouged cheeks, and bright red lipstick. Baggy flying coveralls could not disguise a shapely figure.

"Sure, she's a lady," grinned Tibbets as he presented

the newcomer. "And they don't fly any finer than Dora Dougherty."

Dora was a veteran pilot who had worked for Tibbets on the B-29 testing program. She had handled the bomber with great skill and assurance at a time when many men pilots were doubtful of its capability. Dora once deliberately cut an engine on takeoff and yet became airborne. On another occasion, she landed a B-29 with an engine on fire. At Wendover, Dora flew a transport. Sometimes Tibbets wished he could send her up with a B-29. But Dora never complained about any assignment.

Many crewmen were complaining about the training schedules, the long hours, the continual security checks. And, above all, why didn't somebody explain what this was for?

In the words of Captain King, the feeling was growing "that there were 'them' and 'us.' "

Or: Tibbets, Ferebee, and van Kirk; and the rest of the 393rd.

The trio worked and relaxed together. Occasionally, Lewis joined the group. But the once-close relationship between Tibbets and Lewis was cooling. Tibbets felt Lewis was increasingly trying to take advantage of their past association. He was no longer amused by Lewis's determined forays after women, his partying, the aggressive way he approached everything: cards, volleyball, even conversation.

But in the air Lewis continued to excel. In the end, that was what Tibbets cared about.

Beser did not like flying with Lewis "because we had nothing in common." As for the pilot, he had not discovered why the radar officer "brought along a bunch of boxes and tried to look important."

Beser enjoyed the mystery surrounding his function. He was regularly—and unsuccessfully—pumped about his visits to the restricted Tech Area, and the flights he and Tibbets made together to Albuquerque. No flight plans were filed for these journeys.

At Los Alamos, Beser received further instruction

in the intricacies of electronic countermeasures. He would return to Wendover with Los Alamos technicians. They would spend days in the Tech Area helping Beser practice analyzing the intensity variation of successive return waves, or identifying the location, speed, and course of a reflecting object.

After Beser had become familiar with some of the bomb's secret radar system, a security agent was assigned to guard him day and night whenever he left the base. The man took his job so seriously that he even stood guard outside a public toilet in a Salt Lake City restaurant while Beser relieved himself. The radar officer reacted characteristically.

"Listen, Mac. People will think there's something funny about me, with you standing there."

"You listen, Lieutenant. I'm supposed to be in the john with you—not outside!"

Beser gave up. From now on, he must share every social occasion—a date, a drink with friends, a visit home to his family. In time, he came to accept his shadow.

Only at Wendover did he feel really free. His bodyguard's duties ended when Beser set foot on the base.

Grim winter came early in 1944. The November wind whistled across the salt flats, numbing everything in its path.

Perry and his cooks tried hard to make Thanksgiving dinner memorable, offering pumpkin pie and an exotic fruit punch to accompany the roast turkey. The mess officer then produced an abundant supply of Cuban cigars to complete the repast.

Cuba was, in fact, very much on everyone's mind. The latest rumor said that crews would soon fly south to sunny Havana to continue some form of special training.

Tibbets, as usual, remained tight-lipped. Groves was in regular telephone contact with him, wanting to be briefed on progress, chivvying and demanding. Tibbets would mention some of the difficulties he faced in bringing all the bomber crews to readiness. Groves would listen, grunt, and reply, "Work them hard. That's what you are there for."

Scientists flew in and out of Wendover daily, making new demands involving frequent changes. They asked for the bomb bays to be modified. Conventional bombs were held in place by shackles, but it was decided that for a plane carrying just one large, long atomic bomb, what was required was a single, safe, reliable hook from which the nine-thousand-pound bomb could be suspended. No such hook could be found. Bombardier Kermit Beahan was sent to Britain, and brought back the specifications for the one used by the RAF in their Lancaster bombers. It was adapted and fitted to the 393rd's B-29s.

There were constant changes, too, in the bomb's shape and weight. After each change, the scientists flew back to Los Alamos, telling Tibbets before they left that they were satisfied, that no more changes were contemplated, and that he could plan his training program with confidence. A few days later they would return, asking for new modifications as they discovered further aerodynamic-flow or other problems necessitating another alteration in the shape.

Tibbets often found himself in sympathy with the exasperation felt in the base machine shops where the changes had to be made by service personnel. At times they became almost openly hostile to these unknown civilians who descended on them and scrapped a long night's work with the briefest of apologies. Matters were not helped by security's insisting that the scientists pass themselves off as sanitary engineers—a piece of flummery which led to some very ribald comments. Prohibited from answering some of the questions his own engineering officers and men asked, Tibbets knew that to many of them he seemed cold, aloof, and hardnosed. The loneliness of leadership which his mother had once warned him about was becoming increasingly clear.

His command had assumed impressive proportions.

Besides the 393rd, he now had the 320th Troop Carrier Squadron, the 390th Air Service Group, the 603rd Air Engineering Squadron, and the 1027th Air Matériel Squadron.

Between them they fetched, carried for, and served the 393rd. To police them was the 1395th Military Police Company; supporting them were now some fifty agents from the Manhattan Project. Under Uanna's instructions, they continued to try to get the airmen to talk about their work, but they rarely succeeded. The word was out: if Wendover was bad, Alaska was worse.

But that did not solve the problems associated with the daily management of some twelve hundred servicemen. There was an outbreak of venereal disease. The security men were concerned that a number of men had shacked up with local married women whose husbands were away in the service. There was a renewed spate of fistfights and drunken brawls in Salt Lake City involving base personnel.

On one memorable night in the city's Chi Chi Club, a tipsy Captain Eatherly knocked out an infantry major who had ordered him to leave. Eatherly escaped through the club's back door as MPs arrived at the front.

This time Eatherly avoided arrest. But he was being regularly summoned to Tibbets's office to explain his misdemeanors. There was a wad of speeding tickets he had collected. Tibbets made him pay. Another incident concerned liquor permits. In Utah a state permit was needed to buy liquor. The permits were good for a bottle a week. Police found Eatherly with fifteen permits. Tibbets blasted his pilot and squared the law.

Eatherly continued to spend many of his nights shooting dice at a hundred dollars a throw at the State Line Hotel in Wendover. Sometimes he lost—and won back —his month's salary in a few hours. Security agents reported his gambling to Uanna, who complained to Tibbets, "The guy's a psycho."

Tibbets said, "Maybe. But he's a hell of a pilot. That is all that matters."

Eatherly had demonstrated his flying skill strikingly in mid-November. While he was making a final approach to the field, one of the activating switches in his B-29 went into reverse, a serious mechanical failure. The B-29 began to roll "until it was standing straight up on a wing tip." Eatherly calmly righted the plane and made a perfect landing.

That night, he lost a sizable sum in a poker game. Eatherly shrugged aside such losses, hinting of a huge ranch back in Texas whose income could meet any of his debts. He claimed he had left the ranch at seventeen to become a pilot, and that he later fought the Japanese in the Pacific. He told the stories well.

Nobody suspected they were pipe dreams, the first signs of the instability which would eventually have Claude Eatherly committed to mental hospitals. His fellow fliers recognized only that he seemed to have a yearning to be famous.

• 13 •

Second Lieutenant Tatsuo Yokoyama had allowed a full hour for the walk from his gun battery on Mount Futaba to Hiroshima Castle. There he was due to attend the monthly review of the city's defenses. He would not be expected to speak, merely to listen as the local commanders discussed the situation. He doubted if any of them even knew his name. That did not upset him; it would be enough if—like last month—the minutes of the meeting were to note again "the alertness of the Mount Futaba battery during practice."

The days were over when he would arrive at the meeting in a motor-pool car shared with other junior officers. Only the most senior officers were now entitled to use precious gasoline, and then strictly on military business.

Yokoyama did not mind the walk. It was his way of

keeping in touch with the changing situation in the city.

The tangle of black-lettered signs directing military traffic to the port were now faded. It was almost three years to the day since the commander in chief of the Japanese fleet, Admiral Isoroku Yamamoto, had boarded his flagship, anchored in Hiroshima Bay along with other Japanese battleships, to hear the first radioed reports from his forces attacking Pearl Harbor and British Malaya. A few days later, he was given the news of the sinking off Singapore of the *Prince of Wales* and the *Repulse*. But now the revered Yamamoto was dead, killed in 1943 when the plane in which he was traveling was shot down by American fighters, and Hiroshima Harbor contained not one battleship.

Nor were there truckloads of troops winding their way through the streets of Hiroshima to the *gaisenkan*, the "Hall of Triumphant Return." Almost every soldier fighting in the Pacific had embarked through Hiroshima's *gaisenkan;* now it was empty, waiting for the triumphant return of the troops.

Three years ago, the jetties had been lined with thousands of civilians chanting exhortations to those departing troops; now the only civilians in the area who were not directly employed by the port authority were those tending the vegetable patches that sprouted amidst the cranes and sheds.

Everywhere in the city there were slogans urging people to grow more vegetables, even to cultivate weeds. There were also posted warnings of severe penalties for black-marketeering, profiteering, and spreading irresponsible rumors.

Hiroshima's narrow streets had undergone changes in this past year. There were fewer trucks, and no taxis; apart from streetcars, bicycling or walking was the only way to get around.

Cafés offered a tasteless green tea, often served lukewarm because of increasing fuel shortages. Coke balls for the hibachi stoves were regularly dampened in water to make them burn longer. Some restaurateurs had devised a method of balling up pages of the city's newspaper, the *Chugoku Shimbun,* dipping the wads in water, and burning them with the coke. Four wadded pages were sufficient to boil a pint of water in ten minutes.

There were thousands of improvised gardens. Flat roofs were coated with layers of soil to raise beans, carrots, squash, spinach, and Chinese cabbages. Wooden barrels, drums, even worn-out pots and pans were used for growing leeks and radishes.

Neighborhood associations had been formed to handle bulk rations, issued only to ticket holders; there were also tickets for free medicine and dental treatment. During the first week of December, the associations would distribute to each family in their care a cake of bean curd, one sardine or small horse mackerel, two Chinese cabbages, five carrots, four eggplants, and half a pumpkin. The stalk end of the pumpkin was highly prized. Usually an inch or two long, it would be thinly sliced and stewed as an extra vegetable.

Bramble shoots were peeled and sucked as a starter; sorrel was soaked in brine and used with a rice substitute for a main course. Reeds from the Ota River were cut and parboiled. Grubs found in fruit bushes and fig trees were boiled and served with imitation soy sauce. Beetles and worms of all kinds were roasted on slivers of wood.

Kindergartens and elementary schools were now being closed, their pupils and teachers evacuated to the countryside to avoid air raids and to ease the city's rationing problems.

The women of Hiroshima had never looked so drab. Most of them dressed like the men: both sexes favored a badly cut, high-buttoning jacket and trousers. The government encouraged this apparel.

Only the girls in the red-light district continued to wear kimonos. There were thousands of prostitutes in the rat-infested houses of joy. But the nights were gone when ten thousand soldiers en route to the Pacific would swarm through the area.

For those who remained in Hiroshima, even the task of washing was an unpleasant business. The only soap available was made from rice bran and caustic soda. It created a rash. Tooth powder was now a black-market commodity; the accepted substitute was a vile-tasting salty paste.

Movie houses and theaters were popular. The films and plays were often inferior, but the collective heat generated from several hundred people squashed together was a pleasant experience.

Many people solved the problem of keeping warm by baking flat stones or tiles in their ovens, wrapping them in layers of old newspapers, and placing the bundles next to their skin. As the stones cooled, the newspapers were removed layer by layer. Then, when the heat was finally dissipated, the stones were reheated.

Yokoyama had no doubt: the city was coping. And to anybody challenging him, he would have had a ready answer: Hiroshima was intact.

Yokoyama continued walking toward the castle. From ahead came a loud, concerted shout. Yokoyama broke into a run. Rounding a corner, he saw a house collapse into the street. Instinctively, he looked skyward. There were no airplanes.

Through the dust, he saw a group of youths belonging to the Patriotic Volunteer Corps, boys and girls brought in from the country to work as laborers. The group gathered around the house adjoining the collapsed building. Some of them began to saw through the pillars supporting the house; others attached a stout rope to its ridgepole. One of the boys told Yokoyama they were creating a firebreak in case of air attack.

In many parts of Hiroshima, this demolition work had begun to cut swathes through the city. There had not been such an upheaval since the catastrophic floods of August 6, 1653. On that day in the seventeenth century, hundreds of houses had been ripped from their foundations by nature. Now, enthusiastic youths were achieving what subsequent typhoons had been unable to accomplish.

For Senkichi Awaya, the mayor of Hiroshima, the order to create firebreaks was the hardest he had implemented since taking office in July 1943. If it had been issued by the army, the fifty-one-year-old civil servant would have vigorously challenged the command.

But it had come from the Department of the Interior in Tokyo.

A few days ago, Awaya had telephoned Hiroshima Castle and informed the duty officer of the order. Almost immediately, the regional army headquarters there had issued instructions as to which sections of the city were to be demolished; soldiers would be available to supervise and help with the work.

Throughout the morning of December 6, Mayor Awaya's frequent meetings were punctuated by the crash of falling buildings. Finally, hardly able to hear himself speak, he had stood at his second-floor office window and gazed down the street at the clouds of dust rising near the Aioi Bridge. He wondered whether the bridge itself, the most striking in Hiroshima, might also eventually be demolished on the army's orders.

He was reassured by his chief assistant, the diminutive, immaculately dressed Kazumasa Maruyama. Without the bridges, the army's movements within the city would be drastically curtailed; in an emergency it would be necessary to be able to move troops quickly.

Together the two men watched the destruction. Outside the Town Hall, householders seeking compensation and new accommodations were already forming a line. Maruyama reminded the mayor how limited was the help the city could offer. "We can give them only a few yen."

"Just three years—now this. And all because of the army."

For Mayor Awaya to have uttered such words in public would have invited imprisonment, even execution. But in the comfortably furnished mayor's parlor, he and Maruyama now talked openly about such matters. In the sixteen months they had worked together, each man had revealed himself to the other as a devout pacifist and fierce antimilitarist.

Vastly different in their backgrounds—Awaya was from upper-middle-class stock, while Maruyama was proudly working-class—the men were bound by strong personal ties.

Awaya had acted as go-between for Maruyama during his assistant's delicate negotiations with his future wife's parents. As a devout Christian, one of many in Hiroshima, Mayor Awaya had found it difficult to feel his way through the complicated byplay of such discussions, an integral part of Japanese marriage. But the mayor had completed the marriage contract to everyone's satisfaction.

Awaya wished his wife and the four children still at home in Tokyo could be with him; when he had moved to Hiroshima, they had remained behind so that the children's education would not be disturbed.

Awaya was one of the most popular mayors the city had known: free from any taint of corruption, easily accessible, and energetic in handling cases of civil injustice. But he knew he was under suspicion because he was a Christian, and that attempts had been made to subvert his staff. Only here, in his office, with Maruyama, could he dare to express himself freely.

This morning, a familiar topic was again raised, what Awaya called the "terrible decline in our city which can be traced to the folly of the militarists in *showa* fifteen," a reference to the events of 1941.

In just twenty days' time, December 28, the Hirohito reign of *showa* would enter its nineteenth year. Both men agreed that *showa* was now an ironically inept name. (The word means "enlightened peace.")

Awaya raised a theme he increasingly brooded over. "We may have to pay dearly for the mistakes that have been made."

Both men knew how inadequately prepared the city

was for an air raid. There were insufficient shelters; the water pressure to the fire hydrants was low; the few evacuation routes out of the city could easily become clogged.

Nor did Awaya feel the fire lanes would provide adequate protection. "Whole areas within the lanes could simply burn themselves out. The lanes can hope only to stop the city being destroyed all at once."

There was one aspect, however, that Awaya believed they should be grateful for. "The rivers dividing our city provide excellent natural firebreaks. And if necessary, the citizens could take refuge in those rivers from the heat generated by fires."

Four hundred years old, built on a mound surrounded by a moat, Hiroshima Castle was the centerpiece of a vast military complex. Within its keep were the divisional and regional army headquarters, along with some forty thousand men. The area also contained an infantry training school, a hospital, and ammunition and supply depots. Under the castle was the civilian defense headquarters, the unit responsible for alerting the city to air attack, and the central fire control for the antiaircraft batteries.

The perimeter of this multipurpose installation was adjoined by dozens of small factories producing armaments. The larger factories were located on the banks of the rivers.

Yokoyama's visits to the castle provided him with visible reaffirmation of the power of the army; there were always rows of fieldpieces and armored vehicles on display. Within the grounds that the army had garrisoned for nearly a hundred years, the mood was optimistic. Officers and men talked only of great victories to come. Nobody drew attention to shell casings made from inferior metals, or the near-empty fuel tanks of the half-tracks and armored cars.

The mood of senior officers at the defense review meeting was buoyant. One followed another to expound a similar theme. Hiroshima, like all other Japanese cities, was ready to meet the enemy. There was loud agreement with the words of the elderly officer who spoke last. "Let the American bombers come—and soon. They will fall from the skies under our guns!"

His eyes swept the room, lighting on the coterie of young antiaircraft officers that included Yokoyama. "The honor will fall to you to strike the first blows. The enemy is arrogant. He believes he can enter our skies with safety, to bomb our women and children. He will be shown otherwise. Do not fail. We will repeat the success of Pearl Harbor."

• 14 •

In Tokyo, Major General Arisue was showing signs of strain; his face was a shade grayer, the pouches under his eyes darker. He was suffering from lack of sleep, proper meals, and fresh air. These past two months had made severe inroads into his considerable stamina.

His Lisbon contact was unable to provide further details about the mysterious American war project. And without hard information, Arisue could not brief his agent in Brazil, who was packed and ready to slip into the United States.

Increasingly, his department was under pressure from the high command. Data were urgently requested on the B-29s that had started to raid Tokyo and other cities. The arrival of the huge bombers had astonished the Japanese. They had never seen aircraft so big, so fast, so well armed. Information was requested about their bases. Arisue had pinpointed the Marianas, and cursed the lack of spies he had on the islands. He was unable to answer specific questions on the number of American bomber squadrons based there, the supply backup they possessed, the sort of intelligence which would help produce an accurate profile of American strength.

His special listening posts were monitoring nothing of importance in the brief air-to-air conversations between enemy pilots over Japan; ground defenses had been largely unsuccessful in shooting down B-29s. Arisue's tough interrogator, Lieutenant Colonel Oya, was finding it difficult to get even the few American airmen who had been captured to talk.

The latest, Colonel Brian Brugge, Oya had seen soon after he was shot down nine days before, on December 3. Brugge was an important catch; he was deputy chief of staff of the Seventy-third Bomb Wing, based on Saipan.

According to Oya, the stubborn West Pointer refused to cooperate. "We interrogated him thoroughly. He kept a tight lip. He wouldn't crack. Later, he began to suffer from malnutrition. He disliked Japanese food. He died."

Arisue was unhappy that his enthusiastic interrogator had not been able to extract any useful information from this senior American officer. Then, at his lowest ebb, knowing his reputation was being seriously challenged in certain quarters, Arisue received a further piece of unsettling news.

For some days he had been sure that his archrival, naval intelligence, was in contact with a Swedish banker, Per Jacobsson, in Bern, Switzerland. He knew that the purpose of this move was to make contact through Jacobsson with the Americans, leading, hopefully, to a negotiated peace.

In Japanese eyes, there was a fundamental difference between a negotiated peace and surrender. Even so, Arisue's first reaction had been to expose the plotters. Caution stayed him. They undoubtedly included some of the highest-ranking naval officers. If he failed to prove a case against them, he would be in serious trouble. However, he could not help but wonder. Supposing Japan could not win the war? Supposing a negotiated peace was the only answer?

Even two months ago, such thoughts would have been unthinkable for Arisue. But throughout this day they gnawed at him. He sent for situation reports; he questioned staff officers; he studied projections of enemy intentions. Whichever way he turned, the one inescapable truth faced him: the war was going badly. Japan, in his later words, "was short of everything except courage."

By evening, he had come to the conclusion that there was no way Japan could achieve victory Equally, he knew that so long as the country kept fighting, it was not defeated.

With these thoughts in mind, without consulting anyone. General Arisue decided he would prepare the groundwork for a negotiated peace He knew that if he were discovered he would be branded a traitor and executed But by nightfall he was making hi first moves to establish a link in Bern with Allen Dulle European director of the Office of Strategic Services, the American intelligence agency.

• 15 •

Seated at a writing desk in his suite in the Carlton Hotel. a few convenient blocks away from the White House financier Alexander Sachs had little time to study the newspapers or listen to the radio programs marking the third anniversary of Pearl Harbor.

Sachs, the man who had been instrumental in alerting President Roosevelt to the possibility of atomic weapons. was about to reenter the scene.

Yet. for Sachs and millions of Americans December 7 was a day when the media were particularly compelling. Commentators continued to return to a single theme in recalling Pearl Harbor: the country could neither forgive nor forget Japan's treachery; the "Day of Infamy" would have to be avenged.

Vastly better equipped on land sea and in the air, American forces were about to pull a drawstring around the enemy. The Japanese air force was spent; if the kamikaze planes still struck terror in those who were facing them in increasing numbers, newspapers played down the suicide planes as a passing phenomenon, a last, reckless throw by a desperate enemy.

Tokyo Rose's taunt of "Come and get us" was now receiving a confident rejoinder on Stateside radio stations. "We're coming, Rose, we're coming!"

Nobody doubted that America's youth was paying a high price for the long journey to Rose's Tokyo lair. An average of five thousand Americans were dying each week in the relentless push across the Pacific. But as the newspapers pointed out, the numbers were grimmer for the enemy. The decisive aircraft carrier engagement off Guam had become known as the "Great Marianas Turkey Shoot," while the loss of the islands had cost the Japanese fifty thousand dead.

The mood this morning throughout America was uncompromising. The enemy, in the words of one commentator, "must be hit with everything we've got."

Alexander Sachs knew that "everything we've got" was likely soon to include an atomic bomb. Five years after first calling on Roosevelt to authorize its construction, Sachs now wanted the president to put a curb on when and how the bomb would be used.

The financier had been successfully lobbied by the group of scientists beginning to have second thoughts about the weapon. Among them were Albert Einstein and Leo Szilard, who had been so vocal in 1939 about the need for America to equip itself with an atomic arsenal. They now argued that the world situation had changed. The Nazi capability to produce atomic bombs could be discounted. They believed Japan could be beaten by conventional weapons. Any brief military advantage that nuclear bombs would bring America could be outweighed by political and psychological losses. The damage to American prestige, argued Szilard, could be immense if the United States were the first to drop the bomb. If America did so, then Einstein foresaw a worldwide atomic armaments race.

Roosevelt had rejected these arguments. Perhaps he

felt the scientists underestimated the enemy's ability to keep fighting under almost any circumstances.

Sachs had agonized for days over his draft for a startling proposal. But now, in his neat handwriting, he had outlined the conditions he believed Roosevelt should insist upon before ordering the bomb to be dropped.

Following a successful test there should be arranged:

a) A rehearsal demonstration before a body including internationally recognized scientists from all Allied countries and, in addition, neutral countries, supplemented by representatives of the major faiths;

b) That a report on the nature and the portent of the atomic weapon be prepared by the scientists and other representative figures;

c) That thereafter a warning be issued by the United States and its allies in the Project to our major enemies in the war, Germany and Japan, that atomic bombing would be applied to a selected area within a designated time limit for the evacuation of human and animal life;

d) In the wake of such realization of the efficacy of atomic bombing an ultimatum demand for immediate surrender by the enemies be issued, in the certainty that failure to comply would subject their countries and people to atomic annihilation.

Sachs spent over an hour alone with the president. No record was made of their conversation.

A few months later, when Roosevelt was dead, Sachs would claim that the president had accepted his proposals. His implication was clear: those in favor of using the bomb had later persuaded the president to change his mind. It is more likely that Roosevelt, a skilled exponent of the tactic, had led Sachs to believe he had heard what he wanted to hear.

Groves thought Sachs's suggestion that Hitler and

the Japanese militarists could be swayed by a memo about an explosion in some distant place naive in the extreme. Further, the financier's proposal totally removed the surprise element that Groves believed essential. The project chief had always maintained that, forewarned, the enemy would mount an effective counterattack, destroying the plane carrying the atomic bomb either in aerial combat or by ground fire.

However, on December 7, scientists working on the Manhattan Project were satisfied that the Japanese were not far enough advanced in theoretical physics or technology to manufacture an atomic bomb. Therefore, some argued, it would be "unthinkable" to use the weapon against Japan.

The battle lines had been drawn. Even now, the more radical among the scientists were planning fresh strategies to halt the project.

• 16 •

On December 17, the five squadrons at Wendover became formally unified under Tibbets as the 509th Composite Group, attached to the 315th Bombardment Wing of the Second Air Force. The group's strength was 225 officers and 1,542 enlisted men.

Ferebee and van Kirk joined the 509th's headquarters staff as group bombardier and group navigator. They rarely flew now, spending their time preparing and analyzing training programs. When they did fly, they usually went with Lewis, taking the place of his regular bombardier and navigator.

Lewis's crew continued to return one of the best flying records. Their main competition came from Eatherly's crew and crew No. 15, commanded by the effervescent Major Charles Sweeney.

Beser liked to fly with Sweeney "because of the way he kidded everyone along." He was forming lasting judgments on many of the fliers, for "the day was coming when I'd have to trust my life to them."

The radar officer had warmed toward Tibbets; he saw, correctly, a shy man behind the aloof commander. He had become aware that Tibbets had a marriage problem, and decided that Tibbets was "only truly happy in the air, but there he was magnificent."

Beser thought Lewis, on the ground, sometimes acted "like Peck's bad boy; in the air he occasionally got overexcited."

Van Kirk and Ferebee were tagged by Beser as "professionals who never have any problems."

This December morning, at thirty thousand feet over the Salton Sea bombing range, Tibbets and Ferebee were trying to solve a problem that had worried them for a week.

The bombardier had failed to drop dummy practice bombs consistently into the aiming circle, now reduced to three hundred feet. There seemed no reason why some bombs fell into the circle while others landed outside it.

Tibbets was concerned, and he reminded Ferebee why precision was so important. "Tom, when the time comes, we have to be as near on target as we can get. Radar is out because it's still too uncertain. So it's got to be visual. You've got to be able to see the target and then hit it on the nose. And that means we've got to drop within that circle every time."

Tibbets had come on the practice flight to see why the aim was erratic. The weather was perfect: clear skies, easily computed wind drift. With Lewis holding the B-29 steady on the run up to the aiming point, Tibbets watched Ferebee crouching over the Norden bombsight.

The sight had been totally stripped and reassembled, a mechanically perfect instrument.

Ferebee called out that he had the AP in his cross hairs. He lifted himself a few inches off his seat to bring his face closer over the viewfinder. Below, through the optical sight, he could see the bombing circle clearly. Satisfied, he eased himself back on his seat, his head still glued to the viewfinder.

"Bomb away."

Lewis put the aircraft into the mandatory 155-degree turn. By the time ground control reported on the drop, the B-29 was nearly eight miles away.

The bomb had fallen outside the circle.

Tibbets ordered Lewis to fly back toward the AP. He told Ferebee to repeat his actions. He watched intently as the bombardier began to line up the circle in his sights. At the last moment, he rose off his buttocks again.

Tibbets shouted, "That's it!"

He had solved the problem. At the crucial moment, Ferebee, like any other bombardier, lifted himself off his seat to bring his eyes to the sight. The movement was no more than an inch or two. But it was enough. Each time he lowered his eyes to the sight, his head was at a slightly different angle against the viewfinder. If he had been bombing from a few thousand feet, this small movement would have had little effect. But from thirty thousand feet, nearly six miles up, with his head at a slightly different angle each time, it meant the error could ultimately work out to be several hundred feet by the time the bomb hit the ground.

Within hours, Tibbets had ground crews construct and fit a padded headrest to the bombsight. Using it, Ferebee's head was forced into exactly the same position each time. From then on, he bombed with consistent accuracy.

· 17 ·

In the cold dawn light, mess officer Charles Perry surveyed his resources: rows of plump farm turkeys and cured hams, mounds of vegetables, trays of mince pies, and, dominating the kitchen tables, scores of huge

Christmas puddings. Silverplate had ensured that this first Christmas of the fledgling 509th would be a memorable one.

The elements had also contributed to the festive mood. Overnight, heavy snow had fallen, covering the ground inches high. At the main gate, shivering MPs fashioned a couple of snowmen, complete with hats and tree branches for carbines.

Beyond the gate, in their home, the Tibbets family were unwrapping their Christmas presents. Tibbets had given Lucie a gift he had purchased at the last moment in the base commissary. He was always at a loss about what to buy his vivacious wife; it was one of the many small reasons that their marriage was foundering. Lucie felt that her husband was unromantic; a warmhearted Southern belle from Georgia, she found the practical and pragmatic Tibbets often cool and distant. She knew there was no other woman in his life, but she could not understand why he seemed to place his work ahead of herself and the children. Once she had complained to Beser, who often used to baby-sit for the Tibbetses, that "Paul never seems to have time to sit down and talk or play with the children. And when he does talk, it's only about work."

Tibbets had tried to explain that he was by nature "a loner"; he had not added what many of his officers knew: that he really was happy only when he was flying.

His preoccupation with work carried over to his choice of Christmas presents for his small sons. Paul, Jr., and baby Gene both received models of B-17s. There had been a run on the toy bombers at the PX.

This morning the children found several B-17s in their stockings—presents from Lewis, van Kirk, Ferebee, and Beser.

Breakfast over, the Tibbets family went to the morning service at the base church.

Chaplain William Downey greeted his commander warmly. He could not remember when Tibbets had last attended church. Once, shortly after he had arrived on the base, Tibbets had told him that "when I pray I go directly to God without a middleman."

Downey had not been offended; he knew many men like that. He respected their views. And in doing so, the chaplain had earned respect for himself. Articulate and refreshingly earthy, Captain Downey was the ideal spiritual adviser for the high-living 509th. He wasn't shocked by their escapades. Though he wasn't much older than many of the men he cared for, he somehow gave the impression of being a tolerant, worldly-wise man, ready to have a drink, crack a joke, be a "regular guy," without ever losing his dignity.

Even Beser, normally critical of all organized religion, thought Downey was a "helluva sky pilot. If he hadn't been a Lutheran, he would have been a fine rabbi."

By noon on Christmas, the officers' club was full of officers and their wives.

Paul and Lucie Tibbets held gracious court; for the moment, their private tensions and troubles were put aside. Tibbets reminisced with Ferebee and van Kirk about Europe, and wondered how London was shaping up to the "Bob Hopes"—the nickname of the flying bombs raining down on the British capital—"You bob out of the way and hope they miss you."

Before long, a number of the officers were happily crocked and gathered around the club radio singing carols along with Bing Crosby in Hollywood.

The singing was followed by a newscast which brought them sharply back to reality. American troops in Europe were trying desperately to repel a surprise German counterattack that was to become the overture to the Battle of the Bulge. German troops in GI uniforms were creating confusion in the American lines. The news from the Pacific was encouraging: the Japanese homeland was beginning to feel the weight of American bombs.

Lucie Tibbets whispered the hope of any wife. "Honey, maybe you won't have to go after all."

• 18 •

The end of the year was hectic for Groves. His days stretched well beyond their regular fifteen hours; the box of candy he kept in his office safe with the atom secrets needed frequent replenishing. Steadily munching his way through chocolates, Groves issued orders that would eventually change warfare.

He sent for Tibbets on December 28. From a beginning of wariness on both sides, their relationship had passed through several phases to the present state of acceptance by Groves of Tibbets. The project chief found the flier could be as flinty as he was; he learned not to tamper with Tibbets's judgments on flying matters.

The top-secret notes of their conversation show how far he now trusted the 509th's commander.

Tibbets gave June 15, 1945, as the date he would be ready to deliver an atomic strike.

Groves accepted this without demur; the question was then raised "as to what the weather conditions would be over Tokyo between June 15th and 15 July."

It was the first time the Japanese capital had been openly spoken of as a target for atomic attack.

But there might be a weather problem. The notes recorded that "rain could be expected rather frequently [over Tokyo] up to August 15 [1945]. It is not desirable that missions be made in rain."

Apart from weather considerations, Groves set out the governing factors in target selection:

The targets chosen should be places the bombing of which would most adversely affect the will of the Japanese people to continue the war. Beyond that, they should be military in nature, consisting either of important headquarters or troop concentrations, or centers of production of military equipment and supplies. To enable us to assess accurately the effects of the bomb, the targets should not have been previously damaged by air attacks. It is also desirable that the first target be of such size that the damage would be confined within it, so that we could more definitely determine the power of the bomb.

Groves doubted if Tokyo would meet all these requirements. The likelihood was that the city would be heavily bombed in the coming months with conventional weapons.

Personally, he favored Kyoto as a target. Kyoto was the ancient capital of Japan, a "historical city and one that was of great religious significance to the Japanese." With an estimated population of a million, Kyoto, Groves reasoned, "like any city of that size in Japan must be involved in a tremendous amount of war work." Therefore, it would be a legitimate target.

Further, he found Kyoto was "large enough to ensure that the damage from the bomb would run out within the city, which would give us a firm understanding of its destructive power."

At a meeting in Oppenheimer's office at Los Alamos on December 19, Groves had decided the gun-type firing mechanism of the uranium bomb was so reliable it need not be tested before it was used on the enemy. However, the more complicated mechanism in the plutonium bomb would need proving. That was to be done at the Alamogordo firing range in the New Mexico desert on a date still to be decided.

Alone in his office on December 30, Groves decided to take a momentous step. He wrote a memo to General George C. Marshall, chief of staff.

It is now reasonably certain that our operations plans should be based on the gun-type bomb, which, it is estimated, will produce the equivalent of a ten thousand ton TNT explosion. The first bomb, without previous full scale test, which we do not believe will be necessary, should be ready about 1 August, 1945.

Groves had committed the Manhattan Project to a date.

• 19 •

A sailor carefully erased the legend *I.58* from the conning tower of the submarine and painted the flag of the *kikusui* immediately above the Rising Sun emblem. The *kikusui* was the battle standard of the ancient warrior Masashige, who had fought against overwhelming odds, knowing he had no chance to survive.

With the *kikusui* flag gleaming wetly in the winter sunlight, Commander Hashimoto completed the transformation of his submarine by ordering a seaman to raise the boat's new war banner, Masashige's *hiriho kenten,* meaning "God's will."

Banner and flag signified that the submarine was now a human torpedo carrier, the latest weapon devised by the Imperial Japanese Navy. The human torpedoes, or *kaitens,* were the underwater counterpart of the kamikaze.

Since January 1943 at the top-secret Base P, an island in Hiroshima Bay just south of Kure, the navy had been experimenting with the use of human torpedoes, projectiles which could be launched from a mother craft and steered by volunteers toward an enemy ship. The navy hoped these weapons would offset the increasing losses they were experiencing, and help halt the American advance on Japan.

Hashimoto's submarine had been chosen to be one of the flag carriers for Operation *Kaiten.* To accommodate the weapons, workmen had removed the housing for the reconnaissance plane the submarine sometimes carried, its catapult, and its deck gun. That made room on the boat's deck for six *kaitens.*

The torpedoes, shaped like miniature submarines and weighing eight tons each, had explosive warheads. They had a range of thirty miles and a top speed of twenty knots. They were not recoverable. Once a *kaiten* pilot squirmed through a narrow tunnel from the parent submarine into his torpedo and was cast off, there was no returning. Either he exploded against his target or he was blown up by the enemy before reaching it.

It took several hours to winch the *kaitens* onto the submarine's deck, where they were shackled securely.

Late in the morning, the pilots for these craft came aboard and were greeted by Hashimoto. He was struck by the youthfulness of the *kaiten* crewmen; there was also an air of fanaticism about them that chilled him. He, too, believed in the emperor and the traditional concept of dying. But these youths were intoxicated with their patriotism; they told him proudly how they had literally fought for the privilege of making this *kaiten* mission, and how they longed for death. *Kaiten* means "the turn toward Heaven."

As the moment of departure approached, the pilots sat astride their craft, white towels wrapped around their heads and brandishing their ceremonial swords. To Hashimoto, it seemed they were "trying hard to be strong men."

Fenders and berthing wires were detached from the submarine's long, narrow casing. Water on the starboard quarter began to boil. Foam surged around the boat as the ballast tanks were blown to full buoyancy. The freeboard began to increase.

Farewell shouts came from the groups of dockyard workers on the wharf. The pilots raised their swords higher.

Hashimoto watched approvingly as the last ropes were released by the shore crew and hauled in by the seamen on the deck. Weeks of hard practice had paid off; the men moved today with dexterity and skill.

The electric motors silently drew the submarine from the shore, her bow now pointing away from Hiroshima toward the sea. A flotilla of motorboats accompanied the submarine, their occupants chanting in unison the names of the pilots. The submarine increased speed, the escorts fell away, the chanting faded. The boat trembled as the diesel motors started their rhythmic pounding.

In his log, Hashimoto noted on December 29: "Passed through Bungo Channel and turned south, proceeding on surface. Through evening haze took farewell look at the homeland."

Two and a half weeks later, the cry rang out: "Smoke on the port beam!"

The lookout's shout brought the men on the conning-tower bridge scrambling down the ladder into the control room.

"Dive! Dive! Dive!"

Moments after Commander Hashimoto's order, the submarine was sealed, the main vents opened, and the needle of the depth gauge turned steadily as the boat's bow tilted toward the seabed.

Regularly, ever since reaching the area of the Marianas two weeks earlier, Hashimoto had been dodging antisubmarine aircraft patrols flying from Guam. Now, two hundred feet below the waves, undisturbed by the Pacific swell, he and his crew listened for the throb of ships' propellers.

Somewhere above them, approaching, were two enemy ships, probably destroyers.

Hashimoto wondered whether their presence was connected with the daring attack he had launched three days ago. Then, under cover of darkness, he had surfaced eleven miles off Guam and fired four of his human torpedoes against the mass of shipping in Apra Harbor.

It was *I.58*'s first strike and Hashimoto's first use of *kaitens*. Just before entering his suicide craft, one of the *kaiten* pilots had pressed into the captain's hands a farewell note Hashimoto would treasure all his life.

Great Japan is the Land of the Gods. The Land of the Gods is eternal and cannot be destroyed. Hereafter, no matter, there will be thousands and tens of thousands of boys, and we now offer ourselves as a sacrifice for our country. Let us get away from the petty affairs of this earthly and mundane life to the land where righteousness reigns supreme and eternal.

With the four human torpedoes launched, Hashimoto had submerged to periscope depth. As daylight came, he saw great clouds of smoke rising from the harbor. He stole away to safer waters. Later, he had led the crew in prayer for the souls of the four warriors.

Now, the presence of the subchasers above them reminded the crew that they, too, could be swiftly dispatched to join their dead companions.

Hashimoto ordered the submarine rigged for silent running so that nothing could give away their presence. Orders were relayed in sign language or in whispers; nobody moved unnecessarily. All equipment not essential to survival underwater was switched off.

The crew strained their ears for the sound of propellers. It came closer: constant, on course, the high-pitched note of steel blades turning steadily through water. The ships were moving slowly, and it sounded as if each blade was striking the water separately. The screws passed overhead and began to fade.

A look of relief crossed the faces of the men around Hashimoto.

He shook his head, warning.

The sound increased again. Hashimoto drew a circle with his finger in the air: the ships were circling. He guessed that the hunters were hoping their echo sounders could get a fix and give cross bearings. It would be easy then to calculate the setting for their depth charges.

The propeller noise grew fainter, almost disappeared, then returned as a new circle began.

Somebody scuffed the deck plates with his boots. Hashimoto glared fiercely.

The propellers passed overhead, faded—and this time did not return. The ships had either given up the search or extended it elsewhere.

For two more hours, the submarine remained silent in its position. Then Hashimoto ordered it to resume course for Kure.

There it would arrive safely on January 20, having passed on the way other *kaiten*-carrying submarines heading for the waters around Guam.

• 20 •

Tibbets knew he was facing a clear choice. He could either have Lewis court-martialed—or hope the pilot had learned a lasting lesson. Even now, days later, the details of Lewis's adventure made Tibbets shudder.

On December 17, the day Tibbets had solved Ferebee's problem with the bombsight, Lewis had "illegally borrowed" a C-45 twin-engine transport plane. With no copilot or proper maps, and a faulty radio, he had set off on a twenty-five-hundred-mile flight to New York because he "wanted to be home for Christmas." His traveling companion was the 509th's senior flight engineer, hitching a ride to his wedding. Over Columbus, Ohio, the plane's radio, altimeter, and compass had all failed within minutes of each other. Lewis had nosed the transport groundward, "trying to navigate by street lights." A blizzard had blocked out that hope. For two hours in zero visibility, Lewis had searched for Newark Airport, New Jersey. He had eventually landed there with practically no fuel left in his tank.

Christmas over, Lewis had met the new bride and groom at Newark. He had lent the girl his flying jacket and cap as a disguise and ignored the regulations forbidding civilians to fly in military aircraft. Over Buffalo, another snowstorm had forced Lewis to land. Finally, on December 29, he and the newly married couple had landed at Wendover.

Tibbets was staggered that Lewis did not realize he "had broken every rule in the book." The nearest Lewis came to contrition was a sheepish "Gee, I wouldn't want to do that flight again!"

Eight days later, the time had come for Tibbets to make a decision about Lewis. He had taken soundings from a number of sources. The consensus was that Lewis was "a goddam fool, but also a goddam fine pilot."

Tibbets admitted that only an exceptional flier could have flown the trip Lewis did: it had required icy nerves and courage to handle the crippled transport in such atrocious conditions.

He decided not to court-martial Lewis, but "any past favors I owed him were repaid. He had used my name to get that plane. From now on, I was going to treat him like a flunky; he would do exactly what I wanted, when I wanted—or God help him."

This meant that Lewis would draw many of the disagreeable assignments: early-morning flights, night duties, and weekend work. Lewis did not mind. He thought it "a tribute. Paul was giving me all the stuff that nobody else would tackle."

Having made his decision about Lewis, Tibbets now resolved another matter that could not be further delayed: which men he would choose to send to Cuba for "special training."

For days, rumors about the long-awaited trip had prevailed. In subzero Wendover, the vision of the Caribbean was almost unbearable. Plane commanders spent hours hanging around headquarters trying to pick up a whisper; gamblers like Eatherly had offered to make book on the departure date, but there were no takers; even overseas veterans like Classen began to reminisce about tropical life. Amid all the speculation, they did discover one fact: in two days' time, Tibbets would be promoted to full colonel. But that did not make their commander more forthcoming.

Rumors reached fever pitch when the fliers learned that Tibbets was spending this morning studying the flying reports on all fifteen bomber crews. In Cuba, those chosen would carry out long-distance navigational training exercises over water at night, and continue their high-level bombing practice.

Tibbets summoned the group's mess officer, Lieutenant Charles Perry. His orders from Tibbets were clear: arrange a round-the-clock chow line serving the best food in Cuba.

Beser was told he was going. He saw one drawback to the trip: his bodyguard would be traveling with him. He began to lay plans to shake off the man in Havana.

Finally, ten plane commanders were informed they would be flying out later in the day. The Cuba-bound echelon was assembled for a pep talk from Tibbets. "The same rules apply in Havana as here. Don't ask questions. Don't answer questions. Do your job. The final selection for a historic mission could be made from you men."

Before leaving, Eatherly was consulted on the legends about hot-blooded Latin ladies. He said they were all true. The flight surgeon was reported to have packed extra cartons of condoms; the studs in the group boasted they would use them up on their very first night in Havana.

At noon on January 6, Eatherly took off. Nine other B-29s followed him into the air on the long journey south. Late in the afternoon, they landed at Batista Field, twelve miles from Havana.

Tibbets flew down in a transport, bringing Ferebee, van Kirk, and a small headquarters staff. Another transport brought a detachment of MPs, Uanna, and his agents.

All outsiders were barred from the 509th's compound, but many got close enough to peer inquisitively at the planes. The crews reveled in the curiosity they attracted. Eatherly solemnly told a bystander that the

509th was there to protect the island against an expected coup by "unfriendly powers" planning to seize the lucrative gambling concessions. Eatherly was in high spirits. For most of the flight, he had played cards with some of his crew and had won several hundred dollars.

The fliers and ground crew all tried hard to impress the other American servicemen on the base that they were no ordinary outfit. They were coming to think of themselves as special, a feeling that Tibbets had encouraged; the foundation was being laid of the spirit which was to sustain them in the trying time ahead.

Tibbets astonished everybody by refusing even a cup of coffee until every man had been assigned quarters and been fed by Perry's cooks. Only then did Tibbets accept a meal tray.

He had little appetite. He had learned this evening that General Curtis LeMay was on his way to Guam.

A year earlier, Tibbets, Lewis, and Sweeney had taken turns teaching LeMay how to pilot a B-29. LeMay was a difficult pupil, a flying general who found it hard to accept that because an aircraft was 99 feet long, 29 feet 9 inches high, with a wingspan of 141, feet, it was different from any other bomber he had flown. But he finally learned to listen, respect, and obey his instructors. At the end of the course, LeMay had predicted, "We can win the war with this plane."

Now he was going to Guam intending to do just that. If LeMay succeeded, Tibbets knew he would not be needed to drop an atomic bomb.

• 21 •

General Curtis LeMay spent his first three days on Guam trying to find the answer to a paradox in his new charge, the Twenty-first Bomber Command of the Twentieth Air Force.

Why was the B-29—the world's most superior bomber, available for the first time in sufficient numbers to strike terror into the enemy—not realizing its potential?

Here in the Marianas everybody had a different answer. The training manuals said the B-29s could operate at 38,000 feet and cruise at 350 miles an hour for 3,500 miles.

The manuals were wrong.

In the Pacific, the bombers showed signs of severe strain in prolonged flights at over thirty thousand feet. Bombers frequently failed to complete missions because of mechanical difficulties.

Then there was the weather. It was impossible for the air force meteorologists to provide accurate forecasts for the thirteen hundred miles of sky between the Marianas and Japan. Fierce jet streams crisscrossed the void, buffeting the bombers and using up their precious fuel. Over Japan, the targets might be visible one minute, then obscured the next as high winds drove in heavy clouds. Bombs dropped from thirty thousand feet were blown far from their aiming points, and results using even the latest radar equipment were proving unsatisfactory. Eleven targets selected for bombing in January remained almost undamaged. Intelligence monitoring of Japan Radio showed that morale was high and war work so far virtually unimpaired by the air attacks.

LeMay accepted the complaints about the weather, engine strain, and other malfunctions. But solving them would not answer the basic problem. The tactics being used were the ones he had developed in Europe to pierce the German defenses. Later his high-flying methods were used by B-29s operating out of China, raiding Japan from airfields around Chengtu.

China had been a costly and hazardous venture, but LeMay had made contact with a fanatical guerrilla leader. In return for medical supplies and materials, LeMay had persuaded him to radio regular weather forecasts from that area of northern China where the partisans were fighting the Japanese. The reports were invaluable for LeMay's pilots. They often drank a toast to this man.

His name was Mao Tse-tung.

LeMay had already contacted Mao fom the Marianas and arranged for him to radio weather reports to Guam. The man who would soon become the leader of one of the most powerful nations on earth was, on this late January day, proud and willing to act as a barometer for the American general he persisted in calling "Culltse Lee May."

But Mao's weather reports were only a partial answer to LeMay's problem with the B-29s, and the solution LeMay proposed was revolutionary. If it succeeded, he believed he could break Japan. If it failed, his career would be in ruins.

First, LeMay intended to strip his B-29s of their arsenal of machine guns and cannons. Then he proposed to strike in darkness—having his bombers over their targets between midnight and 4:00 A.M. If necessary, they would bomb by radar, in preparation for which LeMay decided to initiate a series of intensive retraining courses. These would ensure that even the least apt radar operator was brought up to the standard he required.

Most important of all, the bombers would go in at between five thousand and nine thousand feet. LeMay was going to gamble that intelligence was right, that the Japanese had not developed a night fighter or converted their antiaircraft guns to radar control. He hoped that, manually operated, the weapons would react too slowly to his low-level assault.

Removing the guns because of the hoped-for absence of night fighters would also increase each bomber's payload. That, too, was crucial, for LeMay intended the B-29s to carry only incendiaries, and thus put the torch to Japan's vulnerable wooden buildings.

While formulating his plans about the new tactics he

meant to employ, LeMay went on listening, something he was very good at. This very lunch hour on January 20, while listening to a weather officer explaining his problems, LeMay had overheard a naval officer from CINCPAC saying that Admiral Chester Nimitz was raising hell over some flying unit in the States that was trying to get itself shipped to the Marianas.

It sounded an unlikely story to LeMay. The unit was something called a "composite group." And LeMay knew there was no such designation in the air force.

· 22 ·

Groves had decided that it was not yet necessary to inform General Douglas MacArthur about the atomic bomb. He approved of the letter Fleet Admiral King had prepared on January 27 for Admiral Chester Nimitz. It was short and to the point and should end the irritating queries emanating from CINCPAC. Written on King's official stationery, the letter read:

My dear Nimitz:

It is expected that a new weapon will be ready in August of this year for use against Japan by the 20th Air Force.

The Officer, Commander Frederic L. Ashworth, USN, bearing this letter will give you enough details so that you can make the necessary plans for the proper support of the operations. By the personal direction of the President, everything pertaining to this development is covered by the highest order of secrecy, and there should be no disclosure by you beyond one other officer, who must be suitably cautioned.

CHINA

SOUTHERN JAPAN

0   Miles   100   200

SEA   OF   JAPAN

HONSHU ISLAND

Tokyo

Kyoto   Yokohama

Shimonoseki   Hiroshima   Saijo   Kobe   Nagoya

Kokura   Kure   Osaka

Fukuoka

Nagasaki   SHIKOKU

Kagoshima   ISLAND

KYUSHU

ISLAND

East

China

Sea

NORTH PACIFIC OCEAN

KOREA

Yellow

Sea

C   H   I   N   A

EAST

Shanghai

CHINA

SEA

AMAMI
O-SHIM

OKINAWA

RYUKYU

Taipei

Canton

TAIWAN
(FORMOSA)

Hanoi

Macao   Hong Kong
(Port.)   (Br.)

Gulf

of   HAINAN

Tonkin   (China)

PHILIPPINE

SEA

C. Engaño

LUZON

PHILIPPINES

FRENCH INDO-CHINA

MINDORO   SAMAR

Saigon

SOUTH   CHINA   SEA

LEYTE

PANAY   CEBU

Pt. Camao   PALAWAN

NEGROS

SULU   MINDANAO

SEA

Map by William Jobar   BORNEO

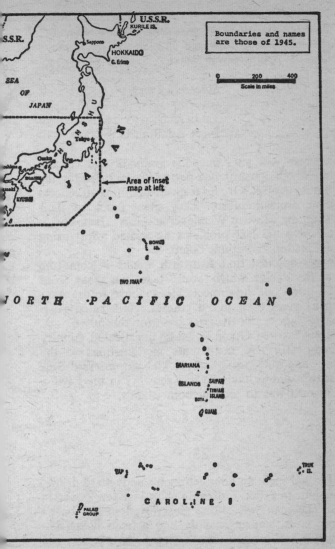

Boundaries and names
are those of 1945.

0   200   400
Scale in miles

U.S.S.R.

KURILE IS.

S.S.R.

Sapporo

HOKKAIDO

C. Erimo

SEA

OF

JAPAN

Tokyo

J A P A N

Osaka

KYUSHU

Area of inset
map at left

BONIN
IS.

IWO JIMA

N O R T H   P A C I F I C   O C E A N

MARIANA

ISLANDS

SAIPAN

TINIAN
ISLAND

ROTA

GUAM

YAP

PALAU
GROUP

C A R O L I N E I

TRUK
IS.

The Western Pacific

I desire that you make available to Commander Ashworth such intelligence data as applies to the utilization of the new weapon.

Sincerely yours,

E. J. King,
Fleet Admiral, U.S. Navy.

Ashworth was an Annapolis graduate and combat veteran whom Parsons had personally engaged for the Manhattan Project. Groves respected both naval officers for their professionalism. They spent much of their time shuttling between Wendover and Los Alamos helping to solve the last problems associated with fuzing and detonating the atomic bomb.

Groves doubted that Ashworth would welcome the trip to the Pacific which would take him away from his test work, but the project chief planned to use Ashworth as more than just a courier. He wanted Ashworth to choose the overseas base for the 509th.

Groves favored Guam. It had sophisticated military workshops for any last-minute modifications to the weapon, and a deep-sea harbor. Tibbets preferred Tinian. It was said to have the best runways in the Pacific.

Ashworth was to look at both islands.

• 23 •

Beser had spent an hour getting his bodyguard drunk, urging him to relax and enjoy their last few hours in Cuba. The man was sitting glassy-eyed in the base's officers' mess, staring stupidly into a fresh daiquiri—the eighth he had consumed in an hour. He was too drunk to notice that Beser had gone.

Beser had hurried to the base motor pool to collect a truck. A Silverplate authorization had overcome the initial objection of the transport officer to part with the vehicle. Then Beser had driven into the old quarter of Havana and supervised a gang of Cubans loading crates into the truck.

Now, the whole secret operation, which so far had gone "like a dream," was being threatened by an MP at the gate to Batista Field. "Lieutenant, I want to see inside this truck."

Beser eyed the policeman: he couldn't be bribed; he would have to be threatened. Crooking his finger—he had borrowed the gesture from a university professor—Beser told the MP to come closer. "What's your security rating, son?"

Beser was barely twenty-three. He sounded like a middle-aged general.

"I don't know, sir."

"Then you had better find out—quick! Move, soldier!"

The MP backed off.

Beser slammed the truck into gear, and it bounded forward into the air base. He drove several times around the administrative blocks to make sure he was not being followed. Satisfied, he then drove to the part of the apron where the 509th was located.

A group of fliers was waiting for him. Beser jumped down from the driver's cabin, and a human chain formed between truck and bombers. The unmarked boxes were stacked in the cavernous bomb bays of the B-29s.

It took almost an hour to transfer the cargo. Each box contained twelve bottles of the best-quality whiskey.

Beser had discovered a Havana wholesaler offering the liquor at a quarter of the price it cost in the United States. The 509th had needed no persuasion to lay out the money for this bonanza.

The escapade was typical. In the past three weeks, the 509th had established a reputation as hell-raisers. Havana, used to the carousing of servicemen, was astonished by the group. They lived and loved at a frenetic pace, fought those who challenged them, and led charmed lives when authority intervened.

An MP patrol picked up drunken 509th mechanics in a street brawl and took them to the military lockup. Their arrest was reported to the 509th's duty officer. He checked his rosters; the men were scheduled to service a bomber in the morning. He demanded their release. When the MPs refused, the officer used "Silverplate" to rouse the local commander. He checked his records, found the code rated the highest priority, and ordered the mechanics set free. The legend grew that the 509th were "The Untouchables."

Tibbets had surprised the rest of the 509th at Wendover by flying back early from Havana to supervise personally the training of the crews he had not sent to the Caribbean. He was determined that when the day came, every one of his fliers would be capable of carrying out an atomic strike.

He worked the five crews still at Wendover hard, sending them back and forth to the Salton Sea bombing range. Without actually saying so, he conveyed to the fliers the impression that although they had not been sent to Cuba, they might still be chosen for the big upcoming mission.

Tibbets received regular reports from Cuba. He was particularly pleased to see that his engineering crews were already showing their mettle: the 509th's planes were losing less than half the number of engines through malfunction that other air force squadrons based on the island were losing. It was what Tibbets had come to expect from his men.

But he was not willing to do what executive officer John King wanted: "turn the squadron into a spit-and-polish outfit."

Tibbets knew that King meant well, but he also realized that the officer did not understand his methods: the easy familiarity he had with the enlisted men, the way he invariably called all his officers by their first names. King was "Regular Army; he had never experienced the unique camaraderie of flying as a team, where lives depend on each other."

Tibbets would never allow anyone to stifle what he

believed was a requisite for any fighting air squadron: spirit. To maintain that spirit, Tibbets was spending more time than ever with his men. His wife and small sons rarely saw him. When he did see the children, he was usually too tired or preoccupied to play with them. The shiny new model bombers the boys had received at Christmas were broken, and he never found time to fix them. His wife looked accusingly at him. Their marriage continued its downhill progress.

Tibbets could see what was happening—and hated himself for making no move to stem the destruction of his family life. The truth was, as he would later admit, that he did not know what to say to mend matters.

He was also not prepared to give up watching over his fliers to be with his family. When he had first married Lucie, he had warned her that "I was a different kind of cat from the ordinary man," and that nothing would stand between him and his work.

In the first flush of marriage, she had accepted that. But now, isolated, reduced to listening to long technical conversations her husband had with the officers he occasionally brought home, Lucie Tibbets knew there could be no future for them together.

Even though he was aware of her feelings, Paul Tibbets was "only able to cry inside myself. She never knew, nobody knew, what I was feeling."

Tibbets and Beser, who had returned with the others from Cuba on February 3, felt they were passing their lives on an endless treadmill between Wendover and Los Alamos.

This morning in early March, they found the sentries at the compound gate more nervous than ever. Both men's ID cards were checked more thoroughly than usual, even though Tibbets and Beser were now familiar faces.

When they eventually entered the site and were greeted by Ramsey, they found the usually unruffled scientist, in Beser's opinion, "hot and bothered."

It was Oppenheimer who told Tibbets the reason for

the increased tension. Groves had just ordered that the first plutonium bomb must be ready for testing at Alamogordo by the middle of July, and the first uranium bomb must be available for war purposes by early August.

The deadline placed an additional burden on men and women who had been working under great strain for two years. Tempers flared. There were angry exchanges between the scientists and security men.

The weather did not help. The spring rains were late in coming, and an arid wind blew from the desert over the settlement, withering the grass and drying up the pond in the center of the compound.

Water shortages had always been a problem. Now, water for personal use was rationed. Workers and their families were advised to brush their teeth with Coca-Cola.

Of late on his visits to Los Alamos, Beser had tended to avoid any scientist who raised a doubt about the validity of his work. In Beser's opinion, such men were misguided. He preferred the views of Dr. Louis Slotin, a young researcher who had worked on the "crit" experiments. "Whether you die by a bullet or a bomb, you are still dead."

The words exactly matched his own views at a time when thousands of Americans were dying from Japanese bullets on Iwo Jima.

Beser was at Los Alamos to learn more about the fuzing mechanism of the bomb, and how the Japanese might interfere with it electronically, causing a premature explosion.

Tibbets had come to see Oppenheimer to finish up the details for the arrival at Wendover of a new special unit—the First Ordnance Squadron—which would have technical responsibility for the atomic bomb when the 509th was overseas.

After settling on March 6 as the date when the squadron would come to Wendover, Tibbets and Oppenheimer were joined by Ashworth. The navy commander had recently returned to Los Alamos after a thirteen-day visit to the Marianas, where he had delivered Fleet Admiral King's letter to Admiral Nimitz and explained to the Pacific commander the role of the 509th. Nimitz had made one comment: he wished the bomb were available now to be used on Okinawa, the last major island to be invaded before mainland Japan.

Ashworth told Tibbets that Guam was unsuitable as a base for the 509th. Instead, he agreed the group should use North Field, Tinian; the field had four eighty-five-hundred-foot-long runways.

"I'll only need one," responded Tibbets.

• 24 •

From the upper floor of his small private hospital, Dr. Kaoru Shima had a good view of Hiroshima. It was one which was beginning to depress him. A slash of wasteland stretched away on each side of the Aioi Bridge, marking one of the fire lanes crossing the city.

Dozens of houses, shops, tearooms, and bars had been demolished in the vicinity of the Shima Surgical Hospital, leaving its medical director and nursing staff with the feeling they worked "on the brink of destruction."

The morning newscast had reinforced this feeling. For the first time, Japan Radio had given a hint that the fighting on Iwo Jima was going badly.

Iwo's eight square miles were just seven hundred miles from Tokyo, close enough for the Americans to covet the Japanese island as a fighter-and-bomber base.

For days, the radio and newspapers in Japan had dwelt on the impregnability of the island's defenses. They had pointed out that the enemy's seventy-four days of preinvasion bombardment had done little to destroy those defenses; the Imperial Japanese Army was sheltering in caves and deep tunnels, often protected by as much as thirty-five feet of concrete. And when the Americans had landed on Iwo, they had been led into a trap. Lured ashore by light opposition, the invading forces had gained a foothold on the island, only to have that hold nearly crushed by murderous cross fire from the entrenched army. Japan Radio had talked of slaughter on an unparalleled scale. But now, in early March, the latest bulletins were speaking of a "strategic withdrawal." Dr. Shima, an old hand at assessing the truth of such claims, knew that Iwo Jima was doomed.

Hiroshima's fire lanes were a constant reminder to him that, as a prelude to invasion, air raids must be expected, and that he would then have to deal with casualties. Only he knew how meager were his resources; in practical terms, he would be able to offer little more than comfort to victims of a major attack. His dispensary was in need of replenishment. He suspected that many of the city's twenty-two other hospitals and clinics, and also its thirty-two first-aid centers, were in a similar position.

The materials now pouring into Hiroshima contained few medical supplies, and most of those would go to the large Ujina Army Hospital, the Red Cross Hospital, and the Mitsubishi Shipyard Hospital. Dr. Shima's private clinic was low down on the army's list of priorities.

The clinic survived solely because of the driving force of its owner. He was also frequently called upon to perform operations in country hospitals. The sight of the doctor pedaling his bicycle, with his bag of instruments strapped to his back, was a familiar one in the area.

The construction of the fire lanes often added time to his journeys, as demolished buildings blocked streets and he was forced to make long detours. But Dr. Shima never complained. To those who did, he had an unfailing answer. "Be glad you are alive."

• 25 •

Fleet Admiral William D. Leahy, Roosevelt's chief of staff, was not impressed with what he had heard of the Manhattan Project. The idea of a single bomb destroying a large city—and ending the war—was farfetched to him. Speaking as "an expert on explosives," he planned to inform the president that the project was a dud, that the bomb would never explode.

Roosevelt had no lack of people prepared to offer him the benefit of their advice. Leo Szilard was one of those asking for an appointment. Szilard now believed it was no longer the Germans who threatened the world; "our worry [is] about what the Government of the United States might do to other countries."

Secretary of War Henry L. Stimson advised Roosevelt not to see the Hungarian scientist. Others were not so easy to avoid. Over a year earlier, Harry S Truman, then a senator from Missouri, had begun asking awkward questions. Stimson had silenced him at that time, but now he had to be more tactful. Any day, Truman could be president. Stimson knew that the ailing Roosevelt was hanging on to life by sheer willpower.

Stimson had told Truman almost nothing. There had been no mention of an atomic bomb. The secretary of war knew that Truman was not satisfied, but he was buying time for the project.

Recently, Roosevelt had asked him to conduct a review of the current situation.

Late in the afternoon of March 2, the two men met in Roosevelt's office. Stimson saw that the president, only days back from the taxing Yalta Conference, looked more gaunt than ever. He was one of the few men who knew about the small box of green tablets Roosevelt kept in a desk drawer for treatment of his hypertension and failing cardiovascular system.

Anxious not to tire Roosevelt with a detailed summary, Stimson put the situation simply. Production of the weapon was on schedule. The bomb would be ready by August, as Groves had promised. The weapon could save the million American lives Stimson believed would be lost before Japan would surrender.

Roosevelt seemed pleased. But Stimson wondered whether the president would live to see those million soldiers return home safely.

The Deficiency Subcommittee of the House Committee on Appropriations—congressional watchdog on how public money is spent—was not placated by the prepared statement Under Secretary of War Robert Patterson had given them.

In secret hearings, the subcommittee had tried to obtain further details of how almost two billion dollars had been spent on a project they could discover nothing about. Patterson had doggedly refused to say. He pleaded security considerations.

Committee chairman Clarence Cannon of Missouri warned that "as soon as the war is over Congress will conduct a most thorough inquiry into the project."

Patterson was himself unaware of most of the Manhattan Project's ramifications. But his political instincts sensed trouble. He knew that an essential rule for survival in Washington was to write a memo. He returned to his office and dictated one to an aide. General W. D. Styer. It was remarkable for its political expediency:

At the beginning of the project I told General Groves that the greatest care should be taken in keeping thorough records, with detailed entries of decisions made, of conferences with persons concerned in the project, of all progress made and of all financial transactions and expenditures. From time to time I have repeated these instructions and have been assured by General Groves that he and his assistants were keeping complete records. I have told him that the most exacting accounting would be demanded by Congress at some time in the future.

The size of the project, its secrecy, and the large sums of money being expended make it necessary that the utmost pains be taken in keeping records, to the end that a complete and detailed history of the project will at all times be available. This should cover fiscal, scientific and industrial phases of the work.

While I have no reason to doubt that General Groves is giving thorough attention to this matter, the importance of keeping full, accurate and intelligible records is so great that I want you personally to examine into the matter and let me have your conclusions. I want you to take any corrective measures, to make sure that a complete current history of the project is being set down on paper by competent personnel.

Patterson had covered himself.

Increasingly, Groves saw himself as a strategist, and because the use of the atomic bomb raised important political questions, also as a statesman. Recently, he had taken steps to work against his government's policy of collaborating with the British on all matters to do with atomic research. Churchill had raised the subject privately with Roosevelt at Yalta. and the president had agreed that Britain should be kept more fully informed on the project. That did not please Groves; he didn't trust the British to keep the atomic secrets away from the Russians. He had decided that America's Allies should get as little information as possible.

He knew more about the weapon than almost anyone else. His performance had been herculean. Factories he controlled were among the largest in the United States. He had authorized the patenting of many thousands of new inventions which accrued from the atomic research. Yet the entire project was being threatened by some of the very scientists whose pioneering work had been invaluable. Groves could not understand them.

Now, another voice had joined the dissidents. On his desk as he talked on the scrambler phone with General George C. Marshall in early March was a memo written the day before to Roosevelt by James F. Byrnes, director of the Office of War Mobilization. Byrnes had an office in the White House and virtually ran the nation's economic affairs while Roosevelt and Stimson concentrated on foreign and military policy. Byrnes was known as "the assistant president."

A copy of Byrnes's memo had been sent over from the White House to Groves for comment. That alone should have reassured him of the strength of his position. The memo was a sensible reminder to the president that there would be a momentous political row if the project failed.

For a man used totally to having his own way, the memorandum's words were chilling.

. . . expenditures approaching two billion dollars with no definite assurance yet of production . . . if the project proves to be a failure, it will then be subjected to relentless investigation and criticism . . . even eminent scientists may continue a project rather than concede its failure. Also it may be feasible to continue the experiment on a reduced scale. In any event, no harm could come from an impartial investigation and review by a small group of scientists not already identified with the project. Such a review might hurt the feelings of those now engaged in the project. Still, two billion dollars is enough money to risk such hurt.

In Groves's mind, the suggestion of an outside review placed Byrnes firmly in the opposition camp. Groves did not believe there was anybody competent enough to carry out such an investigation. It looked like another attempt to stop the project.

Groves finished briefing Marshall without mentioning the Byrnes memo. He was about to hang up when the army chief of staff asked if he had given any thought to how the bomb could be used to best advantage.

Groves had, but he kept his ideas to himself. He told Marshall he thought it was time for the planners to prepare preliminary studies of suitable targets.

There was a moment's silence. Then Marshall spoke. "I don't like to bring too many people into this matter. Is there any reason why you can't take over this and do it yourself?"

Groves eagerly accepted the offer. In his most optimistic moment he had never expected he would have the opportunity to choose atomic objectives.

He could consult, he could heed advice, but in the end he would have the responsibility for recommending which Japanese city would serve as the first target for the atomic bomb.

Secretary Stimson's advice to Groves was clear; Groves should advise Roosevelt to reject Byrnes's proposal for an independent inquiry. Maintaining secrecy was all-important. Congress and the Senate should be given the minimum information needed to secure appropriations. In the past two days, members of both houses had begun asking further questions about the Manhattan Project, following leakages about Under Secretary of War Patterson's appearance before the Deficiency Subcommittee.

Groves was delighted with Stimson's support; it enabled him to dismiss, almost defiantly, Byrnes's mild suggestion of a review.

Next, Groves dealt with Congress and the Senate. He set about the task in cavalier fashion. He was prepared, he wrote Stimson, to allow two senators and two representatives to take a peep at the project.

I would propose to show them those things outside the secret processing areas which have been under constant observation by the construction contractors and their personnel. They would see the size and scope of the installations and have an opportunity to assure themselves of the reasonableness of the various living accommodations which have been provided. I would also like to show them some portions of the processing areas to demonstrate the scope and complexities of the project.

To qualify even for this strictly limited inspection—in reality, a reluctant bit of public relations to raise more money—Groves laid down conditions more appropriate for an inspection of the bomb itself than a mere glimpse of dormitories and kitchens.

There was no possibility of anybody's being allowed near Los Alamos. The visits would be to some of the less-secret atomic sites whose usefulness to the project was already diminishing. And even then:

No notes should be taken by any of the visitors. Joint conversations regarding their visits should be held only while on the project and then in secure rooms. Information ascertained would not be usable for future formal or informal conversations or addresses, until the rules of security are changed by the Secretary of War. Some questions the members might ask would necessarily have to be unanswered and the refusal to answer must be unquestioned.

· 26 ·

Tibbets remained impassive as Major William Uanna spoke without interruption for many minutes, reading from one file after another. His summary was brutal and to the point. "Colonel, you've got one convicted murderer, three men who are convicted manslaughter cases, and several felons. They are all on the lam from the pen. Now, what are you going to do?"

Tibbets restated the question. "I know what *I* want to do. The question is, what are *you* going to recommend I do?"

Uanna was prepared. "I'll do whatever you want."

"Even break the law?"

"Even that."

Tibbets began to explore other areas. "How did these guys get into such a secret outfit as the First Ordnance?"

Uanna suggested that sheer chance had brought the criminals into the ordnance squadron that had just joined the 509th at Wendover. After escaping from various prisons, the convicts had presumably decided the safest place for them to remain undetected was the army. They would have had little difficulty enlisting under false names.

"This is wartime, Colonel. The army doesn't ask too many questions. It's just glad for the manpower."

Uanna's inquiries showed that the special technical talents of the men had been spotted by "scouts" for the Manhattan Project. The seven technicians—mainly tool-and diemakers—had been transferred to the First Ordnance Squadron.

The squadron would "baby-sit" for the atomic bomb when the group went to Tinian. Each of its members was a specialist. Together, they were capable of carrying out, under scientific supervision, any last-minute modifications to the bomb that might be required. It had taken months to find the right personnel. The majority were skilled in metallurgy and allied disciplines. Twenty-seven of them held science degrees. They had been warned that from the moment they joined the squadron they might not see their family or friends until the war was over. Each was allowed to write a daily letter; the mail was sent through a special post-office box in San Francisco.

The squadron had arrived at Wendover on a heavily guarded train. Its men were directed to a special fenced-off compound on the field, watched over by a detachment of Uanna's agents.

Uanna explained to Tibbets how he had spotted the criminals in the squadron. "They were happy about all this security. Only years in prison make men like that. We started digging."

Tibbets looked thoughtful. "We have them locked up here just as securely as if they were back in the pen?"

Uanna agreed that was the case.

"I want to see them."

Uanna raised no objection.

The escaped murderer was sent for. Tibbets studied him. "Do you know why you are here?"

"No, Colonel, I don't."

Tibbets picked up a file. "Listen, fella. I know your real name, your federal penitentiary number, the number of years you were serving, the day you broke out."

Tibbets tapped the file. "It's all here. Who you murdered, the police statements, your trial, your sentence, how you came to us. Everything."

The convict was too stunned to speak.

Tibbets thrust the file toward him. "Here. See for yourself."

Tibbets saw the man tremble. He withdrew the file and closed it, then looked carefully at the technician. "This is the only record which exists of your past. The major and I are the only people who know that you are an escaped murderer. Now, it seems to me that you are real good at your present job. And we need good men. So look here. We're going to give you a chance. Go back to your job. Do your work exactly as you have been doing it. If we have no trouble with you, you will have no trouble from us. When the war is over, we will give you this dossier and a match to burn it."

The dazed convict left the office, too overwhelmed to speak.

One by one, the other criminals were marched in, confronted with their crimes, and made similar offers.

When the last man left, Tibbets turned to Uanna. "Major, I'm not a police department. I'm not interested in bringing people to justice. I'm interested in ending this war. All I want to do is get the proper work out of these men."

The arrival of the First Ordnance caused considerable excitement. Lewis put it succinctly. "If we think we're something special—these guys are something else!"

Even the slaphappy 509th had never seen such an untidy-looking outfit. Some of its members were middle-aged; one or two spoke with a distinct foreign accent. Some were Jewish technicians who until a few years ago had worked in workshops in Berlin and Munich.

The squadron seemed capable of anything and was totally self-contained. They brought and erected their own workshops, connected their own electric power, installed their own special tools. The line crews of the 509th, themselves expert at most things, realized that their peers had arrived.

The squadron's members emerged from their compound only at mealtimes. Then they were accompanied by several burly agents. They all sat in a corner of the mess hall, and when strangers approached, they fell silent. The curious were firmly rebuffed.

The evening of March 7, some of the men from the First Ordnance Squadron went down to the flight line to meet the regular shuttle service from Albuquerque which Dora Dougherty was now running. If they noticed a woman was flying the transport, they made no comment.

There was only one passenger. He led the First Ordnance men over to a B-29.

The regular flight crew had been told to answer any questions the man put to them. He seemed to be interested in the technical performance of the bomber, and spent some time examining the bomb-bay doors.

At the end of his inspection, the man turned to the

ordnance men. "These ships are not good enough for the job. They will have to be replaced."

With that, he walked past the gaping flight crew, boarded Dora's transport, and was on his way back to Los Alamos.

By lights-out, the whisper had spread. Beser would remember a fellow officer telling the story. "Hear about this nut who flew in, said scrap our aircraft, and flew out again? Just like he was a five-star general, not a guy in a naval captain's uniform. Doesn't he know there's a war on—nobody can scrap aircraft just like that!"

"We'll get those planes." Beser knew how much power Captain William Parsons wielded.

Parsons had initially been considered as an alternate to Groves to head the Manhattan Project. He had come to Wendover to check out the planes that would fly the atomic strike. He found that constant test-flying and training had almost worn out the bombers. They were to be exchanged for the very latest models. These planes would have fuel-injection engines, electronically controlled reversible propellers, and generally would be much better than their predecessors.

Tibbets would soon have the best fleet of bombers that America could provide.

• 27 •

In the early evening of March 9, the first of 325 B-29 bombers took off from Guam. This B-29 was a pathfinder, a torchbearer for LeMay's gamble.

Eleven other bombers followed it into the air. Between them, they would pinpoint the northeastern sector of Tokyo. LeMay code-named the operation "Meetinghouse." In China, a meetinghouse was a place where important decisions were made.

The pathfinders were to sow their incendiaries carefully in a giant "X" whose arms would cross several square miles of one of the most congested cities in the world.

Chomping on a cigar, the chunky LeMay watched the main bomber force take off. In a few hours, either his bold plan would be vindicated or he would be in disgrace.

None of the 325 bombers climbing into the dusk was armed. Their bomb bays were filled with a total of two thousand tons of incendiary bombs.

LeMay had ended his briefing of the crews with: "You're going to deliver the biggest firecracker the Japanese have ever seen!"

Few fliers had reacted with enthusiasm. Doubtless many of them recalled the first American air attack on Tokyo, in 1942; three of General James Doolittle's fliers whose planes had been forced down by the Japanese had been tried for murder, found guilty, and executed.

LeMay's crews were also concerned about their orders to attack at such low levels without armaments. Intelligence was not comforting. Around Tokyo the Japanese were reported to have 331 heavy-caliber guns, 307 automatic-firing weapons, 322 single-engine fighters, and 105 twin-engine interceptors.

LeMay had confidently predicted that this defensive arsenal would be outwitted by his surprise tactics. Now he must wait for confirmation from General Tom Power, his chief of staff, flying in a lead bomber with orders to radio back news of the attack.

The pathfinders arrived over Tokyo at midnight. The city was in darkness. The weather forecast was correct: skies were clear; a chill, twenty-eight-mile-an-hour wind had sent most people to bed early.

Flying downwind, the pathfinders marked the target area with magnesium, napalm, and phosphorus, sowing their canisters in straight lines across wooden buildings and narrow streets.

At 12:30 A.M., the main task force arrived over Meetinghouse. No fighters scrambled to meet them;

ground fire was minimal. As LeMay had predicted, Tokyo's defenses were caught totally unawares by his low-level assault.

The B-29s began to bomb systematically along the spreading arms created by the pathfinders. They dropped loads of pipelike canisters to fuel the growing inferno.

Fifteen thousand feet above the flames, Power's plane circled the target. The chief of staff radioed a commentary back to Guam. "It's spreading like a prairie fire . . . the blaze must be out of control . . . ground fire sporadic . . . no fighter opposition. . . ."

The conflagration spread and intensified, sending great whirls of superheated air high into the sky. The bomber pilots felt they were flying, one reported, "in Dante's Inferno." Turbulence from the firestorm raised the huge bombers hundreds of feet higher into the air, then sucked them down again. Fliers were sick from the bouncing. Then a new sensation made them vomit afresh: it was the sickly-sweet stench of thousands of bodies burning.

Finally, as planned, at 3:30 A.M. the last B-29 dropped its seven tons into the furnace and fled southward.

Power radioed his final report. "Target completely alight. Flames spreading well beyond Meetinghouse. All Tokyo visible in the glare. Total success."

The fires were a funeral pyre for some one hundred thousand souls. Almost half a million more were injured. Two hundred and fifty thousand buildings were destroyed in an area of about sixteen square miles.

Of the 325 bombers that created this holocaust, 14 were lost.

LeMay's gamble had worked. He immediately ordered further low-level sorties against Nagoya, Osaka, Kobe. and Okayama.

During the past two months, all LeMay's efforts had been devoted to developing these tactics. There had been no time for anything else—certainly not to listen to the recurring rumor that some crack new outfit was coming to the Marianas.

But now, in his moment of triumph, the rumors took on substance. LeMay was told that part of North Field, Tinian, was being annexed on direct orders from Washington to house a "special bombing group."

LeMay reckoned that unless it arrived soon, there might be little left for this new outfit to bomb except ruins and paddy fields.

• 28 •

In Tokyo, General Army Headquarters was in turmoil. Following the incendiary raid, the high command was evacuating to the more protected, tree-shaded grounds of the military academy at Ichigaya Heights, in the west-central area of the city.

The journey across Tokyo was unusually difficult, for LeMay's raiders had created universal panic.

In the immediate aftermath of the attack, with air temperatures in the blitzed area reaching two thousand degrees, the frenzy to escape had turned ordinary citizens into savages. Thousands jumped into the Sumida River, to die either from drowning or when the fires sucked out the oxygen from their lungs. Police and firemen were trampled in the panic. Great mounds of dead were piled in the streets of northeast Tokyo.

In the past twenty-four hours, thousands had trudged out of Tokyo with nothing but the clothes they wore. Behind them, they left charred families and friends. This exodus posed a serious problem. The refugees could spread panic, cause confusion, and lower morale.

Major General Seizo Arisue was glad it was not his concern to deal with such matters. His immediate interest focused on the reaction of naval intelligence to the raid.

They had withdrawn their peace feelers to Allen Dulles. It did not take Arisue long to discover why.

Far from being demoralized by the attack of LeMay's bombers, the admirals had stiffened their will to resist.

Naval chief of staff Admiral Soemu Toyoda announced that the only way Japan could survive "with dignity" in the face of such terror was to fight on, to launch determined counterattacks, to make America realize the Japanese nation would never surrender. The navy, he let it be known, was considering means of carrying the war to American shores.

The talk at army headquarters was even fiercer. Staff officers, thirsting for revenge, devised a plan to saturate the Marianas with *shimpu* attacks, but the problems of getting the kamikazes to within striking distance proved insurmountable.

Gauging the strength of this bellicose mood, Arisue decided this was not the time to talk peace with the enemy. He also decided to suspend his own efforts to reach Dulles.

Word of the destruction in Tokyo had not officially reached Hiroshima. The censor's office had so far refused to clear reports on the raid for the nation's press and radio.

The news reached Hiroshima unofficially on March 12 by one of the few trains civilians could still use. Within an hour after the refugees from Tokyo had arrived in Hiroshima, Mayor Senkichi Awaya knew what had happened in the capital. Using his official position, Awaya managed after several hours of anxious waiting to reach his wife by telephone. She and the children were unharmed. He told his wife to bring the children with her and join him as soon as possible in Hiroshima, where they would be safe.

Sachiyo Awaya hesitated. She and the children had all survived the raid; the refugees were probably exaggerating; anyway, the army in Tokyo said it was unlikely the bombers would return, and if they did, next time they would receive a hot reception.

Awaya was aware that at any moment the connection might be interrupted; telephone operators had the authority to terminate any call which was not of a military nature. The mayor spoke urgently. "The enemy will return. That is the nature of war. You and the children must come here."

Still, his wife expressed her reluctance to leave Tokyo. He then advanced an argument that he knew she would find difficult to reject. "It is possible that we will all die together in the battles to come. If that is to happen, I wish us to die together as one family."

His wife promised that as a start she would bring their eldest son. The fourteen-year-old boy could continue his education at a school in Hiroshima.

One week later, between 7:30 and 8:00 A.M. on March 19, Hiroshima experienced its first air raid. Four carrier-based fighter-bombers flew across the city. Only two bombs were dropped; one fell harmlessly in a river, the other killed two people and destroyed their homes.

The planes escaped before antiaircraft fire could be brought to bear on them. The incident caused widespread excitement and speculation in the city. Fierce arguments broke out between skeptics and the proponents of the view that Roosevelt had agreed to spare Hiroshima. In the end, the supporters of this theory triumphantly pointed to the fact that the bombers had not made a second pass over the city. The two bombs they had released were dropped in error—that is why they had sheered away. And, to clinch their case, the proponents pointed to an inescapable truth: while there were a number of air-raid warnings in the two weeks that followed, no bombers had come anywhere near the city.

These recent warnings delayed mayoral assistant Kazumasa Maruyama's regular weekly trip into the countryside to barter for food for his wife and Mayor Awaya.

This morning Maruyama had risen at five and left his wife still sleeping in their tiny bedroom. He listened to the radio before leaving the apartment. The radio was important. Air-raid warnings were broadcast over it. It was the radio, with its first hint of a "strategic withdrawal," that had prepared listeners for the loss of Iwo Jima.

The newscaster this morning was as confident as ever. The Special Attack Corps, the kamikazes, had yesterday struck another mortal blow against the enemy off the shores of Okinawa. Among their many targets was "the pride of the enemy fleet, the warship *Indianapolis.*" The name of the ship did not register with Maruyama, but he deduced that behind the blaring words, the radio was starting to prepare its audience for an unpalatable fact: the enemy had reached the shores of Okinawa.

If Okinawa should fall, Maruyama had no doubt, the enemy would then invade Japan itself.

The thought of what that would mean was too horrible to contemplate. The newspapers and radio spoke of American soldiers as "bloodthirsty devils"; perhaps, after all, he had been wrong to support the mayor's idea of bringing his family to Hiroshima. Perhaps they would be better off near Tokyo, protected by the largest concentration of defending troops.

Still dwelling on the dilemma the broadcast had created in his mind, the mayor's assistant headed out of the city on foot.

Commodities were more useful than money for obtaining a few vegetables and fruit to augment the legal rations. From today, those rations were to be cut further, the rice portion reduced to three bowls a day for twenty days in any month. No food would be issued for the remaining calendar days. The quality of the rice was so poor that Maruyama would never have eaten it before the war. Fish, the other staple of the Japanese diet, was also becoming scarce. American bombers were systematically destroying the fishing fleet.

Maruyama was warmly greeted at the farm. He was the most important customer among all those who came to offer goods in exchange for food. Soon, Maruyama was sitting cross-legged in his stockinged feet in the farmhouse living room, sipping tea.

Normally the farmer plied him with questions about life in the city. This morning it was the farmer who had information to impart, and he was determined to make the most of it.

Maruyama provided the opening by mentioning that the air raid had made many people nervous in Hiroshima.

"The city will not be bombed again."

Maruyama smiled wanly, but he knew he must not offend the farmer; he was a touchy man and could sell his produce to whomever he liked. Maruyama said he hoped his host was right and that the city would be spared.

"It will. You see, when the war is over, Americans will build their villas here! It is such a beautiful city."

Maruyama complimented the farmer on being privy to such interesting information.

"I cannot tell you how I learned it. But I can tell you this, Mr. Secretary, that a client almost as important as you told me."

Nodding gravely, Maruyama stood up. It was time for business. He opened the bundle of old clothes he had brought. As each item was displayed, the farmer reached into his own sacks and laid out his purchasing price in produce.

Maruyama estimated that, with the clothes, he had purchased enough food for the mayor as well as for his wife and himself for three days—perhaps five if his wife was extra careful. He exchanged deep bows with the farmer, carefully bundled up the produce, bowed a last time, and retraced his steps to Hiroshima.

He had traveled less than a mile when a peasant rushed out of his cottage and shouted that the radio had just announced another air-raid alert.

Unable to resist, Maruyama did his own bit of rumor-mongering. "Don't worry. Hiroshima won't be bombed again. Haven't you heard? The Americans want to build their villas here! Maybe even Roosevelt will come!"

He walked briskly on toward the city.

· 29 ·

Group bombardier Tom Ferebee was relaxed as he announced laconically, as he always did at the initial point, that straight ahead and thirty-two thousand feet below he could see the small desert town of Calipatria in Southern California.

Beyond the town lay the Salton Sea and the 509th's bombing range.

There were now three minutes to go before the brand-new bomber reached the aiming point. It was the first of the replacement aircraft that Parsons had deemed necessary. It had arrived at Wendover on March 9 and had been closely examined by Tibbets, van Kirk, and Ferebee.

The new bomber *was* different. Though a lot of the armor plating as well as the guns had been left out, it was built more ruggedly. Tibbets admired the reversible propellers. Ferebee liked the quick-action bomb doors; they were designed to close in two seconds after a bomb was released. This would allow the plane to carry out its 155-degree turn even faster. Van Kirk appreciated his navigator's seat; it was more comfortable than the one he was used to.

A team of engineers and mechanics had flown in with the aircraft. At Tibbets's request they had made a number of minor adjustments. But one of the engineers was not satisfied with the way the bombsight gears were working. Ferebee said he could adjust matters after a test drop or two. The engineer fussily explained that was not the way he did things. He put in a monitoring set and was given special clearance to make this one flight to observe the operation of the Norden sight.

Tibbets assigned Lewis to try out the new bomber on what was by now a regular milk run from Wendover to the Salton Sea. Ferebee was on board partly because this time they were to drop one of the precious "fuzed units." These were dummy bombs the exact shape of the atomic bomb and containing the proximity-fuze firing mechanism. Each of these mechanisms cost the equivalent of a Cadillac.

In addition to the engineer, there was another new face on board, Second Lieutenant Morris R. Jeppson of the First Ordnance Squadron. In the roomy cabin he shared with the navigator and radioman, Jeppson had rigged up a control panel to monitor the bomb's complex internal electronics before it was dropped from the plane.

A religious and reserved young man, Jeppson quietly went about his work, oblivious of all the banter around him. He knew the fliers were curious about his presence, and he sensed they were eager to pump him about the First Ordnance. But he admired the way they restrained themselves. He liked that sort of discipline.

Jeppson was a physics graduate who while in the service had studied at Yale and Harvard and at the Massachusetts Institute of Technology. His talents were noticed, and he was assigned to the First Ordnance.

He took an immediate liking to Lewis. The pilot was friendly, suggesting where he could store his equipment and telling him what he should expect on the flight. So far, it had been uneventful. The feedback from the cables running from his control panel to the bomb revealed that the weapon was "acting normally."

"Two minutes to AP."

Lewis acknowledged Ferebee's words. He prepared to slam shut the bomb-bay doors the moment the bombardier announced the blockbuster was on its way down.

The engineer had a duplicate of the bombsight Ferebee crouched over. If the bombardier's instrument malfunctioned, the bomb could still be dropped by Ferebee's ordering the engineer to pull a lever.

For his own purposes, the engineer synchronized his movements with every adjustment Ferebee was making.

"One and a half minutes to AP."

Suddenly the B-29 leaped higher into the air.

"Je—sus!"

Ferebee's strangled cry was followed closely by another from Lewis. "You've dropped the bomb too soon!"

Ferebee corrected him. "I didn't. That engineer must have done it."

Lewis yelled at the engineer over the intercom. "Did you touch anything?"

"I thought we were at the drop point!"

Ferebee's next words stopped Lewis's flow of invective. "It's falling straight into the town!"

He watched, transfixed, as the bomb plummeted earthward. Though it contained only a small amount of explosive, with its ballast and electronic equipment the blockbuster weighed over nine thousand pounds; it could do considerable damage.

"Bob, hold her steady."

Lewis held his original heading.

Jeppson calculated that the bomb needed about a minute to reach the ground.

Thirty seconds passed.

Then Ferebee spoke. "It's going to miss."

The bomb fell half a mile beyond Calipatria.

Within hours, Manhattan Project agents had sealed off the area and were searching for the unit. It had buried itself ten feet underground. It was recovered, and bulldozers filled in the hole. No one in Calipatria knew how close the town had been to being hit.

The flight back to Wendover was a tense one. The wretched engineer's attempts to apologize met with icy silence.

At Wendover he was bundled into a car and driven to Salt Lake City. There he was put on a train by project agents and told he would never again be allowed near the air base.

Tibbets glanced in angry disbelief at one of his most trusted officers, a short, trimly built lieutenant colonel.

Uanna, seated beside Tibbets, continued to question the officer. "You admit you took a B-twenty-nine without authority to fly home on a weekend pass?"

The officer maintained his aggressive pose. "I have the authority to take a plane."

Uanna's reproof was mild. "Nobody in the entire air force has the authority to take our most top-secret bomber for pleasure purposes."

Tibbets took over. "You took the plane and left it unguarded for two whole days on a civilian airfield?"

"Yes. But the plane was locked."

"And then you gave your father a conducted tour of an airplane that few servicemen on this base are allowed to go near?"

"My father's interested in flying. I didn't think there was any harm."

Tibbets exploded. "I don't want to hear about your father's interests! And it seems to me that you have never been able to think!"

"Colonel, I'm prepared to apologize—"

"Apologize! You think that settles matters? You've broken every goddam security rule. And you call yourself an officer! I'm going to make an example of you!"

The officer waited uneasily.

His decision made, Tibbets wasted no time in delivering sentence. "You've got just sixty minutes to pack. A plane will be waiting for you. Its destination is Alaska. You're going to spend the rest of your war talking to penguins!"

"Colonel—"

"Another word and I'll have you court-martialed. Now, get out!"

The disgraced officer left.

This was the third case of the week in which security regulations had been breached. Two days earlier, on March 20, a couple of lieutenants on duty at the telemetering station at the Salton Sea bombing range had left their highly secret ballistic-measuring equipment and driven across the border into Mexico "for a little fun." They, too, had been swiftly sent to Alaska.

Privately, Tibbets sympathized with the three officers, but even if he had wanted to, he could not have shown them compassion. That might have opened a floodgate, and the carefully wrought security protection he and Uanna had built up could have been swept away.

Tibbets knew his actions did not make him popular. But as he had once told van Kirk, he wasn't "trying to win a goddam beauty contest."

Transferring a senior and two junior officers to the icy wilds of Alaska would be a deterrent. But it would not alleviate the tensions. For six months, Tibbets had driven his men at a relentless pace. And, until a few days ago, Tibbets himself had not been that familiar with "the object of all this slave driving," the top-secret nuclear mechanism inside the bomb. Then, Parsons had flown to Wendover with schematic drawings of the uranium bomb in order to discuss with Tibbets a new series of fuzing tests. Tibbets already knew the bomb would be about ten feet long, twenty-eight inches in diameter, and weigh something over nine thousand pounds, but what he learned from Parsons caused him to be "amazed by the sweet simplicity of the thing."

The bomb's uranium core would weigh only about twenty-two pounds, split into two unequal segments kept six feet apart inside the barrel of a cannon, which was itself inside the bomb's casing. Between the two pieces of uranium 235 was a "tamper," a neutron-resistant shield made from a high-density alloy. The tamper was to stop the two pieces of uranium from reacting with each other—to help prevent premature "crit"—which would cause an unscheduled nuclear explosion.

The smaller piece of uranium 235 would weigh five pounds. This was the atomic "bullet" which, when the gun was activated by the proximity-fuzing system, would be fired down the gun barrel at the "target," the larger piece of uranium 235 fixed to the muzzle of the cannon just a few feet away. The "target" would weigh about seventeen pounds.

When fired, the force of the uranium "bullet" would make it sever the pins previously holding it in place, break through the tamper, and ram it into the "target" —causing the nuclear explosion.

After the description, Tibbets was jolted when Parsons told him that despite all the planning and testing, the scientists at Los Alamos still did not know if the uranium bomb would actually work. Tibbets remembered how "Parsons just sat there and said there was no way of being certain the weapon would go off— until it was used. He didn't think the risk of failure was high. But it was there."

Ever since, Tibbets had been mulling over what Parsons had told him. That, coupled with the security breaches by the three officers, made him edgy. Then, in the evening, he was called from dinner to interview a man who had checked into Wendover's State Line Hotel. Security agents had discovered he was using a false name. For thirty minutes the man resisted Tibbets's questions. Then one of the agents spoke. "We're going to turn you in as a spy. Spies in this country go to the electric chair."

The man talked. He admitted he was using an alias, in the hope of selling phony magazine subscriptions on the base. He was escorted to Salt Lake City and warned to stay out of Utah.

The episode further worried Tibbets. Inside the base, it was now an open secret that the group was going to drop "a big bomb" on Japan. Tibbets thought it was only a matter of time before there was a serious security leak.

• 30 •

Even here in Warm Springs, Georgia, President Roosevelt could not shake off the cares of war. At noon, a messenger appeared in his study with a leather pouch. The mail from Washington had arrived to intrude upon the rest that his doctors had ordered for the chief executive.

In some ways, he had reason to be cheerful. The Allies were winning. Germany was on the verge of collapse. In the Pacific, landings had been made on Okinawa by 183,000 soldiers and marines.

But already the death toll was high. This morning, as usual, the president had the latest casualty figures— 6,481 Americans had died in battle during the past week, bringing the total to 196,669 American lives lost in the fight against the Axis.

He was still studying these figures when Madame Elizabeth Shoumatoff, the portrait painter, arrived.

Roosevelt was dressed, as she had requested, in a Harvard tie and a vest, neither of which he liked. He allowed her to slip his cloak over his shoulders. Its dark cloth contrasted with the curious luminosity of the president's features. His skin had become parchmentlike, and this morning was aglow with an intense brightness that seemed to come from deep within.

Suddenly, he raised his left hand to his forehead and pressed hard against the skin. His hand fell back on his lap, and his fingers began to twitch. He dropped his cigarette and raised his right hand to massage the back of his neck. He closed his eyes and began to moan softly. Then his head slumped forward, and he slid down in his seat, limp as a puppet.

The president's doctor arrived in moments.

At 3:35 P.M., April 12, 1945, Franklin Delano Roosevelt was pronounced clinically dead.

The free world had lost a statesman, America a

leader, and the Manhattan Project, at this most crucial stage, its benefactor.

Oblivious of what had just happened in Georgia, Harry S Truman, thirty-fourth vice-president of the United States, this afternoon acting in his capacity as president of the Senate, appeared to the assembled senators to be taking copious notes of the debate in progress. Many thought it was typical of the way Truman did things: he was a meticulous fact-gatherer.

In reality, he was writing a letter to his mother, full of chatty news. He ended with a reminder.

Turn on your radio tomorrow night at 9:30 your time and you'll hear Harry make a Jefferson Day address to the nation. I think I'll be on all the networks, so it ought not to be hard to get me. I will be followed by the President whom I'll introduce.

At 4:56, the Senate recessed, and Truman dropped into Speaker Sam Rayburn's office for a bourbon and water. He was still there when Roosevelt's press secretary, Steve Early, telephoned and asked Truman to "please come over and come in through the main Pennsylvania Avenue entrance."

Truman did not ask why. He assumed Roosevelt was back from Warm Springs and wanted to raise some minor point with him.

Truman was shown up to Eleanor Roosevelt's second-floor study. She walked toward him and grasped his arm. Her voice was calm and measured. "Harry, the president is dead."

Dumbfounded, Truman instinctively looked at his watch to remember the moment he had heard the unbelievable news. It was 5:25 P.M.

Mrs. Roosevelt spoke again. "Harry, is there anything *we* can do for you? You are the one in trouble now."

She invited him to use the study telephone, and left to attend to the funeral arrangements.

At 7:00, Truman went to the Cabinet Room in the White House to be sworn in. The Cabinet watched in silence as Chief Justice Harlan Stone explained the brief ceremony to Truman.

Stone consulted a piece of paper and asked Truman to confirm that the "S" in his name stood for "Shippe."

Truman's twangy drawl cut through the doom-laden atmosphere. "The 'S' stands for nothing. It's just an initial."

The chief justice erased "Shippe" from the oath. An aide whispered to Stone that they still could not begin, as they did not have a Bible. They all waited in strained silence until a frantic search of the White House produced one.

At 7:09 P.M., the Bible was handed to Truman, who repeated after Stone the presidential oath of office. "I, Harry S Truman, do solemnly swear that I will faithfully execute the office of President of the United States and will to the best of my ability preserve, protect, and defend the Constitution of the United States."

Truman impulsively kissed the Bible. Then he motioned for the Cabinet to join him at the long table. He made them a promise. "It will be my effort to carry on as I believe the president would have done."

For Truman, the new president, for all the men in the room, Franklin D. Roosevelt was still "The President."

Truman asked Roosevelt's Cabinet to stay on in office. But he gave a hint of things to come when he closed the meeting with another promise: "I will assume full responsibility for such decisions as have to be made."

The Cabinet filed out. At the door, Stimson lingered. When he spoke to Truman, his voice was unsteady. "Mr. President, I must talk to you on a most urgent matter."

Truman nodded.

"I wish to inform you about an immense project that is under way—a project looking to the development of a new explosive of almost unbelievable destructive power."

Stimson paused.

Truman waited, but the secretary of war did not elaborate.

On the first morning of his presidency, Truman awoke at his customary hour of 6:30. This Friday the thirteenth was going to be a hot, sticky day. Then it struck him that a president of the United States did not concern himself with forecasts unless they affected important issues. Whatever the weather, he now had to run the country.

At the White House, Truman showed himself a swift decision maker. That morning he dealt quickly and surely with certain domestic issues and was briefed by members of the Cabinet.

At 2:30, James Byrnes arrived. Truman had two questions he wanted Byrnes to answer. First, would Byrnes give him a written report on the Yalta Conference? Byrnes had taken copious notes there for Roosevelt, and he immediately agreed to provide a memorandum.

The second question was more surprising. Truman began by reminding Byrnes that because of the way he had become president, there now was no vice-president. According to the Constitution, if Truman died or became seriously incapacitated and unable to remain president, the secretary of state would succeed him.

Truman asked if Byrnes would like that post. It was a surprising offer in view of their previously cool relationship. As the unofficial "assistant president," Byrnes had been far closer to Roosevelt than Truman, and at times had used his power to snub the vice-president. But in asking Byrnes to become first in line of succession to the presidency, Truman was displaying the political skill that made him so formidable. He wanted Byrnes on his side; he was prepared to buy him.

Byrnes accepted.

Then, speaking in a voice Truman felt was one of

"great solemnity," Byrnes made an announcement more startling and mysterious than Stimson's had been on the previous evening. "Mr. President, we are perfecting an explosive great enough to destroy the whole world. It might well put us in a position to dictate our own terms at the end of the war."

• 31 •

Beser, like most of the 509th, had heard the news of Roosevelt's death over the radio. Some of the men had been listening to NBC's "Front Page Ferrell"; others had been tuned to CBS's "Wilderness Road"; by far the majority had been following the adventures of ABC's highly popular "Captain Midnight."

At 5:49, the first flash interrupted all three programs. By 6:30, local radio stations in Utah were broadcasting details of the poignant cable Eleanor Roosevelt had sent to her four sons: two of them were in the navy, sailing off the coast of Okinawa.

DARLING: PA SLIPPED AWAY THIS AFTERNOON. HE DID HIS JOB TO THE END AS HE WOULD WANT YOU TO DO. BLESS YOU. ALL OUR LOVE. MOTHER.

Beser turned off the radio. His reason for doing so was understandable. "By switching it off, I believed I could deny the truth. President Roosevelt had been leading us for so long that his death was impossible to immediately accept."

That evening, members of the officers' and enlisted men's clubs on the base made their gesture: there would be no gambling or drinking until Roosevelt was buried. Eatherly surprised many by being one of the most vociferous supporters of this pledge.

Bob Lewis touched a popular emotional chord with his words. "I never met the guy. But I felt that I had lost a great buddy."

For many of these young men, who could hardly remember when he had not been president, the thought of an America without FDR in the White House was impossible to comprehend. Gradually, though, the talk at Wendover, as elsewhere, turned to the new president. Of most immediate concern to the 509th was his attitude toward the prosecution of the war. Everybody at Wendover knew where Roosevelt had stood. Many of them could quote from his speeches with their recurring theme that the enemy must be pursued to its lair. Roosevelt had almost lived to see the pursuit reach Berlin.

But would Truman be so keen to conquer Tokyo?

A well-rehearsed team, pilot Charles Sweeney and bombardier Kermit Beahan brought the B-29 toward the aiming point. For this test, they were using the makeshift range that had been laid out on the salt flats a few miles from Wendover.

Thirty-two thousand feet below, grouped near the AP, scientists and technicians from the First Ordnance Squadron waited to see if the latest adjustments they had made to the bomb's proximity-fuzing system would work.

Today's bomb was filled with ballast and a pound of explosive, enough to cause a small aerial explosion so that the scientists could see whether the fuzing mechanism worked at its present height of two thousand feet.

Sweeney's crew, No. 15, had been briefed by Tibbets on the test flight. He had reminded them of the importance and value of each fuzed unit, particularly as the system was still proving troublesome.

Though Tibbets had not said so, he was paying the chubby-cheeked Sweeney and his fliers a rare compliment. In selecting them for a flight of considerable consequence for the scientists, he was openly acknowledging what almost all the other crews now accepted: crew 15 was probably the best in the 509th.

The only challenge to this claim came from the vociferous Lewis and his crew.

The relationship between Lewis and Sweeney had been cool from the days both men had worked on the original B-29 test program. Lewis suspected that the Boston Irish Sweeney had "kissed the Blarney Stone"; certainly, Sweeney had a great deal of charm, which he used to get the very best from all those he worked with. It didn't work with Lewis, a failure that Sweeney philosophically accepted. Professionally, he felt that Lewis was "lucky" to be in the 509th, and even luckier to act, on occasion, as copilot to Tibbets.

This sort of personal tension had increased the competitive spirit between the two crews.

Tibbets watched the situation carefully. He never appeared to favor any crew unduly. After Sweeney had been assigned the test flight, Lewis had been asked to perform a series of takeoffs and landings with a nine-thousand-pound bomb filled with high explosives in his bomb bay. The exercise was not so pointless as it sounded to the crew. Tibbets wanted Lewis, and later the others, to become "psychologically prepared" for the possibility that one day they might be forced to land carrying an actual atomic bomb.

Tibbets was aware of the view prevailing within the higher echelons of the Manhattan Project: unlike conventional bombs, the atomic bomb was far more valuable than the aircraft carrying it, or the crew. He conveyed this thought to Lewis. The pilot performed his exercises with the gentle care of a veteran Red Cross transport pilot.

Approaching the aiming point, Sweeney watched Lewis circling far below. Then Beahan called out, in a Texas accent even Eatherly agreed was "broad," that the AP was almost in the center of his bombsight's cross hairs. Beahan, an overseas veteran like Ferebee, was a highly efficient technician, known to his fellow fliers as "The Great Artiste." Crew 15 held him in such reverence that they boasted he could "hit a nickel from six miles up."

Beahan asked for a minute course change. Copilot Fred Olivi, a bulky twenty-three-year-old Italian from Chicago, watched Sweeney respond. Olivi thought it was "almost magic" the way Sweeney and Beahan worked together.

The crew braced themselves for the familiar upward thrust following the bomb's release.

This flight would make another entry in the strictly illegal diary Sergeant Abe Spitzer was keeping of his time with the 509th. He was the radio operator and, at the age of thirty-five, looked upon by the rest of the crew as an old man. They would have been surprised at the gentle-voiced Spitzer's acid observations on some of the men he worked with. But even Spitzer had to admit that, in the air, crew 15 was a closely coordinated unit.

"Bomb away!"

Beahan's words were followed by a leap upward from the B-29, cut short when Sweeney went into the usual 155-degree turn. Simultaneously, an explosion rocked the bomber.

Sergeant "Pappy" Dehart, the tail gunner and another Texan, shouted, "It's blown up!"

The bomb's fuzing mechanism had detonated prematurely, less than a hundred feet below the B-29. The spent unit continued toward the ground.

Sweeney brought the aircraft under control and landed. Tibbets was waiting for him. He put into words the unspoken fear of them all. "Let's hope that doesn't happen when we've got a real one on board."

Over the weekend of April 21, the 509th had made their usual journey into Salt Lake City, and already the complaints were being received in the duty office.

Eatherly had set the pace, racing his roadster hub-to-hub against that of his flight engineer. They passed a whiskey bottle back and forth, from one car to the other, as they traveled at close to ninety miles an hour. The bottle was empty when they reached Salt Lake City.

A number of fliers took rooms in the Hotel Utah, and soon noisy parties were under way. A redhead was seen running naked down a hotel corridor, pursued by several pilots in their shorts.

On Monday morning, the Salt Lake City police department was phoning Wendover with a mounting list of breakages, assaults, and traffic violations.

Tibbets managed to placate the civilian authorities. But the symptoms were clear: the 509th had reached breaking point.

The time had come to leave Wendover.

In Tibbets's mind, there was another good reason for their departure. He had come to the conclusion that the scientists were "tinkering" with the atomic bomb; they seemed "more concerned with producing a *perfect* weapon instead of being satisfied with the one they had and using it to end the war. They wanted to improve the design, run more tests, make endless changes before they would let the bomb be used in combat."

This troubled Tibbets; he could imagine the physicists "still tinkering" when the war was over, "and the whole damn thing would have been a waste of time."

The 509th's base was reserved on Tinian. Weeks ago, orders had been given that a ship be standing by at Seattle to carry the ground echelon to the Pacific. All Tibbets had to do was telephone Washington, use the Silverplate code, "and we could be in the war."

The thought of seeing action again was exhilarating. But the prospect of what would happen to him if he actually ordered the 509th to be mobilized worried Tibbets. "Groves might have me stripped of my command, posted to Alaska, even sign court-martial papers."

Nevertheless, Tibbets asked the base telephone exchange to connect him with Air Force Command Headquarters in Washington. Once plugged through to his liaison officer, his message was brief. "This is Silverplate. We are ready to move."

The matter was soon arranged. The group's main

ground-echelon force would leave Wendover for embarkation at Seattle on May 6. The bomber crews would fly out to the Pacific later.

Soon afterward, Tibbets received a priority call from Washington, ordering him to fly there at once. His caller offered a gratuitous piece of news. "Colonel, you're in big trouble with Gee-Gee."

Gee-Gee was one of Groves's nicknames.

Tibbets arrived in Groves's office early in the evening.

"As I came through the door, he erupted. Who the hell did I think I was, ordering my outfit overseas? For ten solid minutes he raked me over the coals, up one side and down the other, never repeating himself. I never had such a flaying. I had never seen him so mad. Then, suddenly, he stopped and gave me a big smile and said, 'Goddammit, you've got us moving! Now they can't stop us!' He was tickled to death I had done it. Without my planes, there was no way the scientists could keep tinkering with their toy."

• 32 •

The invitation to dinner with his commanding officer, Colonel Hiroshi Abe, came as a pleasant surprise to Tatsuo Yokoyama. The antiaircraft gunnery officer's relationship with Abe had until now been distant and formal.

Then, a week ago, Abe had invited Yokoyama to dine at his home near Hiroshima Castle this Saturday night. There was one condition: an air raid would cancel the invitation. In the past weeks there had been a number of alerts. And once, a stream of bombers had passed high over the city.

But since the two bombs had been dropped over a month ago, on March 19, Hiroshima had remained free of attack.

After evening gunnery practice, Yokoyama dressed in his best uniform and told his sergeant where he could be reached.

The sergeant, the gun post's gossip, smiled broadly and said he was sure Yokoyama's evening would be undisturbed, "because Truman's mother is a prisoner in Hiroshima!"

Yokoyama was astonished.

The sergeant was insistent. "She was on a visit to the city when the war started. She has been here ever since!"

"Who told you this?"

The sergeant said he knew "somebody" on Lieutenant General Shoji Fujii's staff. Fujii, the district commander, was keeping Truman's mother in Hiroshima Castle as a hostage against air attacks.

Common sense told Yokoyama to dismiss the story. But increasingly, the most outlandish tales turned out to be true. There had been the yarn about fifteen-year-old boys being taught to fly as kamikaze pilots in the Special Attack Corps. He had not believed what he had heard until he had actually seen some of them at Hiroshima Airport. He had also discounted the tale that old women were being shown how to sharpen bamboo poles and use them like spears, until he saw women practicing on the grounds of East Training Field.

He decided to check the Truman story with Colonel Abe.

Abe's house was a small, compact dwelling near the castle. He was a widower and lived there with his daughter. Yokoyama was surprised to see he was the only guest.

Abe was a good host, with a plentiful supply of sake. Mellowed and relaxed, Yokoyama asked about President Truman's mother.

Abe laughed uproariously. He said he wished the story were true; then she could answer some questions about her son.

Lowering his voice, Abe told his guest still another

story. "Truman's mother is from Hiroshima! That is why we have not been bombed. She has told her son to spare this one city in all Japan."

Yokoyama asked why, then, was Hiroshima being prepared for attack? What was the purpose of the fire lanes?

Abe told him, "It helps create a mood of militancy. People who lose their homes will be ready to fight even harder for their lives, Japan, and the emperor!"

Yokoyama asked if this meant that after all these months of practice he and his men would have no chance to fight. If this were so, he would respectfully request a posting to Tokyo or one of the other cities where air attacks were now frequent.

Abe calmed his guest and invited him to eat. Dinner was served by Abe's daughter, a plumpish, moon-faced girl in her late teens. After dishing up bowls of rice and slivers of meat and fish, she left the men to eat and talk.

Yokoyama again brought up the question of a transfer.

His host looked at him carefully. "I have not invited you here to discuss such matters, but rather something that is important to me."

Yokoyama became respectful and silent as his host explained that he had long been impressed by the younger man's qualities. Abe revealed he had even made inquiries about Yokoyama's family background. "It is very satisfactory. You have honorable parents."

Knowing what was coming, for such inquiries could mean only one thing, Yokoyama waited.

Abe's next words were harsh and matter-of-fact; a businessman making an offer. "Marry my daughter, and your future will be assured. I will see to that."

Bowing gravely, Yokoyama promised his host to discuss the matter with his family. Such talks were essential before the proposed marriage could be formally contracted.

It would mean a trip home to Tokyo. Yokoyama

found that prospect almost as exciting as the reason for making the journey.

When Yokoyama reached Hiroshima Airport on April 28, he found the army transport he planned to take to Tokyo had left early. It worried Yokoyama that he had missed the flight. He knew how much trouble Colonel Abe had taken to get him a seat on the plane.

Yokoyama tried to hitch a lift on the next transport to the capital. He was told to wait. He sat on the ground outside the operations room and waited for his name to be called.

Hiroshima's airport was being extended. It was too small for the growing demands of the military. It was crammed with their aircraft. Yokoyama watched a transport taxi by. From a nearby hut a group of youngsters filed out to the plane in their cut-down overalls. Waiting to greet them was a handsome young flying officer, Second Lieutenant Matsuo Yasuzawa, one of the air force's most experienced instructors. Every pilot Yasuzawa trained now was meant to be a kamikaze. These youngsters were his latest intake. Their average age was sixteen years.

Yasuzawa was flying them to an airfield about a hundred miles from Hiroshima, on Kyushu, where they would receive their final training. Afterward, they would leave for Okinawa, where this first month since the Americans had invaded, nearly a thousand kamikaze pilots had died. They had sunk or damaged over a hundred American ships.

Yasuzawa realized how important holding Okinawa was to Japan. He hated having to remain behind as an instructor. He had recently been stopped by a senior officer just as he was about to take off in a training plane with the intention of ramming into a B-29 that was bombing his airfield. Yasuzawa was considered too valuable to lose; apart from instructing experienced pilots how to fly more advanced aircraft, Yasuzawa had the ability to take a raw recruit and teach him the rudiments of flying in ten days. The kamikaze pilots were being given only ten hours' tuition. They barely knew how to fly. To make sure they did not lose their nerve at the last moment, the cockpits of their suicide craft were sometimes screwed down shortly before take-off. Once they were airborne, the young pilots had no alternative but to die.

Today, as he settled himself at the controls of his well-used transport, Yasuzawa felt he would end the war preparing schoolboys for combat while never experiencing it himself.

Soon after Yasuzawa's transport trundled into the air, Yokoyama watched a navy fighter-bomber land and taxi toward the communications room. Officers ran to meet it. Out of the cockpit climbed an immaculate figure in a spotless white naval uniform. It was Captain Mitsuo Fuchida, the pilot who had led the raid on Pearl Harbor and was now the Imperial Japanese Navy's operations officer.

Listening to the respectful greetings of the other officers, Yokoyama gathered that Fuchida was in Hiroshima to attend one of the regular army-navy liaison conferences. Yokoyama bowed deeply as Fuchida walked briskly past him. The flying ace did not return the greeting. Yokoyama doubted whether Fuchida even noticed him.

Shortly afterward, an officer told Yokoyama there would be no seat available for him that day to Tokyo. He left the airport, his mind still filled with the image of Fuchida. It would be something to cheer him on the long journey he now faced by train to the capital.

Across the city, in their Hiroshima home, Mayor Senkichi Awaya listened sympathetically as his wife and eldest boy told of the rigors of their nightlong train journey from Tokyo. Several times the blacked-out train had been forced to stop until American bombers passed.

Although Mrs. Awaya had agreed to bring their son to Hiroshima weeks ago, only recently had it become convenient to transfer him from his school in Tokyo to the one attached to Hiroshima University. They had decided the other three children would remain in the capital. Their eldest daughter was married and living in Kobe.

The mayor's assistant, Maruyama, sought to reassure Mrs. Awaya. "They will all be safe as long as they stay out of the center of the cities. And here, you will be safe. Hiroshima is not a large city. They will bomb other places first. By the time it is our turn to be attacked, the war will be over."

The train carrying Yokoyama to Tokyo left at 4:00 P.M. Six months had passed since he had last made the journey. Nothing had prepared him for the changes he now saw: city after city bore the marks of incendiary bombing. As he came closer to Tokyo, even the darkness could not conceal the destruction.

Leaving the Shimbashi railway station, Yokoyama set out to walk to the southern suburbs where his parents lived. His route took him past the Imperial Hotel. Designed by the brilliant American architect Frank Lloyd Wright, the Imperial had survived the great Tokyo earthquake of 1923, but now it was a gutted ruin. Farther on, the Ginza—the business and nightlife heart of Tokyo—was a scorched wasteland of ashes and craters.

Yokoyama realized that he had been misled: in Hiroshima the newspapers and radio had given no inkling of the scale of the destruction in Tokyo. For the first time he felt he had been betrayed by the army. He could now see clear evidence that Japan was incapable of winning the war.

Eventually, he reached his parents' home. The house was intact, but Yokoyama wondered how long it would remain so. The American bombers seemed intent on working their way outward until all of Tokyo was destroyed. Wearily, he entered the house convinced that Japan must make peace or face extinction.

His parents were waiting for him. After they made him comfortable, he told them the purpose of his visit, explaining about Abe's marriage proposal. Yokoyama described what little he knew of his commander and his daughter. His parents listened gravely. Finally, Yokoyama's father spoke. Normally, a marriage joining two military families was a desirable thing, but these were not normal times; values were changing. Nobody could be sure what the future attitude of people would be toward members of the armed forces. To have been in the army might be a disadvantage. To be married to the daughter of a ranking officer could even be a liability.

Yokoyama's parents would promise no more than to consider the matter further after they had made the necessary inquiries about Colonel Abe's antecedents.

Professor Tsunesaburo Asada's wife bowed gracefully to her husband as she boarded the train for Nara, bound, along with the families of other important Japanese scientists, for the comparative safety of the countryside. In the past fortnight, Osaka had been attacked three times by formations of B-29s; 20 percent of the city was destroyed.

Mrs. Asada turned and bowed again from the train. Then she was lost behind the press of people crowding the windows to wave to loved ones on the platform.

Asada did not wait for the train to leave. He had work to do. His long period of research had begun to pay off. One of Japan's latest and most advanced long-range bombers, the Ginga, carrying a single seventeen-hundred-pound bomb, had flown to Saipan and attacked the main American air base on the island. The bomb was fitted with Asada's proximity fuze, similar to the one that had exploded prematurely under Sweeney's bomber.

Asada's fuze had detonated its bomb exactly as planned, thirty-five feet above the Saipan airfield. It had caused considerable destruction. Scores of parked B-29s were destroyed or damaged. The pilot of the Ginga reported to Asada that a large part of the air base was "an ocean of fire." The photo-reconnaissance pictures showing the wrecked American planes reminded the scientists of similar ones taken at Hickam Field, Pearl Harbor. But it was a short-lived moment of triumph.

The air force could not repeat the attack because its base on Iwo Jima was now in American hands, and the round trip to Saipan from Japan was outside the sixteen-hundred-mile range of the Ginga bomber.

Nevertheless, Asada's proximity fuze had been proved a success. The navy had ordered twenty thousand of them to be manufactured. Eventually, twelve thousand would be produced, many of them fitted to bombs and stored secretly on Kyushu awaiting an American invasion. When that came, it was planned, the bombs would be exploded at mast-height above the warships and troop-carrying landing craft so as to cause maximum casualties.

Asada was praised by senior naval officers for his invention. He was pleased, though secretly he thought some of the approbation was an attempt to humor him. His death ray remained far from ready for use. But he was still optimistic and spending most of his time on the project.

Meanwhile, the navy now had another new weapon.

It was the brainchild of Dr. Sakyo Adachi, a scientific colleague of Asada's attached to the naval meteorological department. Adachi had remembered what every Japanese high school pupil knew: although the great trade winds blow from east to west, from America to Japan, there is another wind, the Japan Current, which blows in the opposite direction.

Adachi filled a balloon with gas and attached to it a small canister containing high explosive. The trial balloon bomb was launched and tracked for some distance by a Zero fighter. It climbed steadily into the Japan Current and then headed eastward on a journey which would take it across the Pacific, passing north of Hawaii, and eventually to the coast of the United States.

Other balloon bombs followed.

Radar was not yet advanced enough to warn of their approach.

The Japanese, of course, did not know if the balloons had reached their target. But navy chief of staff Admiral Toyoda, mindful of his promise to carry the war to the American shore, ordered full-scale production of the balloon bombs.

Soon, all of America's West Coast cities would be targets. Given favorable weather conditions, the balloons might even reach Salt Lake City and Chicago.

In the coming weeks, some six thousand balloon bombs would be launched. Of those that would arrive in the United States, most would fall in the deserts of California and Nevada and the forests of Oregon. It would never be officially revealed how many victims they had claimed. And nobody will ever know how many Japanese balloon bombs still lie unexploded in remote areas of North America.

The first wire-service flash of Roosevelt's death had reached army intelligence chief Arisue in Tokyo before most people in Warm Springs were aware of the event.

Since then, he had been busily building up a psychological profile of Truman. Most of his information came from the Japanese military attaché in Bern, Lieutenant General Seigo Okamoto, who had been the link in Arisue's abortive attempts to contact Allen Dulles.

Aided as well by wire-service copy and transcripts of monitored broadcasts, Arisue came to an unexpected conclusion: Truman was going to be even tougher than Roosevelt.

The new president would, in Arisue's estimation, "overwhelm the old man" who had been prime minister of Japan for the past ten days.

On April 5, a serious political crisis, brewing for weeks, had finally erupted in Tokyo. On that day, General Kumaki Koiso, the compromise premier following Tojo's forced resignation, had suggested to the military that they allow him a share in their decision making. The generals had refused. Koiso had resigned.

He was replaced by Admiral Kantaro Suzuki, a hero of the Russo-Japanese war, whose frail body bore three bullet marks—a legacy of the days he had fallen foul of right-wing extremists in the army.

Arisue was astounded that Suzuki had accepted a post where the risks of death were even greater. He would have been more astonished to know that the emperor himself had charged Suzuki with the task of finding a means of ending the war. Those means did not, of course, include outright surrender.

Within hours of accepting office, Suzuki had received alarming news. Japan's ambassador in Moscow had cabled that the Soviet Union did not intend to renew its neutrality pact. It would be allowed to lapse automatically in one year. Finding an acceptable means of ending the conflict became even more urgent.

The prospect of Japan's negotiating a peace was very much on Arisue's mind. On the very day Roosevelt was being buried on the other side of the world, he had learned that naval intelligence was again trying to contact Allen Dulles in Switzerland.

Arisue understood the reasoning of his naval counterparts; it coincided with his own. Truman was a hardliner; it would be better to settle with him *now,* while Japan still had some bargaining power left. The American bombing offensive, the sea blockade, the relentless ground-fire barrage which had now crept to within 350 miles of Tokyo—to Okinawa, where a fierce and bloody battle was raging for the last major island between the enemy and Japan's westernmost mainland island, Kyushu—all these would ultimately weaken Japan to the point where the unacceptable unconditional surrender would be all that was left.

But Arisue and the other moderates did not believe Japan should surrender unconditionally. He believed that, by negotiation, Japan should attempt to hold some of the territory her forces had occupied in the war, and even if this proved impossible, there must at absolute minimum be a guarantee by the Allies of the emperor's safety and continuing omnipotent rule.

Arisue did not trust the navy to achieve even this fundamental requirement in its maneuvering in Switzerland. He cabled military attaché Okamoto in Bern and told him to redouble his efforts to contact Dulles.

• 33 •

On Truman's desk was a letter from Stimson. It had arrived the day before, April 24.

Dear Mr. President,

I think it very important that I should have a talk with you as soon as possible on a highly secret matter. I mentioned it to you shortly after you took office, but have not urged it since on account of the pressures you have been under. It, however, has such a bearing on our present foreign relations and has such an effect upon all my thinking in this field that I think you ought to know about it without much further delay.

Truman had arranged an appointment for his secretary of war at midday. The president would be happy to have any information that might help him keep the Russians in their place. He had shown his mettle three days earlier when Molotov and Gromyko, en route to the opening session of the United Nations in San Francisco, had stopped by the White House. Truman had told them the Soviet Union was reneging on its Yalta agreements. His language was so blunt and without diplomatic euphemisms that Molotov had bridled. "I have never been talked to like this in my life."

Truman's reply was crisp. "Carry out your agreements, and you won't get talked to like this."

Promptly at noon, the secretary of war arrived. Stimson said he was expecting one other person. Five minutes later, Groves appeared. He had slipped in through the back door to avoid arousing speculation among the journalists stationed in and around the executive mansion.

Stimson said the meeting was to discuss details of a bomb equal in power to all the artillery used in both world wars.

Groves winced inwardly. He had earlier told Stimson not to lay too great an emphasis on the bomb's power; he did not want the new president to become alarmed at the sheer magnitude of the weapon.

But Stimson was determined to lay out all the facts. He began to read from a prepared memorandum.

Within four months we shall in all probability have completed the most terrible weapon ever known in human history, one bomb of which could destroy a whole city.

Although we have shared its development with the United Kingdom, physically the U.S. is at present in the position of controlling the resources with which to construct and use it and no other nation could reach this position for some years. Nevertheless, it is practically certain that we could not remain in this position indefinitely.

Stimson explained that the theory behind the making of an atomic bomb was widely known. He went on to conjure up a nightmare that could come to pass.

We may see a time when such a weapon may be constructed in secret and used suddenly and effectively. . . . With its aid, even a very powerful unsuspecting nation might be conquered within a very few days by a very much smaller one. . . . The world in its present state of moral advancement compared with its technical development would be eventually at the mercy of such a weapon. In other words, modern civilization might be completely destroyed.

Truman paused, then posed a question: was Stimson at least as concerned with the role of the atomic bomb in the shaping of history as with its capacity to shorten the war?

"I am, Mr. President."

While they were speaking, the United Nations was about to hold its opening session in San Francisco. Stimson had anticipated Truman's raising this matter. He continued to read from his memo.

> To approach any world peace organization of any pattern now likely to be considered, without an appreciation by the leaders of our country of the power of this weapon, would seem to be unrealistic. No system of control heretofore considered would be adequate to control this menace. Both inside any particular country and between the nations of the world, the control of this weapon will undoubtedly be a matter of the greatest difficulty and would involve such thorough going rights of inspection and internal controls as we have never before contemplated.

Groves had never heard Stimson speak like this. For a moment he may have wondered whether the secretary had been contaminated by his contact with all those "longhairs" who had tried to make Groves's life such a misery these past months. Then, with a sense of relief, Groves heard what Stimson went on to say.

The secretary stated that, in spite of all this, he still favored using the bomb against Japan; that if it worked, it would probably shorten the war.

The meeting ended with Truman's agreeing to the formation of a specialist panel, to be known as the Interim Committee, to draft essential postwar legislation and to advise Truman on all aspects of atomic energy.

Stimson agreed to be its chairman.

• 34 •

At precisely 6:55 A.M. on April 30 in Hiroshima, Dr. Kaoru Shima was awakened by a five-hundred-pound bomb exploding two blocks from his clinic. It had fallen on the Nomura Life Insurance Building. By the time the doctor had leaped out of bed and rushed to the window, nine other bombs had fallen in a ragged line across the city, killing ten people, injuring another thirty, and damaging twenty-four buildings.

So swift and unexpected was the attack that no warning had been broadcast over the local radio, and no antiaircraft fire directed against the lone B-29 which had dropped the bombs.

Dr. Shima rushed to reassure his patients and staff. Next, he made several telephone calls to Hiroshima Castle. He then waited until the usual morning staff meeting before speaking about the matter further. Dr. Shima knew it was important not to disturb the normal routine of the clinic.

As he sat cross-legged on the floor sipping tea and discussing case histories and further treatment, his calmness soothed his staff. It was only at the end of the meeting that he mentioned the bombing.

Though the army had imposed a news blackout about the attack, Dr. Shima had discovered that the city's military leaders believed the raid was a fluke.

He explained their view to the staff: the enemy would not have sent a solitary bomber halfway across the Pacific simply to drop a few bombs on Hiroshima. The B-29 had doubtless become separated from a larger force, missed its original target—probably Kure —and simply scattered its bombs on the nearest available city, which, unhappily for them, happened to be Hiroshima.

The staff was not altogether reassured by this explanation. One raised the perpetual fear that the bombers would return in force.

Dr. Shima knew that the city's good fortune in thus far escaping mass air attack had increased the expectation among many of its people of such a calamity's occurring. Dr. Shima knew that by "imagining the worst," people felt they could actually ward off disaster.

He himself was a fatalist, believing that whatever lay ahead, nothing he could do would alter matters. He now offered his staff a simple reaffirmation of his beliefs. "If we are attacked tonight or sometime in the future, we can do nothing to prevent it. What we can do is to remain calm and cheerful and set an example to our patients."

Alone in his office that night, Dr. Shima did something that an increasing number of Japanese were doing. He tuned his radio to receive the shortwave transmission relayed directly from Guam, bringing, in impeccable Japanese, news of the war that Japan Radio could never broadcast.

The penalty for listening to such enemy broadcasts was death. But for men like Dr. Shima who had come increasingly to distrust the claims of continuing victories made by Japanese Radio, the risks were worthwhile.

Radio Guam had been first with the news that Iwo Jima had fallen; this morning, the modulated voice of the unknown Japanese-American speaking from fifteen hundred miles away spoke of the terrible losses the Japanese were experiencing on Okinawa. Then the broadcast dealt with the latest raids on Tokyo and other cities. He warned that Japan would be razed to the ground unless it surrendered.

The broadcast left Dr. Shima with a feeling of acute despair. He returned the radio dial to the local station, switched it off, and left his office to go home to bed.

Shortly after dawn that same day, in Kure, the wife of submarine commander Mochitsura Hashimoto tried to awaken her husband. An air-raid alert had just sounded, and it was time for the family to go to the shelter.

Cradling her three small sons in her arms, Hashimoto's wife called with increasing urgency for her husband to wake up.

Hashimoto continued to sleep. Nothing short of an earthquake would awaken him after his last, traumatic voyage.

On April 2, the day after the Americans first landed on Okinawa, Hashimoto was ordered to attack enemy shipping in the area. The outward journey had been a foretaste of what lay ahead. American bombers had mined the coastal waters of the Inland Sea, making it hazardous even before reaching the waters of the Pacific. And when Hashimoto finally arrived off Okinawa, he was promptly bombed by American planes. During the seven days he remained near the island, he was attacked at least fifty times. The longest period he could allow on the surface was a scant four hours in the middle of the night, barely enough time to ventilate the boat and recharge its batteries.

Hashimoto had just missed seeing the American cruiser *Indianapolis* limping from the scene of battle. It was returning to San Francisco for repairs after having been badly mauled by a kamikaze.

At Okinawa, submarine *I.58,* like the *Indianapolis,* took a beating. Even so, Hashimoto was furious when he was ordered back to base. Only when he reached Kure on April 29 had he learned that his boat was the sole Japanese submarine to return safely from Okinawa. He was also informed that *I.58* would have to remain in dock for a major inspection.

Too tired to really care, Hashimoto had stumbled home to bed, giving firm instructions to his wife that nothing should be allowed to disturb him.

Now, all her urgent calling did not awaken him. Then she realized it was too late—the familiar drone of aircraft engines was overhead.

Kure Harbor held most of Japan's remaining warships. It was a priority target for American bombers, which regularly attacked the area in spite of its well-entrenched defenses. This morning, the bark of anti-aircraft fire mingled again with the noise of exploding bombs.

Clutching her children, Mrs. Hashimoto lay down beside her still-slumbering husband and listened to the sounds of war.

• 35 •

Precisely at 9:00 A.M. on May 8, 1945, President Truman broadcast live to the American nation. In London and Moscow, Churchill and Stalin gave their people the news at the same time. "The Allied armies, through sacrifice and devotion and with God's help. . . ."

Victory in Europe was a fact.

Truman's words, delivered on this, his sixty-first birthday, confirmed what every American wanted to hear: Germany had surrendered unconditionally. For the first time in modern history, the entire armed forces of a nation became prisoners of war.

In the national rejoicing for V-E Day, most ordinary Americans momentarily forgot Japan. Truman did not. In the twenty-four days he had been president, he had thoroughly briefed himself on his predecessor's position on a Japanese surrender. Truman had come to the same conclusion: just as with Germany, only unconditional surrender was acceptable for Japan. Pearl Harbor and Japanese atrocities against American prisoners of war made such an uncompromising attitude virtually inevitable.

However, inside the State Department, some officials were arguing that the American government should modify this position, and that a way should be found to make peace with Japan before the Russians intervened and established a Soviet influence in the Pacific. Opposing this view were those who felt that any leniency was unwarranted and would allow the Japanese militarists to survive.

While the internal debate continued, U.S. monitors listening to Japan Radio had picked up a report of a recent statement by Suzuki, the new prime minister of Japan. Although secretly charged by the emperor to bring an end to the war, Suzuki had delivered an astonishingly militant speech to the Diet, telling them that unconditional surrender was totally unacceptable. Japan must fight to the very end.

Suzuki made a passionate appeal to the people.

Should my services be rewarded by death, I expect the hundred million people of this glorious Empire to swell forward over my prostrate body and form themselves into a shield to protect the Emperor and this Imperial land from the invader.

Truman's first public pronouncement on Japan since becoming president answered Suzuki.

The Japanese people have felt the weight of our land, air, and naval attacks. So long as their leaders and the armed forces continue the war, the striking power and intensity of our blows will steadily increase, and will bring utter destruction to Japan's industrial war production, to its shipping and to everything that supports its military activity.

The longer the war lasts, the greater will be the suffering and hardships which the people of Japan will undergo—all in vain. Our blows will not cease until the Japanese military and naval forces lay down their arms in unconditional surrender.

Just what does the unconditional surrender of the armed forces of Japan mean for the Japanese people? It means the end of the war. It means the termination of the influence of the military leaders who brought Japan to the present brink of disaster. It means provision for the return of soldiers and sailors to their families, their farms and their jobs. And it means not prolonging the present agony and suffering of the Japanese in the vain hope of victory.

Unconditional surrender does not mean the extermination or enslavement of the Japanese people.

It was a clear statement of the American government's position: Surrender unconditionally, or face Armageddon. Short-wave broadcasts beamed it to Japan.

Truman's warning was dismissed as propaganda. Japan Radio repeated the nation's determination to fight on.

Truman could only reflect: They have been warned.

Shortly before dawn, Mayor Awaya and his family, along with many other households in the district, were awakened by the sound of trucks, loud knocking, and cries of fear.

The Kempei Tai, the dreaded military police, were continuing the roundup they had begun in early May of people suspected of voicing in private the opinion that the government should make peace. Almost four hundred prominent public figures had been arrested in Hiroshima in the past fortnight.

The Kempei Tai throughout Japan had begun arresting all suspected radicals following the broadcast of Truman's speech on May 8.

Since then, the American broadcasts had been a constant reminder to those in Japan who dared risk their lives listening that the truth was other than as broadcast by Japan Radio.

Many of the American broadcasts were made by Captain Ellis Zacharias, USN, speaking in fluent Japanese. His voice was becoming as familiar to some Japanese as was that of Tokyo Rose to American servicemen in the Pacific.

Few of his listeners suspected that Zacharias's words were being carefully studied by government officials in

Tokyo for a sign that the United States might, after all, change its mind about unconditional surrender. To the bulk of his listeners, Zacharias was simply an astonishingly well-informed foreigner with a rare understanding of how the Japanese thought and expressed themselves. He did not threaten or bluster; he simply presented the inescapable facts.

In Hiroshima, the Kempei Tai had carried out their customary predawn arrests. Operating from headquarters on the grounds of Hiroshima Castle, the eight-hundred-man-strong Kempei Tai unit had full powers over every civilian and soldier in the city. The interrogators were provided with an official manual, entitled *Notes for the Interrogation of Prisoners of War,* which contained specific instructions on how to apply a variety of tortures to the body and mind.

The Kempei Tai in Hiroshima were able to perfect their techniques on local civilians whom they had arrested. But what the interrogators hoped for were American prisoners. All units in the area had been alerted that if any enemy fliers were shot down, they must immediately be delivered to Kempei Tai headquarters at Hiroshima Castle.

· 36 ·

The evening of May 8, Tibbets sipped a few soft drinks in the officers' mess at Wendover and retired early. He had moved into the club after his wife and children had vacated their house just outside the base gates; all the 509th's families had now departed in preparation for the group's move to Tinian. Lucie Tibbets and the boys had gone home to her parents. Tibbets, caught up in an ever-increasing merry-go-round of flying between Wendover, Washington, and Albuquerque, felt it was "best" that his family was away. He was being driven hard; his mind was a whirl of conferences and high-level telephone conversations, often conducted in code, with Groves. He was having to cope with the strain of running a complex organization in which he was the only one who knew the precise details of the end product. Every problem ultimately ended up on his desk; every hour he had to make decisions, whether they involved flying-fitness reports, engine reports, bombing reports, security reports, or sickness reports. His life, he felt, was "just one damn report after another."

Lucie wrote that she and the children had settled in "just fine" with her mother. Tibbets was pleased, but without his wife, life at Wendover was even emptier. The departure of the eight-hundred-man-strong main ground echelon for Tinian two weeks earlier had left the base seeming "like a ghost town."

Tibbets was glad of an excuse to get away to Omaha to do what he called "a little shopping."

On the south side of Omaha, covering hundreds of acres, the Martin bomber plant was carefully guarded. Flying over the plant, Tibbets glimpsed the guards at the main gate and the men patrolling the high fence that surrounded the area.

He landed and taxied his transport to the aircraft reception area, passing several B-29s being towed out of the assembly sheds. He was happy to see that here, at least, it was just another working day and that the airplane workers had not taken time off to recover from their victory-in-Europe celebrations.

At the reception area he presented his ID card to a waiting manager and was taken to a long, cavernous building. There, his credentials were checked again. Nobody without proper authority was admitted.

The code name Silverplate ensured that Tibbets was going to be able to do something few other fliers in the air force could: he was going to choose his own personal B-29, the one he intended to use on the first atomic mission.

The senior assembly-line foreman escorted Tibbets down the production line. Regularly, they paused to clamber up the scaffolding to look at a bomber. Once, Tibbets turned to the foreman and said the B-29 they were inspecting looked fine.

The foreman shook his head. "First shift."

"First shift" signified a bomber whose assembly had been started by a shift that had just returned to work after its days off—by men who were still recovering from two days of drinking and partying or just plain relaxing. They were not quite at their best; they sometimes produced a bomber "where all the nuts and bolts haven't always been double-checked."

Tibbets moved on.

The foreman stopped at another B-29. Gangs of riveters and fitters swarmed over the fuselage. They gave Tibbets a brief, curious stare, then continued their work.

Tibbets and the foreman climbed up to the cockpit. It was already fitted with its leather seats. Tibbets sat down and looked out through the domed nose at the bustling factory floor.

The foreman's shout was reassuring. "This is the one for you."

The plane's assembly had been started by men who were working at their peak, where "even the screws on the toilet seat were given an extra turn." The foreman told Tibbets this was the best plane in the factory. His words sealed the transaction.

A delivery date was agreed upon. Tibbets told the foreman that he would send Lewis and his crew to pick up the plane.

• 37 •

There was one vacant chair at the long conference table on May 28. It was next to Tibbets's chair. Senior naval and army officials and scientists from the Manhattan Project looked pointedly at the empty space. Tibbets stared back impassively. Inwardly, he was seething. Inexplicably, Beser had failed to show for this important Target Committee meeting.

The previous meeting, on May 12, had clarified many operational details: the proximity fuzes on the atomic bomb would probably be set to detonate about two thousand feet above the ground; if the weather over the target made it impossible to bomb visually, the weapon should be brought back, this operation inevitably involving some risks to the base and other aircraft; if for any reason it was found necessary to jettison the bomb, care must be taken that this was not done in water near American-held territory, since "water leaking into the gun-type bomb will set off a nuclear reaction."

The May 12 meeting had also discussed specific targets. The emperor's palace in Tokyo had been considered, but was not recommended. However, the committee members "agreed we should obtain information from which we could determine the effectiveness of our weapon against this target."

Finally, the meeting had earmarked four cities for possible atomic attack. They were, in order of preference, Kyoto, Hiroshima, Yokohama, and Kokura. All four cities had been "reserved": bombing of them by conventional weapons was henceforth prohibited. Now, at this third meeting of the Target Committee, these and other targets were to be further considered.

Promptly at 9:00 A.M., Groves took his place at the far end of the room. The meeting opened with an aide's handing out target-description files. Each contained large-scale maps, reconnaissance photographs, and related data; as the meeting was also to review air-sea rescue procedures and navigational aids, maps of the Pacific and Japanese coastal waters were distributed.

Tibbets had wanted Beser present specifically to answer any questions about radar. He had allowed him to fly to Washington in advance so that the radar officer could visit his parents in Baltimore over the weekend. Beser had promised to meet Tibbets outside the con-

ference room before the meeting began, but there was
no sign of him.

Beser arrived after an MP had closed the doors to
conference room 4E200 and posted himself outside
them.

The WAC officer at the reception desk near the MP
eyed Beser suspiciously. "Are you lost, Lieutenant?"

"Not if this is the Pentagon, ma'am."

"This is a restricted area, Lieutenant."

"I know. And I'm late!"

Beser turned toward the guarded door. The MP
stiffened. The WAC raised her voice. "You can't go in
there!"

Beser turned. "Ma'am, if this is the Target Committee meeting, they're expecting me!"

"You want me to believe a *lieutenant* is expected in
there with all *that* top brass!"

"Yes, ma'am."

"Lieutenant, why don't you go get some coffee and
forget you ever walked in here."

"Ma'am, you're making a heck of a mistake—"

"Lieutenant, go!"

"Yes, ma'am!"

Beser left and waited outside the reception area.
Thirty minutes later he was still there when he heard
a whispered conversation going on behind him. He
turned to see an angry major towering over the WAC.
The door of the conference room was ajar. The major
spotted Beser.

"Are you Beser?"

"Yes, sir."

"Goddam, you should have been inside!"

"I know. Somebody should have told this lady that."

"They're waiting for you to answer a question! Get
in there!"

Beser strolled as nonchalantly as he could into the
conference room.

A navy captain was addressing the gathering. He
stopped in midsentence and glared at Beser.

Tibbets motioned for Beser to sit beside him. Beser began to whisper an explanation to Tibbets. "First the train from Baltimore was late. Then I couldn't get a cab at Union Station, and finally this WAC—"

The captain interrupted Beser's soliloquy. "If the lieutenant is quite ready to answer the question?"

Beser looked around helplessly.

Tibbets saved him from further embarrassment by restating the question. "The matter is this. The navy wants to place a submarine three miles off the Japanese coast and put out a loran beam for us to navigate by on our approach to the target. In the event of trouble, the beam could also be used to guide us to the submarine for a possible sea rescue." Loran was a sophisticated radar development that both the navy and air force had started using.

The captain spoke again to Beser. "The question is, Lieutenant, what are your views on this proposal?"

"It's bullshit!"

The captain gaped. Tibbets groaned. The rest of the room remained deathly quiet. From the top of the table, Groves's voice filled the void. "Why do you say that?"

"Sir, I don't believe you can hold a submarine that steady. The tides are going to pull it off track. The boat's going to be fighting the motion of the sea. The submarine must be on the surface for loran to work. And in no way can it remain surfaced three miles off the Japanese coast without coming under attack."

Groves's next words closed the matter. "Those seem good enough reasons. Let's move to the next item on the agenda, the positioning of rescue aircraft. . . ."

Beser turned to Tibbets and whispered anxiously, "Was that all right?"

Tibbets mouthed a one-work reply. "Bull's eye!"

For two days, in the closest secrecy, some of the best civilian, scientific, and military brains in the United States had met to consider the future of the atomic bomb.

The Interim Committee, under the watchful eye of Secretary of War Stimson, was holding its fourth and, as it was turning out, its most crucial meeting in a month.

For this meeting, the committee's distinguished scientific panel was also present. The members were Robert Oppenheimer, Enrico Fermi, Ernest O. Lawrence, and Arthur Compton. Not only did this panel advise the committee, it also acted as a conduit for the ideas of other scientists.

The committee's discussions had continued well into this first day of June. The committee listened intently as the Manhattan Project's scientific director revealed details of both types of bomb, the uranium gun-type weapon and the plutonium bomb, which would undergo testing at Alamogordo in seven weeks' time. Since each bomb was virtually handmade, supplies were strictly limited, and it had been decided not to test the uranium bomb, as "it is expected that it will work."

The uranium bomb, like its sister, would achieve its principal effect by blast; that effect might be felt up to a mile or more away from the explosion.

In answer to another question, Oppenheimer stated the bomb would be ideal for use against a concentration of troops or war plants, and that it might kill "about 20,000 people."

Shortly afterward, the meeting adjourned for lunch.

No notes were taken during the meal, and who said what would forever remain a matter of dispute. According to physicist Arthur Compton, he asked Stimson whether it might be possible to arrange a nonmilitary demonstration of the atomic bomb in such a manner that the Japanese would see the futility of continuing the war.

Both Lawrence and Oppenheimer were said to be skeptical of the suggestion. Oppenheimer was said to have doubted "whether any sufficiently startling demonstration could be devised that would convince the Japanese that they ought to throw in the sponge."

After lunch, Stimson reportedly argued that "nothing

would have been more damaging to our effort to obtain surrender than a warning or a demonstration followed by a dud—and this was a real possibility. Furthermore, we had no bombs to waste. It was vital that a sufficient effect be quickly obtained with the few we had."

The ultimate responsibility rested with Stimson for recommending to Truman whether and how the bomb should be used. Privately, he had already made up his mind. He felt that "to expect a genuine surrender from the Emperor and his military advisors, they must be administered a tremendous shock which would carry convincing proof of our power to destroy the Empire. Such an effective shock would save many times the number of lives, both American and Japanese, that it would cost."

The Interim Committee came to the same conclusion. At the end of its deliberations, it offered three recommendations for the president about the first use of the atomic bomb:

It should be used as soon as possible;

It should be used on a military installation surrounded by houses or other buildings most susceptible to damage;

It should be used without explicit prior warning of the nature of the bomb.

While the president was being advised to act, some of the scientists who had helped make the awesome new weapon were still trying to limit its use. Some preferred that Japan be warned; others insisted that a public demonstration of the bomb's might would be enough to cause Japan's militarists to capitulate.

On June 12, seven scientists from the Chicago laboratory submitted a petition to the secretary of war urging a demonstration before observers from many countries in an uninhabited area. It was the Franck

Report, destined to become the most famous document concerned with the use of the atomic bomb. It was submitted, through channels, to the Interim Committee's Scientific Panel.

On June 16, the panel met in Oppenheimer's office in Los Alamos to consider the report. They acknowledged it was a fair-minded and serious attempt to present all sides of a complex issue. But in the end, the panel reported "with heavy heart" to the Interim Committee that "we can propose no technical demonstration likely to bring an end to the war; we see no acceptable alternative to direct military use."

The committee agreed with the conclusion of its Scientific Panel. In four momentous days, the Franck Report had been delivered, discussed, and discounted.

In the meantime, on June 12 General Groves had received a summons in midmorning to see Stimson at the War Department. Stimson's first request to Groves was for the names of the Japanese cities that had been reserved for possible atomic attack.

Groves hesitated. Only this very morning he had completed drafting a memo to Marshall. It was headed "Atomic Fission Bombs," stamped "top secret," and contained concise summaries of four targets: Kokura, Hiroshima, Niigata, and Kyoto.

These were the latest revised recommendations of the Target Committee. In making that selection, the committee had taken into account the "psychological factors"; it was deemed desirable to make the first use of the bomb "sufficiently spectacular for the importance of the weapon to be internationally recognized when publicity on it was released."

Psychologically, Kyoto was seen as the best target: it had the "advantage of the people being more highly intelligent and hence better able to appreciate the significance of the weapon."

On the other hand, Hiroshima "has the advantage of being such a size and with possible focussing from nearby mountains that a large fraction of the city may be destroyed."

Groves still favored Kyoto. Its intelligentsia would spread the word of the bomb's awesome power. Faced with such evidence, the Japanese government would have to surrender.

Groves believed that bringing about that surrender was a military matter. He therefore told Stimson that he planned to submit the suggested target list to General Marshall the next day for approval.

"I wish to see it."

Groves tried to conceal his alarm. "I would rather not show you the report without having first discussed it with General Marshall, as this is a military operational matter."

Stimson had spent thirty-five years in public service, most of it close to U.S. presidents. He was not used to being opposed, though old age had taught him tolerance. He continued to extend it toward Groves. "This is a question I am settling myself. Marshall is not making that decision. I would like to see the report."

Groves continued to hedge. "It's back in my office."

"Then have it brought over."

"It will take some time."

Stimson's patience ran out. Fixing his eyes on Groves, he made his point acidly clear. "I have all morning. Use my telephone to get it over here right away."

An unhappy Groves sent for the report.

Stimson again asked Groves to name the targets.

"The primary is Kyoto. . . ."

"I will not approve that city."

"Mr. Secretary, I suggest you will change your mind after you read the description of Kyoto and our reasons for considering it to be a desirable target."

"I doubt it."

Stimson explained something Groves had never seriously considered. "Kyoto is an historical city, and one that is of great religious significance to the Japanese. I visited it when I was Governor-General of the Philippines, and was very much impressed by its ancient culture."

A messenger arrived with the target report. Groves launched into the argument in favor of Kyoto: the city was filled with booming war plants; it was an ideal choice. Stimson cut him short, called in Marshall, and repeated his strong objections to Groves's proposal.

Groves later produced the only detailed account of what followed.

> Marshall did not express too positive an opinion, though he did not disagree with Mr. Stimson. It was my impression that he believed it did not make too much difference either way. . . . Personally, I was very ill at ease about it and quite annoyed at the possibility that he might think I was short-cutting him on what was definitely a subject for his consideration. After some discussion, during which it was impossible for me discreetly to let General Marshall know how I had been trapped into bypassing him, the Secretary said that he stuck by his decision. In the course of our conversation, he gradually developed the view that the decision should be governed by the historical position that the United States would occupy after the war. He felt strongly that anything that would tend in any way to damage this position would be unfortunate. On the other hand, I particularly wanted Kyoto as a target because it was large enough in area for us to gain complete knowledge of the effects of an atomic bomb. Hiroshima was not nearly so satisfactory in this respect.

Still "ill at ease and annoyed," Groves retreated to his office. Despite Stimson's strictures, during the time ahead Groves would continue to press for Kyoto even though he was told that the president himself also opposed atom-bombing that city.

Later Groves would claim, by a somewhat dubious

twist of logic, that it was he who was responsible for actually saving Kyoto. "If we had not recommended Kyoto as an atomic target, it would not of course have been reserved and would most likely have been seriously damaged, if not destroyed, before the war ended."

• 38 •

For the past seven days, Lewis and his crew had been waiting in Omaha to pick up the new bomber. Ever since Tibbets had chosen the plane, it had been receiving "special handling," and consequently the plant was delayed in turning it over to Lewis.

While waiting, some of the crew had picked up girls and held a succession of increasingly wild parties at a local hotel. One of the men got involved with a married woman, and they were caught in bed together by her husband. In the ensuing fight, the police were called, and it had taken Lewis's considerable diplomacy to square matters. He had also placated irate motorists after another of the fliers "bombed" passing cars with beer bottles from his bedroom window. When the hotel management complained, Lewis managed to calm them down.

Over the past months, Lewis had become increasingly protective toward his crew. Within the group, the barriers of rank largely disappeared; there was an easy, first-name relationship between officers and enlisted men. Socially, Lewis spent considerable time in the enlisted men's club, removing his officer's jacket and often wearing one of Sergeant Joe Stiborik's instead.

Private Richard Nelson, the nineteen-year-old radioman, found the way Lewis treated him as an equal surprising. Caron believed the pilot was trying to develop a close-knit, interdependent unit in which the men "could rely on each other in combat."

When flying, Lewis still did everything "by the

book"; he punished mistakes with a few choice words. But no outsider was allowed to criticize what he considered "his crew." He told the men, "You got a problem, I'll sort it out."

Before flying to Omaha, Sergeant Robert Shumard, the tall, soft-spoken assistant engineer, came to Lewis visibly upset because one of the MPs at Wendover had shot and killed his red setter dog. Lewis's anger was awesome; he verbally flayed the MP. His reaction only increased the respect and affection the crew had for their unorthodox captain.

Equally, some of them resented the intrusion of Ferebee and van Kirk, even Beser and Jeppson, and, on those rare days when he flew with them, Tibbets. On those occasions, Lewis was "demoted" to copilot. Even then, he tried to make it clear that it was "his crew" that was flying the plane.

Caron felt that Lewis and his overpossessiveness could create a problem when the colonel came to fly the mission. The tail gunner had no doubt that it would be Tibbets who would command the first strike. He liked the days when Tibbets flew with them. "He was just a gentleman, quiet and studious. Now Bob, he was a fine pilot, but he behaved like a cowboy."

This morning of June 14 at the Martin plant in Omaha, Lewis had his regular crew with him. It was a red-letter day for them all. With a good deal of joking and storytelling, they inspected their shiny new B-29. After preflight-checking the plane thoroughly, flight engineer Duzenbury said he was satisfied. Lewis ordered the crew aboard, started engines, and took off. He circled Omaha once, and then set course for Wendover.

At 9:30 A.M., the Joint Chiefs of Staff arrived in Truman's office. With them came Stimson, his assistant, John J. McCloy, and other senior advisors.

For two days, on June 14 and 15, the chiefs, the military heads of the armed forces, had been perfecting their invasion plans for Japan, code-named "Olympic" and "Coronet."

Olympic called for an initial assault against southern Kyushu on November 1, 1945, with a force of 815,548 troops; Coronet was the plan for the invasion of Honshu five months later, in the Tokyo area, with a commitment there of a further 1,171,646 men.

Truman listened intently as General Marshall presented the case for invasion. A "considerable discussion" followed on the expected casualty rate.

Stimson summed up the prospects. "A landing operation would be a very long, costly and arduous struggle on our part . . . the terrain, much of which I have visited several times, has left the impression on my memory of being one which would be susceptible to a last-ditch defense."

The possibility of a political settlement after a warning to the Japanese was raised by Stimson's assistant. McCloy believed there were many Japanese who did not favor the war, and, given the opportunity, their opinions might be influential.

The suggestion caught the meeting unawares.

Stimson agreed that Japan was "not a nation composed of mad fanatics of an entirely different mentality from ours." He also agreed that before the actual invasion some sort of "last-chance warning" should be given which made clear to the Japanese leaders that if they did not surrender, they would be responsible for what followed. Stimson was not yet sure whether or how this warning should be linked to the atomic bomb.

The chiefs listened but expressed no opinion about the atomic bomb—except that if it was used it should be dropped without prior notice. The matter was not pressed, for nobody in the room could yet know what the bomb would actually do. And nobody, in McCloy's words, could even be "certain in spite of the assurances of the scientists that 'the thing would go off.' "

Without positive proof of the weapon's viability, it was impossible to plan a meaningful strategy other than in terms of conventional warfare.

Truman reluctantly approved the invasion plans,

aware that ultimately a million American lives could be lost as a result of his decision.

President Truman's concern about casualties would doubtless have been even greater had he known that Japanese intelligence had anticipated the American plans, and that at the very moment he was giving the go-ahead for the invasion of Kyushu, reinforcements were being rushed to that island.

Those forces, charged with repelling the Americans, now had their headquarters in Hiroshima.

• 39 •

Shortly after dawn on June 19, a dull rumble awoke Second Lieutenant Tatsuo Yokoyama. The sound came from within Mount Futaba. Construction gangs were using compressor tools to burrow out an underground communications complex inside the base of the hill.

Yokoyama's gun post was immediately above the bunker, and it meant that he and his men lived from dawn to dusk with a jarring sound beneath their feet that reminded Yokoyama of earth tremors.

The destruction he had witnessed on his last visit to Tokyo, coupled with his parents' attitude toward the proposed marriage to his commanding officer's daughter, had left Yokoyama badly shaken. To make matters worse, he had been away during the second American air attack on Hiroshima. Nor was he consoled by Colonel Abe, his commander, who said that with each day that passed, the chances of Yokoyama's seeing action increased.

Abe continued to be solicitous, treating Yokoyama as if he were already a member of the family. But Yokoyama was not so sure. His mother had written a guarded letter saying his father was having to delve deeper into the girl's background. Until these inquiries were complete, she urged her son to limit his social contact with his commander. Yokoyama found himself inventing excuses to turn down invitations to dine at Abe's home or visit him at the officers' mess in Hiroshima Castle. The temptation to go was strong. Yokoyama would have given anything to escape the tedium of life on the gun post.

Instead, he would spend this day, as he did all the others, drilling his men—and surveying through his binoculars the signs that Hiroshima was now the linchpin in the defense of the whole of the western half of Japan. By road, rail, and sea, in defiance of American bombers and submarines, men and supplies were pouring into the city. After further training and fitting-out there, they were moved to their forward positions on Kyushu. Remaining in his command center in Hiroshima, in charge of all troops in the west, was the man who had been chosen by his emperor and the high command to save Japan from defeat.

At the foot of Mount Futaba, not far from Yokoyama's protective antiaircraft guns, Field Marshal Shunroku Hata had set up his headquarters.

Hata was one of the most successful, famous, and respected commanders in all Japan. He was close to the emperor and had once been considered for the post of prime minister. Instead, he was given a position perhaps as important: he was named head of the Second General Army and told that only he could save Japan from ignominious defeat.

His arrival in Hiroshima disturbed the officers in Hiroshima Castle. Quiet-mannered but stern, Hata overawed them. The sixty-five-year-old field marshal had more experience of war than all of them put together. They were relieved when he decided not to make his headquarters in the castle.

By the middle of June, Hata's headquarters staff of some four hundred men included many of the best military brains in the country. They planned to wage a war of attrition the like of which the world had never witnessed.

Gradually, under Hata's command, the island of Kyushu was being turned into an armed fortress; from the Goto Archipelago in the north to the Osumi Islands in the south, a system of interlocked defenses was being erected. They stretched back from the coast, layer upon layer, devised to cause the maximum casualties to the enemy. Linking it all was a complicated communications network controlled from Hiroshima and ending at Hata's headquarters.

The city itself was a beehive of war industry; hardly a home was not involved in manufacturing parts for kamikaze planes and boats, for bombs, shell casings, rifles, and handguns.

Recently an order had been given to plaster the walls of the city with a new slogan:

FORGET SELF!
ALL OUT FOR YOUR
COUNTRY!

Hata planned that when invasion came, every man, woman, and child in western Japan would carry a weapon.

Children were shown how to construct and hurl gasoline bombs; enough bottles and fuel were being conserved to make over three million.

Even the infirm were mobilized. In Hiroshima the bedridden and wheelchair-bound were assembling booby traps to be planted in the beaches of Kyushu.

For the main thrust against the invaders—an engagement now commonly referred to as "the great climactic battle"—Hata had under his command some four hundred thousand men, many of whom were already in place on Kyushu. Minoru Genda, the architect of the Pearl Harbor raid, had recently arrived there as commanding officer of a large, newly formed fighter group. In addition, there were about five thousand aircraft standing by, ready to be used as kamikazes.

In Hiroshima, forty thousand troops had their headquarters in the castle. Down by Hiroshima Harbor, at Ujina, a further five thousand soldiers, mostly marines, were perfecting their own novel seaborne kamikaze tactics. Hundreds of small suicide craft, most the size of rowboats, were being fitted with motors, filled with explosives, and concealed in coves around the bay. If an invasion force arrived, the boats would be brought out of hiding, and each, manned by its crew of one, would be steered into a landing craft to blow up on impact.

Hata believed that although it was impossible for Japan to defeat America, so also it could be made impossible for America to defeat Japan. He hoped that once the Americans had sampled the welcome he was preparing, they would come to the negotiating table and drop their demand that Japan surrender unconditionally.

• 40 •

Tibbets looked down on Hiroshima.

Its rivers, bridges, harbor, the castle and adjoining military drill fields were all clearly visible in the reconnaissance photographs before him. So were the roads, railroad, warehouses, factories, barracks, and private homes. Here and there the urbanization was broken up by parks and woods. Beyond the city lay the hills, cocooning Hiroshima on three sides. They provided an almost perfect natural barrier to contain an atomic blast.

He noted the ground defenses, an irregular chain of gun posts stretching from Mount Futaba in the northeast to the harbor in the south.

Speaking quietly and authoritatively, using all his accumulated experience of bombing, Tibbets delivered his judgment on the suitability of Hiroshima as a target. "The various waterways give ideal conditions. They allow for no chance of mistaking the city. Hiroshima can be approached from any direction for a perfect bombing run."

His listeners silently considered this assessment.

Tibbets continued with his careful study, now turning to reconnaissance photographs of other Japanese cities spread out on the conference table in General Henry Arnold's office in the Pentagon.

This June 23 meeting was the latest in a series that were settling the crucial details of how best to defeat Japan.

A few days ago, LeMay had flown in from Guam especially to attend. He had already been told—on a fleeting visit Tibbets made to Guam earlier in June—that it would be too dangerous for the crew to drop an atomic bomb from below twenty-five thousand feet. In Washington, Groves had spelled out to him the probable power of the bomb and the reason the potential targets had been chosen.

LeMay had barely reacted when Groves told him that the actual operation would be entirely under "your control, subject of course to any limitations that might be placed upon [you] by instructions." Only Groves knew that those instructions would be so worded that effective control of the operation would remain in his own hands.

LeMay had announced he would want to carry out the bombing operation using a single unescorted plane. He pointed out that the Japanese were unlikely to pay any serious attention to a solitary aircraft flying at high altitude, and would probably assume it was either on a reconnaissance or weather mission.

Groves had approved the idea. He did not tell Le-May that Tibbets had already come to a similar conclusion and that the 509th's training had been devised with that plan in mind.

LeMay had returned to Guam believing he would soon be responsible for delivering a weapon he didn't yet entirely have faith in. Nor was he convinced that

Tibbets and the 509th were the best choice for the mission. LeMay thought it might be preferable for one of his own Pacific combat-hardened veterans to do the job, a crew that had already proven its worth over Japan.

Tibbets, completely unaware of this, had flown from Wendover to Washington to attend this conference in Arnold's office. Having completed his evaluation of the reconnaissance photographs, he waited for questions from Groves and Arnold, chief of the air force.

They did not come. The two men stared silently at the photographs, their eyes going first to the glossy, thirty-inch-square prints of Hiroshima, then to those of Niigata and Kokura, the two other targets now on the list of Japanese cities reserved for possible atomic attack.

Groves asked Tibbets how he would approach Hiroshima.

Using his hand to indicate a route across the photograph, Tibbets explained that he would begin his bombing run east of the city and approach Hiroshima at an angle of ninety degrees to the rivers bisecting it. He pointed at a spot on the photograph close to Hiroshima Castle, where the Ota River breaks into tributaries.

"Suppose that's the aiming point. Approached crossways, any one of the riverbanks would provide a handy reference point against which the bombardier could check his final calculations. If we flew up one of the rivers, the bombardier would be looking mainly at water through his bombsight. It would be harder for him to tell when he was close to the AP."

Groves permitted himself a rare joke. "Colonel, I think by the time your bombardier gets over the target, he'll be able to spot it blindfolded."

The men around the table sat down, and the discussion continued on other aspects of launching an atomic strike.

Groves was involving himself in such detailed discussions because he had come to believe that

. . . some of the Air Force people . . . displayed a total lack of comprehension of what was involved. They had assumed that the atomic bomb would be handled like any other new weapon: that when it was ready for combat use, it would be turned over to the commander in the field, and though he might be given a list of recommended targets, he would have complete freedom of action in every respect.

The chief of the Manhattan Project felt the matter was "too complicated and all-important to be treated so casually"; that decisions about its use should be vested in him, though he did concede that "the President would also share in the control, not so much by making original decisions as by approving or disapproving the plans made by the War Department."

Watching Groves now, on the opposite side of the table, Tibbets was struck yet again that here was a man "who would move hell on earth to get his own way."

Tibbets had also worked out Groves's tactics: he "didn't like a face-off, preferring to attack from the flank."

Tibbets, on the other hand, believed in a frontal assault on any problem—or on any opposition. He thought that too much of his time was being consumed "messing; a lot of hours were being spent discussing imponderables."

But one imponderable Tibbets thought well worth discussing was that of the likely prevailing weather conditions over the target.

Ever since April, air force meteorologists had been preparing summary charts of the conditions that could be expected in the coming months over Japan. The data were based on information provided by the U.S. Weather Bureau and on old weather maps from the marine observatory at Kobe for the period 1927 to 1936.

The prognosis was poor. From June to September

there was a maximum of only six days a month when cloudiness was likely to be three-tenths or less. For this period, eight-tenths cloud could be expected for at least eighteen days in any month.

Bombing by radar had been considered and rejected. After considerable study, an expert had concluded:

It is apparently quite possible to completely misinterpret the images on the radar screen; a section of rural Japan could be mistaken for a city. With radar bombing and a good operator, the chance of placing the bomb within a given 1,000 foot circle is about 1% to 2%. This figure takes into account the fact that the probability of entirely missing the target area is from 70% to 50%.

By bombing visually, however, "in clear weather the probability that a good bombardier can place the bomb within a given circle of 1,000 feet radius lies between 20% and 50%."

Tibbets's own bombardiers were regularly dropping their practice bombs into a three-hundred-foot circle.

The air force meteorologist then told the meeting that between then and Christmas, August was probably the best time to drop the atomic bomb, "with the early part of the month offering marginally better weather conditions than the latter."

Tibbets liked the meteorologist's next suggestion. "Suppose no weather forecast at all was made, but that the mission started out on a given day, preceded by spotter planes who would radio back weather reports to the bomber while it was in the air. The bomber could then proceed to that target showing the clearest weather."

Tibbets felt this would be a simple and relatively uncomplicated procedure. The 509th could provide the weather planes, and he himself would be free to make the final decision, in the air, clear of any outside interference and pressures and with the very latest weather information, on which Japanese city would be bombed.

Lewis held back sixty-five tons of bomber, its tanks filled with seven thousand gallons of fuel, while he watched the rev counter. The needle climbed to 2200 and remained constant. The bomber shuddered, protesting against the brakes that held it at the end of the Wendover runway.

The copilot, seated beside Lewis, angled the wing flaps for takeoff. Over the intercom, Shumard and Stiborik, in the waist blister turrets, confirmed the flaps were set. Duzenbury reported all four engines were functioning smoothly.

Only then, satisfied that all the checks prior to takeoff had been made, did Lewis push the throttles forward to their full power positions and release the brakes.

At 260 feet a second, the B-29 rushed down the runway, carrying nine men, their equipment and personal belongings on the most exciting journey any of them had ever made.

Beneath them, in the bomb bay, was the remainder of the whiskey that Beser had purchased in Cuba, and a variety of goodies from the Wendover PX. The ever-thoughtful Lewis, looking out for his crew, particularly the enlisted men, had suggested they should stock up on any of the things they might miss in the Pacific.

Nelson had picked up a pile of paperbacks, thrillers and adventure stories. He planned to read a book on every mission he made over Japan. Caron had stowed away some good-quality stationery to write home to his wife. Shumard had purchased a box camera to take some photographs.

Accompanying them were also the crew's "trophies" —a couple of pairs of panties from bar girls in Salt Lake City, a carton of condoms which nobody claimed ownership to, and a garter belt, clipped over the toilet seat.

As usual, Lewis had explained the "house rule" for using the toilet. The first man to use it would be responsible for emptying and cleaning the chemical bucket at the end of the journey.

Lewis had known crew members to "bend their guts to avoid being the first to use the can." This always amused him, as he had trained himself to manage a ten-hour flight without once having to crawl back through the plane's central tunnel to use the toilet.

He eased the bomber into the air and began to circle over the base. He switched on the intercom. "Hold on! We're gonna buzz the tower!"

Caron, in the tail turret, braced himself.

At full power, the B-29 swooped down on the base. Shouting like dervishes, the crew encouraged Lewis to fly ever lower. Lewis tipped the plane on one wing tip. Soon his port wing was inches clear of the ground as the bomber made its madcap way across the airfield. Caron thought they "must have scared the pants off anybody watching, buzzing the field like a fighter plane."

The angry voice of the controller in the tower ordered Lewis to gain height at once.

The bomber continued on its low-level course, careening over the ground, its wing tip still only inches away from destruction. It was, for Nelson, "a magnificent example of flying skill."

Lewis eased the bomber to its cruising height and headed south. Already on Tinian were over twelve hundred men from the 509th and twelve of the group's B-29s.

The excitement on board Lewis's aircraft was unabated. None of the crew had ever before been overseas to a combat area. Most of their knowledge of the war had come from the movies and the *Saturday Evening Post* articles that Caron collected.

To them, war was a "chance to do something for your country," to "bring peace to the world," or, as Lewis preferred it, "to go and beat hell outta the Japs like they tried to beat hell outta us at Pearl and other places."

Lewis was not a bloodthirsty, vengeful young man;

nor, indeed, were any of the crew flying south with him. They were, in Caron's words, "just average guys going to do a job."

Now, flying to what they hoped would be a tropical paradise, Lewis marked the moment of departure from Wendover. "Tinian, here we come!"

ACCELERATION

JUNE 28, 1945,
TO AUGUST 2, 1945

Exhausted from his climb up Mount Lasso in the northern part of Tinian, Chief Warrant Officer Kizo Imai, Imperial Japanese Navy, lay flat on the moist jungle carpet of rotting leaves and fungi, face close to the earth, frayed cap pulled down over his forehead.

Hunger and a sense of duty drove the thirty-year-old officer to crawl regularly to this vantage point; at 564 feet, it was the highest hill on the island.

From here, Imai could see many of the compounds where the twenty thousand Americans on Tinian were billeted. More important, he could watch where they dumped their garbage. They constantly changed the sites. Imai supposed it was to make it more difficult for him, and the five hundred other Japanese troops in hiding on Tinian, to scavenge for food. Starvation had made them desperate. Even when the Americans dumped their garbage in the treacherous currents around the island, the Japanese plunged into the sea at night to grub for it.

Imai's home on Tinian was a cave, "a hole in Hell," where lice, rats, and other vermin added to the misery of life. Unshaven, unwashed, unkempt, he and others like him lived a troglodyte existence, seldom daring to light fires in their jungle hideaways lest they give away their positions. In his cave, Imai had left behind eighteen soldiers—all who survived of the forty-eight men he had originally led into hiding when the Americans had overrun the island eleven months before.

Imai had come to Tinian to help build airfields; three

runways had been completed and a fourth was under construction when, in June 1944, the Americans had struck.

Air attacks and naval bombardments had softened up the islands for six weeks. After Saipan was overrun, heavy artillery based there systematically pounded the northern end of Tinian. In one fifteen-day period, a shell a minute fell on the island. Fighters swooped low over Tinian dropping napalm bombs, the first time they were used in the Pacific.

In between, the Japanese garrison dug in. They believed that the Americans would attempt a landing at Tinian Town. The Japanese fortified the area; many of their guns were British six-inchers, captured at Singapore. And throughout the island, around sugarcane fields and behind thick jungle foliage, machine-gun nests were positioned and small foxholes prepared in which a solitary soldier huddled, cuddling explosives close to his body; if an American tank passed over his foxhole, he was ready to blow himself up along with the tank.

On the fortieth day of the siege, July 24, Imai had peered through the half-light of dawn to see the American battle fleet slowly circling the island, pumping thousands more shells on the ravaged landscape.

Opposite Tinian Town, the armada had halted and lowered its landing craft. The Japanese began firing their heavy guns. The Americans quickly retreated and reembarked. The Japanese were delighted.

Too late, they realized the attack on Tinian Town was a ruse. The bulk of the American forces had landed in the north of the island—a rugged, rocky area that the Japanese had thought unassailable.

With a foothold established, the U.S. marines had stormed inland. It took them eight days to reach Tinian Town and capture the island. Four hundred Americans were killed; over eight thousand Japanese died.

Chief Warrant Officer Imai had fled to the jungle, along with some seven hundred other Japanese survivors. In the months since then, that number had been whittled away to less than five hundred hunted men.

Now, on Mount Lasso, waiting for the garbage trucks to appear, Imai began his other task: noting down how the American forces were deploying themselves. This he did in preparation for an event he still expected to happen "at any moment": an invasion by imperial forces come to recapture the island. When that day came, Imai hoped to lead his men in a banzai charge against the Americans.

Meanwhile, through his binoculars, he could survey almost the whole island. Tinian from north to south is about twelve miles long; its width is never more than five miles. Gently undulating, the island is really a plateau jutting up from the Pacific. Most of its coastline consists of sheer cliffs of rusty brown lava rising from the sea. Tinian is at the southern end of the Mariana Islands, which together form an arc over 425 miles of the Pacific—clumps of coral that, until World War II, few people knew existed.

Scanning the horizon to the north, Imai could see the coast of Saipan, less than four miles away. As usual, the intervening sea was busy with American ships of all sizes and kinds. Some were making their way to the American naval anchorage at Tinian Town, three miles southwest of where Imai lay.

Inland from Tinian Town, originally only a cluster of shacks but now a busy military port, the Americans had completed the work the Japanese had begun: clearing away jungle to make runways, aprons, taxiways. Paved roads led to fuel and bomb dumps, workshops, and warehouses. There was a growing number of hospitals. Imai concluded that the Americans must be expecting a large number of casualties in some impending battle. His belief in the imminence of a Japanese assault on the Marianas grew. In fact, the hospitals were being readied to receive the casualties expected from the invasion of Kyushu.

Surveying the countryside, Imai's attention was attracted by something unusual. Below and about half a mile to the northwest, gangs of soldiers were completing the fencing in of a compound.

Rectangular in shape, half a mile long by a quarter-mile wide, the compound was tucked away in a low-lying area near the coast.

The new fence around the compound was high and forbidding. Behind the wire were different-sized Quonset huts connected by paths and roads. Until this morning the huts had been occupied by army construction gangs whom Imai had previously watched completing work on the giant airfield beyond the compound. Now they were vacating these quarters.

In the center of the compound, a smaller, closed-off area had been erected; thick coils of barbed wire surrounded a group of windowless huts. Armed guards stood at the only gate to this area. There were also several guards at the main entrance to the compound.

Imai felt uneasy. The compound looked like a prison camp; perhaps the inner area was a punishment block. In Imai's mind, this could mean only one thing: the Americans were planning a new drive to round up the remaining Japanese on the island.

Imai touched his weapons: a long ceremonial sword and a pistol. He didn't know if damp had made the bullets useless, but he was sure the sword blade, made by the same secret process that had fashioned the swords of the ancient samurai, was as sharp as the day he had received it, shortly before he had arrived on Tinian, in March 1944.

Peering down on the strange new compound, Imai was determined about one thing: he would rather die than surrender and end up imprisoned there. He was fascinated by the activity around the main entrance to the compound; a continuous procession of trucks was now driving up to the gates. There, the guards stopped and checked every vehicle.

As one of the trucks pulled up, two men got out and removed a large board from the back.

Imai focused his binoculars on the scene. Two white-helmeted MPs, carbines cradled in their arms, came into sharp focus. They looked tanned, healthy, and bored. He moved his glasses slightly to bring the board into view. Imai could read and speak a little English. Although he could not make out all the lettering, he was able to distinguish the numbers and some of the words. They were:

RESTRICTED. 509TH COMPOSITE GROUP
ALL PASSES TO BE SHOWN
AT ALL TIMES

A feeling of relief filled Imai. It was not, after all, a prison camp. But the compound was clearly different from all the others he had observed; it seemed to Imai that this one "must be very important."

Then another and more pressing thought filled the warrant officer's mind. So intent had he been on watching all the activity that he had completely neglected to note where the American garbage trucks had emptied their loads. Now he and the men waiting back in his cave would have to forage in the darkness among the trash cans—a risky business in view of the patrols that guarded each compound.

Nevertheless, Imai's time on Mount Lasso had been worthwhile. Careful not to leave any trail, he hurried back to the cave.

Inside, it was filthy, the ground littered with old food tins and other bits of flotsam scavenged during night forays throughout the island. Stacked in a corner were rifles and a few cases of ammunition. Beside them was a radio transmitter-receiver.

The last message it had received was on the night Tinian fell, when the supreme commander of the Imperial Japanese Army in Tokyo had sent word that help would be coming. Since then, there had been silence. Imai wished somebody knew how to fix the transmitter so that he could send a message to headquarters in Tokyo about the strange new compound on the island. Maybe they could even arrange to have it bombed.

· 2 ·

Tibbets continued to inspect the compound to ensure it would be a suitable final home for the 509th. He had flown from Wendover to do so. He would have been there sooner, but had delayed his departure from the United States so that his senior navigator, van Kirk, who had come with him, could have news before leaving of the birth of his new baby son. It was a gesture in keeping with Tibbets's aim to treat his men with consideration at all times—until they tried to take advantage. Then he could treat them, in his own words, "rougher than any MP master sergeant in a military prison."

Tibbets took his time over the inspection: he wanted the 509th to have "the best going," and not even Groves's personal representative on the island, Colonel E. E. Kirkpatrick, who was accompanying him on the inspection, was going to hurry Tibbets into a decision.

Impassive as usual, restricting his words to a few questions, Tibbets led Kirkpatrick and the commanders of the 509th's squadrons from one hut to another. Kirkpatrick had hoped Tibbets would not be "too finicky about housing." The rule on crowded Tinian was twelve officers or twenty enlisted men in a Quonset hut twenty-nine feet wide by fifty feet long. As group commander, Tibbets would share his accommodation with three or four senior staff officers.

Tibbets responded typically. "Before you settle my living space, I want to make sure the men are comfortable. This will be the fourth move they've had to make since arriving out here. I want it to be the last."

Kirkpatrick thought Tibbets a "bit cocky"—a view he would express to Groves in a secret memo—"inclined to rub his special situation in a bit, but smart enough to know how far he can go. He plays his cards well."

Tibbets thought it essential to establish the ground rules on how the 509th were to live and work. During his one previous visit to the Marianas, he had made it clear what those rules were. He wasn't, he would later insist, "looking for special treatment," but simply seeking to ensure that the group was properly settled within the framework of an existing and complicated air force operation.

On this second visit, he detected opposition—muted but discernible—behind the "glad-handing."

Some of it came from the Seabees, who were being moved from the most comfortable quarters on the island to make room for the 509th. Tibbets sympathized with them. They were all Pacific veterans, many of whom would be called upon to shed more sweat and blood in the invasion of Japan.

Tibbets knew that the invasion would be costly. The long and bitter campaign to secure Okinawa had just ended. It had taken over 500,000 troops three months to subdue the Japanese garrison of 110,000, who had fought fanatically and died almost to a man. If the American casualty figures for Okinawa were any guide —49,151 dead plus 34 warships sunk and 368 badly damaged—the resistance to be expected on the main islands would be formidable.

The latest American intelligence reports indicated that some of the two million battle-hardened troops in China were being brought home to help defend the homeland. Already in Japan were another two million soldiers, untried in battle but eager to fight. The vast mass of the imperial forces had not been beaten.

Tibbets had expressed to LeMay the hope that the atomic bomb would make them "see sense," and avert unnecessary bloodshed. LeMay concurred. The meeting between the two men at LeMay's Guam headquarters on June 27 had been cordial enough, though LeMay still had reservations about being able to pinpoint a target from thirty thousand feet. He told Tibbets the 509th fliers should get some experience, suggesting that, initially, they could drop their practice bombs on the nearby island of Rota, which was still in Japanese hands.

As their meeting was ending, LeMay made an unexpected remark. "Paul, I want you to understand one thing. No flying for you over the empire."

Tibbets was stunned.

Puffing steadily on his ever-present cigar, an action which made him look like a younger, not quite so bulldoggish Churchill, LeMay explained his reasons. "We don't want to risk losing you. I understand you know more about this bomb than any flier in the air force. You're too valuable. You'd better stay on the ground."

Tibbets said nothing. LeMay's order made sense: if he fell into Japanese hands, the entire project would be jeopardized. But Tibbets was determined on one thing: he would fly the first atomic strike, "come Hell or high water."

On Tinian, having completed his inspection of the new compound's living quarters, kitchens, and mess halls, Tibbets examined the "inner sanctum," the Tech Area workshops. There, if all went well, the bomb would be finally assembled. Two of the workshops would be ready in a few days; the other pair would not be complete until August 1.

Tibbets thought schedules were "running tight"; he wished he could remain on Tinian to see things through. But his presence was required as an observer during the critical test-firing of the plutonium bomb at Alamogordo.

His tour of the compound complete, Tibbets expressed himself satisfied. The 509th would move into its new quarters on July 8.

For the moment, there was no more he could do on Tinian. Having briefed the group's senior officers on daily routine matters, Tibbets began the long, weary plane journey back across the Pacific.

• 3 •

Squatting around an upturned crate, Beser and the other players tried to concentrate on their game. Even now, in the sudden tropical darkness, the cloying, enervating heat was stifling. The only garment each man wore, shorts—khaki trousers cut off about six inches below the crotch—was soaked with sweat.

As the evening wore on, the men around the makeshift card table had to raise their voices to make their bids heard. Not far away a stream of B-29s was taking off on another firebomb raid.

Tonight, as usual, the officers in the hut counted the number of aircraft, keeping score by the distinctive sound of engines being boosted to maximum power prior to takeoff. So far, the tally was 249 bombers airborne.

Silence returned to the island. But Beser offered a side bet that another bomber would take off within the next half hour, to make a round total of 250. Nickels and quarters were tossed onto the crate.

Soon afterward, the unmistakable roar of four 2,200-horsepower Wright turbo-supercharged engines starting up shattered the silence, and Beser collected his winnings.

Tired now of their game, he and the others listened to the bomber going through its preflight engine tests. Navigator Russell Gackenbach—the young lieutenant who had survived the security snares on that first day at Wendover—went out of the Quonset hut to watch the takeoff.

It was a pitch-black Tinian night, moonless, with a hot breeze blowing in off the sea.

Gackenbach sensed, rather than saw, the B-29. His ears followed the bomber as it left the apron and taxied to the runway. He glimpsed short stabs of flame from the engine exhausts. The engines were boosted to full power, the stabs grew brighter, then disappeared as the bomber roared down the runway.

Gackenbach cocked his head: one of the engines was out of pitch. He shouted into the Quonset hut. The others had also heard the sound. They joined Gackenbach. The group listened as the aircraft continued to roar down the runway.

"He's airborne!"

Gackenbach's shout of relief was followed by Beser's warning. "He's not going to make it!"

The words were followed by a bright, orange-red flash, low in the sky over the runway, enveloping the bomber.

A split second later, the roar of high-octane fuel exploding over incendiary bombs reached the horrified watchers. The flash spilled across the night sky, briefly lighting up an area of several hundred square yards.

The flames and noise faded as the wail of crash trucks took over.

The 509th officers turned and went back into the hut. They all knew that the most the crash trucks could do was sweep up a few charred remains.

Lewis switched on the intercom and told the crew to prepare for landing. Until now, it had been an eventless journey. Some fifteen miles ahead, Tinian appeared as an indistinct mass, hidden by a morning sun haze.

At his station, a small, windowless cubbyhole just forward of the front bomb bay, radioman Dick Nelson tuned the radio compass to Tinian's signal. Three days in the air, interspersed with brief stopovers where the food and accommodations were poor, had dampened Nelson's enthusiasm. He felt tired, in need of a bath, and, though he would never admit it to any of the men around him, a little apprehensive about the future.

He checked the IFF; the device continued to give out the silent signal which identified the B-29 as an American military aircraft.

The flat voice of a ground controller on Tinian gave Lewis the wind's speed and direction at North Field.

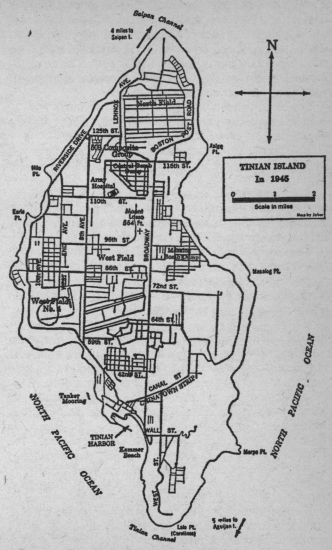

Tinian Island, 1945

Now Lewis gave the crew an enthusiastic view of the island. "It's wonderful! The jungle looks just like in the movies! Those beaches are made for Esther Williams! And the water's the bluest I've ever seen! We're gonna have a great time!"

After some six thousand miles and three days of flying, Lewis called out the landing orders.

When the wheels had been lowered, Stiborik and assistant engineer Shumard, in the waist blister turrets, confirmed the landing gear was locked in position.

"Flap check. Five degrees."

Again, Stiborik and Shumard reported when the flaps were down.

"Flap check. Twenty-five degrees."

The men in the blister turrets confirmed the change.

Moments later, Lewis touched down on North Field and taxied to the 509th's special dispersal area.

Caron's immediate—and abiding—impression when he crawled out of the tail turret was that "we had landed on the world's biggest latrine."

The bomber had parked downwind of one of the giant cesspools dug by the Seabees.

Lewis guessed he would soon get used to the stench. If that was the only drawback to Tinian, it really was Paradise, with its Quonset huts beneath palm fronds, and paths made of crushed coral kept tidy by smiling natives.

To further a feeling of home-away-from-home, and because Tinian was roughly the same shape as Manhattan, the principal roads had been named and signposted as New York streets.

Broadway was the longest thoroughfare, running from North Field past the foot of Mount Lasso down toward Tinian Town; a splendid highway, over six miles in length, lined with living and working quarters.

Parallel to Broadway, on the western side of the island, was Eighth Avenue, running from the beachhead the marines had established when they invaded Tinian, down past the island's second-largest landing

The *Enola Gay* as photographed in September 1945
(Photo: George Caron)

The crew of the first atomic mission. Kneeling: Sergeant
Joseph Stiborik, Sergeant George Caron, Sergeant Richard
Nelson, Sergeant Robert Shumard, Sergeant Wyatt
Duzenbury. Standing: Lieutenant Colonel Porter (ground
officer, not on crew), Captain Theodore Van Kirk, Major
Thomas Ferebee, Colonel Paul Tibbets, Captain Robert
Lewis, Lieutenant Jacob Beser. Missing from photo: Navy
Captain William Parsons, Lieutenant Morris Jeppson.
(Photo: George Caron)

Colonel Paul Tibbets waves before taking off on the first atomic mission. *(Photo: Paul Tibbets)*

Tibbets, on return from atomic mission, wearing the Distinguished Service Cross *(Photo: George Caron)*

Captain Robert Lewis in the aircraft commander's seat of the *Enola Gay* *(Photo: Robert Lewis)*

Tail-gunner George R. Caron (Photo: Richard Nelson)

Caron at his post aboard the *Enola Gay* (Photo: George Caron)

Chaplain William Downey (Photo: William Downey)

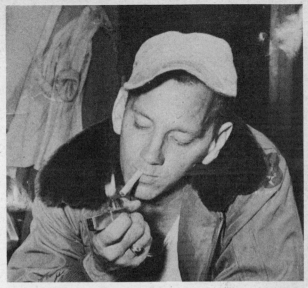

Flight engineer Wyatt Duzenbury (Photo: Richard Nelson)

Duzenbury in the tunnel connecting the rear and forward sections of the *Enola Gay.* Below him is the hatch leading to the bomb bay. (Photo: John King)

Radar operator Jacob Beser *(Photo: Jacob Beser)*

Bombardier Thomas Ferebee *(Photo: Richard Nelson)*

Navigator Theodore "Dutch" Van Kirk (Photo: Theodore Van Kirk)

Inside the top-secret compound of the 509th Composite Group *(Photo: John King)*

The wreckage of crashed B-29s on Runway A was a constant reminder of the dangers crews faced on take-off. *(Photo: Paul Tibbets)*

In August 1945, Tinian Island held the world's largest operational airfield. In the foreground are the four parallel runways of North Field. (Photo: John King)

The *Enola Gay* returns to Tinian. *(Photo: John King)*

General Spaatz salutes Tibbets after decorating him. *(Photo: George Caron)*

This reconnaissance photograph, recently declassified, was used in planning the atomic attack on Hiroshima. (Photo: U.S. Army Air Force)

Mayor Senkichi Awaya of Hiroshima (Photo: Authors' Collection)

Matsuo Yasuzawa, the instructor of kamikaze pilots who landed in Hiroshima just before the atomic bomb fell (Photos: Matsuo Yasuzawa)

Kanai Hiroto, who helped interrogate American prisoners of war in Hiroshima *(Photo: Kanai Hiroto)*

Kizo Imai, one of nearly 500 Japanese soldiers in hiding on Tinian Island in 1945 *(Photo: Kizo Imai)*

The staff of Second General Army Headquarters, Hiroshima. Among those shown are: Field Marshal Hata (front row, fourth from left); Prince RiGu (front row, third from left); Lieutenant Colonel Oya (second row, far right). *(Photo: Lieutenant Colonel Oya)*

Mochitsura Hashimoto, commander of the submarine I.56 (Photo: Mochitsura Hashimoto)

Mitsuo Fuchida, leader of the raid on Pearl Harbor, who arrived in Hiroshima shortly after the atomic bomb was dropped (Photo: Wide World Photos)

Hiroshima—before (Photo: Koichi Sako)

Hiroshima—after (Photo: Robert Lewis)

Shima Surgical Hospital after the atomic bomb exploded directly overhead (Photo: Dr. Kaoru Shima)

Hiroshima Industrial Promotion Hall, before the detonation
(Photo: Hiroshima Central Municipal Library)

Now known as the atomic dome, the Industrial Promotion
Hall has been allowed to remain largely as it was immediately after the detonation. (Photo: Reader's Digest)

strip, West Field, and eventually ending at Tinian Harbor.

Hugging the west coast was Riverside Drive, a gently curving road off which were several small beaches and coves.

Forty-second Street was at a busy crossroads in the southern section of Tinian, close to Wall Street, Grand Avenue, Park Row, and Canal Street, which led to Second Avenue, and another group of familiar-sounding roads, Fifty-ninth Street, Sixty-fourth Street, Seventy-second Street, and Eighty-sixth Street.

The 509th were in temporary quarters just east of Broadway near Eighty-sixth Street. When Lewis and his crew reached their huts, they found them empty. Nine of the 509th's crews were away on a practice mission, dropping high-explosive bombs on Rota.

It seemed to Lewis that he had arrived on Tinian not a moment too soon.

• 4 •

After two weeks of study, the situation was becoming clear. While there were still some gaps, Major General Arisue had been able to make an authoritative assessment of Japan's internal political situation.

It was desperate.

The battles between the militarists and the moderates, so far confined to words, threatened to shake the imperial throne. What concerned Arisue was the prospect of bloodshed after the talking between the two sides finally stopped. In his heart he believed the most extreme elements would even kill the emperor if he opposed their stated intention to lead Japan to victory or to fight until not a single person was left alive in the country.

Opposing these fanatical diehards were the moderates, led by the Marquis Koichi Kido, lord keeper of the privy seal, the man the emperor trusted above all others. It was Marquis Kido who had kept the peace when the two factions had confronted each other at the imperial conference of June 8. But he had been unable to keep the conference from deciding to continue the war to the bitter end. In the emperor's presence, and without his saying a word, they had decided there must be no surrender.

Then, four days later, a moderate, a naval admiral, his path to the throne cleared for him by Kido, had presented the emperor with clear confirmation of what Kido had already told him.

The admiral's report detailed serious shortages of raw materials. In the war industries, the workers—many of them school-children—were beset by lack of experience; output was constantly falling short of expectations. Industrially, Japan was becoming moribund. Except for morale, the overall situation was dire.

On June 18, Prime Minister Suzuki called a meeting of Japan's Inner Cabinet. While Arisue had been unable to obtain precise details of the meeting—held the same day President Truman approved the invasion plans—he did establish that the war minister and the representatives of the army and navy had maintained their stated position: all forward planning must be linked to the demands an enemy D-Day would create.

However, these three hard-liners had agreed on one important concession. While they still opposed direct negotiation to end the war, they now had no objection to talks starting *after* Field Marshal Hata's army had dealt the enemy a crushing blow on the invasion beaches.

To Arisue, the fact that the three had been moved this far from their previously entrenched position was a "major victory for reality."

Outwardly maintaining his careful position between the militarists and the moderates, Arisue had come to favor peace at almost any price apart from unconditional surrender. His overriding objection to such a surrender was that it would likely mean the removal of the emperor, and that was unthinkable.

On June 22, ten days after the admiral had delivered his report on raw materials and morale, Emperor Hirohito had requested the Inner Cabinet to initiate peace negotiations, using, if possible, the good offices of Russia.

To this end, on June 24, a former prime minister, Koki Hirota, called upon the Soviet ambassador in Tokyo, Jacob Malik.

Malik correctly saw the move as an attempt to keep the Russians out of the war. Hirota's efforts came to nothing.

There, for the moment, the diplomatic maneuvers rested. Arisue had increasing evidence that Russia was bent on war. His staff was monitoring Soviet troop movements near the Chinese border: a formidable force was being assembled there, probably preparing to attack the Japanese troops facing them in Manchuria.

Arisue believed that a Russian attack would not be so much concerned with helping the Allies win the war as with establishing Soviet influence in the Pacific. The thought of a Soviet-dominated Japan chilled him.

The intelligence chief felt it was more urgent than ever to come to terms with the United States. He decided he would have to formulate a new approach to America through the one pipeline he had: the Office of Strategic Services in Bern.

His agent in the Swiss city, Lieutenant General Seigo Okamoto, had been standing by for weeks to carry a message to the OSS, which could then relay it to Washington.

Arisue cabled Okamoto requesting he find out the minimum conditions that America would accept for a Japanese surrender.

Even with a dozen radio sets tuned to different stations, the room was almost totally silent except for the gentle whirring of the fans suspended from the ceiling. Each radio could be heard only through the headset of the man seated before it. The men were monitors, the morning shift of a round-the-clock watch being kept on the airwaves of the Pacific and beyond. They were a part of the communications bureau of Field Marshal Hata's Second General Army Headquarters.

The bureau, the nerve center of Hata's headquarters, was housed in a former school, a long, two-story building at the foot of Mount Futaba, near the East Training Field. Special landlines linked the bureau to General Army Headquarters in Tokyo; other lines ran to military centers on Kyushu—Fukuoka, Sasebo, Nagasaki, and Kagoshima; the bureau was also linked to the naval base at Kure, marine headquarters at Ujina, and the regional defense command in Hiroshima Castle.

The monitoring room was the bureau's showpiece; only the large transmitting and monitoring center just outside Tokyo rivaled the listening post at Hiroshima. And never had it been so busy as in these past few weeks, following the arrival in Hiroshima of Lieutenant Colonel Kakuzo Oya, Arisue's specialist in American affairs, transferred to Hata's staff as chief intelligence officer.

The monitoring room could provide the first indication that an actual landing on Kyushu was about to take place. Prior to that, it was expected that the Americans would spend weeks bombarding the invasion area by sea and air.

Hata hoped he would have sufficient warning of an impending landing for Kyushu's kamikaze planes and suicide motorboats to attack the invasion armada. Much of the success of this plan depended on the men manning the monitoring room. All of them were either too old or otherwise unfit for combat service. Each had an excellent command of English.

In eight-hour shifts, they sat, writing pads at the ready, listening to an endless stream of words and music relayed from as far away as Washington, D.C.

The busiest time was from midday to midnight. During these hours, half the sets in the room were tuned to transmission from Okinawa, Iwo Jima, and the Marianas. Many of them were in code, but a sufficient number were made in clear language to provide the monitors with information that could be acted upon speedily. These intercepts included not only military radio traffic but also brief radio tests made by B-29 radiomen just before takeoff.

There was an hour's time difference between Japan and the Marianas—Hiroshima was one hour behind Tinian—and if the radio tests were made around 3:00 to 4:00 P.M. Hiroshima time, then the monitors knew that a raid could be expected that night. They used the number of tests they picked up as a rough guide to the number of aircraft to be expected.

The monitors passed their notes to supervisors who, in turn, sent the information to the central communications room. From there, the entire air-raid alert system of western Japan was informed. The whole operation took only minutes.

As the bombers entered Japanese airspace, the monitors picked up snatches of conversation between aircrews, enabling the supervisors to estimate which areas of Japan the planes meant to attack. The information, along with the intercepts of radio messages to and from ships at sea, was typed up for later analysis. It all helped Hata and Oya to gauge the enemy's strength and intentions with remarkable accuracy.

Since coming to Hiroshima, Oya had visited the monitors regularly, hoping his presence was an indication to them of the importance he placed on their work.

But his real specialty was interrogation. From the days he had first come to work with Arisue, he had shown an aptitude for questioning. It was Arisue's proud boast that if Oya couldn't make a man talk, then nobody could.

Oya still regretted that he had arrived in Hiroshima too late to be the first to interrogate the ten American fliers who had been shot down over Okinawa and brought to the city before the island fell.

So far, they were the only American POWs in Hiroshima. They were kept at Kempei Tai headquarters in the grounds of Hiroshima Castle.

· 5 ·

The sun was still a glowing ball skimming the horizon on July 12 when Charles Perry, the 509th's mess officer, rose from his bunk. He stepped gingerly onto the floor. The night before, one of the other officers in the Quonset hut had set traps to catch the rats which roamed the group's compound. The 509th had moved into their new quarters on Tinian four days ago, and, in spite of the rodents, the consensus was that this time "the Old Man has done us proud." The men accepted Tibbets's absence without question: back at Wendover they had become accustomed to their commander's disappearing.

Perry hoped that when Tibbets returned from the States he would bring a few "presents"—liquor and cigarettes. In the deft hands of Perry, these items were valuable commodities to barter. The usually urbane, sophisticated mess officer was nowadays behaving "like an Arab trader."

Because of his efforts, the group enjoyed a selection of dishes not available to the twenty thousand other Americans on Tinian. It was Perry's proud boast that "in the 509th a PFC eats better than a five-star general."

This morning, as usual, Perry saw that the returning B-29s were "like beads on a string. As soon as one landed, another made its approach. There was always the same number of planes in sight. It was thrilling to watch."

It was broad daylight when the last returning bomber landed. The weary crews, who had been almost thirteen hours in the air, would spend most of the day sleeping. As they went to bed, some of the 509th's crews were preparing, yet again, to practice-bomb the Japanese on nearby Rota. None of them had yet been allowed to fly over Japan.

Their B-29s were parked in segregated areas on North Field and guarded around the clock. The sentries had orders to shoot any unauthorized person who attempted to approach the airplanes after being challenged.

This stringent security had already attracted the curiosity of other squadrons. Their questions remained unanswered. Now, as planes from the 509th took off for Rota, catcalls and jeers from a group of combat veterans drifted across North Field.

The muted resentment which Tibbets had detected was out in the open; the 509th had become an object of derision.

Soon, the taunts would be turned into verse, penned by a clerk in the island's base headquarters.

Nobody Knows

Into the air the secret rose,
Where they're going, nobody knows.
Tomorrow they'll return again,
But we'll never know where they've been.
Don't ask us about results or such,
Unless you want to get in Dutch.
But take it from one who is sure of the score,
The 509th is winning the war.

When the other Groups are ready to go,
We have a program of the whole damned show.
And when Halsey's 5th shells Nippon's shore,
Why, shucks, we hear about it the day before.
And MacArthur and Doolittle give out in advance,
But with this new bunch we haven't a chance.
We should have been home a month or more,
For the 509th is winning the war.

Thousands of copies of this doggerel were mimeographed and distributed throughout the Pacific command. From Hawaii to the Philippines, men read about this strange outfit on Tinian who stirred themselves to make occasional sorties against a tame target, the Japanese on Rota.

In public, the 509th laughed off the poem, but it touched a raw nerve among many in the group. Six weeks had now passed since the ground echelon had arrived on Tinian. For them in particular, the weary waiting, having to parry relentless sniping questions, dividing their time between the beach, mess hall, and movie theaters—all had combined to dent their pride. Some of the 509th even wondered if their compound, with its tough-talking guards, was fenced in not as a security precaution but because the group needed "baby-sitting."

Beser awoke late, having been until the early hours of the morning in the Tech Area workshop where the atomic bomb would be finally assembled. There, Jeppson and members of the First Ordnance Squadron were preparing for the arrival of the bomb's component parts.

Jeppson and the five other specialists on the proximity-fuze mechanism had been among the first to arrive on the island. In their spare time, they had made for themselves a porch out of bomb crates which formed the entrance to the tent they chose to live in; carefully sited on a high bluff where it received maximum breeze, the accommodation was the envy of almost all in the 509th.

Beser was in a hut close to the cemetery where the Americans who had died taking Tinian were buried. It was also where the remains of the crew he had seen crash were interred; Beser had learned that such crashes by B-29s loaded to the maximum with incendiary bombs were a frequent and disturbing fact of life on Tinian.

As he dressed, Beser saw that his Quonset hut was empty. He guessed his fellow officers had gone to the beach. He turned on the hut's radio. The strains of "Sentimental Journey" came through the static. It was followed by a dulcet voice that Beser was fascinated by, but hated.

Tokyo Rose was making one of her regular propaganda broadcasts to the American forces in the Pacific.

Twice already she had startled the 509th by making specific references to the group. The first was shortly after the ground echelon landed on Tinian on May 30, Memorial Day. Tokyo Rose noted their arrival and urged them to return home before they fell victim to the victorious Japanese forces.

Some of the 509th had jeered. Others had shown concern. They wondered how she could possibly know about the most secret unit in the entire American Air Force. Two weeks later, Tokyo Rose mentioned them again. She warned that the group's bombers would be easily recognizable to Japanese antiaircraft gunners because of the distinctive "R" symbols on the B-29 tails. This time, nobody scoffed. The insignias had only just been painted on.

But even if Beser found the omnipresent sources of Tokyo Rose disturbing, he still listened to her beguiling voice.

This morning, as usual, she had the latest baseball scores from the States; news of the dramas and comedies playing on and off Broadway; details of the fiction and nonfiction bestsellers—all interspersed with current selections from the "Hit Parade."

There was no mention of the 509th. Beser switched off the radio, leaving Tokyo Rose to entertain other lonely men thinking of home.

• 6 •

On July 15, over breakfast, Swedish banker Per Jacobsson explained that all the terms were negotiable —except the clause relating to the emperor. Now he awaited his old friend Allen Dulles's response.

Twelve days before, Lieutenant General Seigo Okamoto had received Arisue's instructions to establish the minimum surrender terms the Allies would accept from Japan—other than unconditional surrender.

Okamoto had discussed the matter with the Japanese ambassador to Switzerland. They had called in two senior officials of the Bank for International Settlements—to which Jacobsson was financial adviser.

For several days, this consortium debated what surrender terms they believed would be acceptable to Japan, having received no guidance or encouragement from Tokyo. The group had devised a ploy so daring that even the conservative Jacobsson thought it had a good chance of success.

They proposed that if the American government would accept the terms of surrender that they, the consortium, had devised and believed the Japanese government would accept—then America should publicly advance those terms as emanating from Washington. In this way, Japan would be offered a face-saving opportunity to surrender.

Jacobsson had brought the proposals to Dulles's current headquarters in Wiesbaden, Germany. The suggested terms were: unconditional surrender should be modified so as to include a guarantee of the continuing sovereignty of the emperor; no changes in the Japanese constitution; internationalization of Manchuria; continuation of Japanese control over Formosa and Korea.

Dulles knew the weakness of his present position. Roosevelt had given him a free hand; Truman had shown himself unwilling to grant such latitude. Dulles was not authorized to speak for the new president or the American government. Further, he was aware of the possible repercussions in America that could result from any sign of appeasement toward the Japanese. And yet, Jacobsson's view that if the Japanese could keep their emperor they would probably surrender, interested Dulles.

The Russians were crouched, committed to leap at Japan's northern flank in August—less than a month away. But Dulles believed the Soviet Union would not stop there. Once she was in the Far East, Russia would stay there, permeating the whole area with her influence.

He made up his mind.

He gave Jacobsson a counterproposal. Carefully couched in lawyers' language, it drew a clear distinction between a firm promise and an "understanding." But what Dulles was saying was clear: there was a good chance that America would let the emperor stay, *provided* Hirohito took a public stand *now* to help end the war.

Jacobsson was relieved. Dulles's proposal, if not what the banker wanted, was at least something.

He hurried back to Bern.

Dulles began to make plans to fly from the nearby Frankfurt air base to Berlin. He wanted to report to Stimson, who was due in Berlin shortly to take part in the upcoming Big Three Conference at Potsdam.

• 7 •

From Oppenheimer's office at Los Alamos, a telephone call was made to the guardhouse farther down on the mesa. The call ordered the sentries to let the approaching convoy pass out through the gates unhampered.

Accompanied by seven cars was a closed black truck. Four men sat in each car. Beneath their coats were pistols in shoulder holsters; on the car floors were shotguns, rifles, and boxes of ammunition. The men had orders to shoot to kill anybody who attempted to stop the convoy.

In the car immediately behind the truck rode two army officers. Their field artillery collar insignia were upside down—an indication of the hurry with which Major Robert Furman and Captain James Nolan had assumed their disguises.

In reality, Furman was a Princeton engineering graduate, attached to the Manhattan Project. His normal role was to procure strategic materials and help recruit scientific personnel. Nolan was a radiologist at Los Alamos hospital.

Today, the two men were beginning a journey scheduled to end on Tinian. Until they reached that destination, they had strict orders not to let out of their sight a fifteen-foot-long crate—it contained the atomic bomb's inner cannon—and a lead-lined cylinder two feet high and eighteen inches in diameter in which was the uranium projectile. Crate and cylinder were now being carried in the truck.

Oppenheimer had impressed upon both men the virtual irreplaceability of the material they were accompanying.

Only a mile down the mountain road from Los Alamos, near-disaster struck when the car in which Furman and Nolan were traveling blew a tire and slewed out of control, threatening to plunge with its occupants into a nearby ravine.

The truck screeched to a halt. Security agents cocked their guns.

The car was brought under control; its tire was changed, and the journey resumed. In a cloud of dust the convoy passed through Santa Fe and reached Albuquerque's airfield.

Three DC-3s were waiting. Furman and Nolan were given parachutes and boarded the center plane. The crate and bucket-shaped cylinder were put on the same plane; they, too, had their own parachutes.

The crew had been given one instruction: in the event of an emergency, the crate and cylinder were to be jettisoned before the passengers.

The planes reached Hamilton Field, San Francisco, without incident. A new team of agents then escorted the crate, cylinder, Furman, and Nolan to their next means of transport—a heavy cruiser whose recent battle scars, earned at Okinawa, were hidden under a fresh coat of paint. It was the *Indianapolis*.

* * *

A few hours after Dulles made his plans to travel to Potsdam, in Wendover Paul Tibbets watched a transport plane make its final approach. It descended over the salt flats, banked to avoid the town, and then touched down, rolling past the three B-29s still on the base.

How long the bombers would remain there depended on the news the transport brought. The plane carried a Manhattan Project courier who shuttled between Washington, Wendover, and Los Alamos carrying instructions too secret to be delivered by other means.

The courier brought news that part of the atomic bomb had been delivered to the *Indianapolis*. The other part—the uranium 235 "target," the lump of uranium that would be placed at the muzzle end of the gun inside the bomb—was to be flown to Tinian by the crews still at Wendover.

The operation was code-named "Bronx Shipments." Tibbets often wondered who invented the endless cover names that were given everybody and everything associated with the project. He was still surprised each time Groves came on the telephone with the words, "This is 'Relief,'" or when Ashworth announced himself as "Scathe," sometimes bringing news from the "Coordinator of Rapid Rupture," the pseudonym given to one of the scientists working on the plutonium bomb.

Tokyo's memo confirmed a recent one from "Judge" (Captain Parsons) giving details of how the "target" for "Little Boy" (the uranium bomb) should travel to "Destination" (Tinian). "Little Boy" was just one of a variety of names for the bomb. It was also known as "the gadget," "the device," "the gimmick" (an expression Tibbets favored), "the beast" (often used by scientists now critical of the project), "S-1" (preferred by Stimson), and "it" (used by the 509th, still mystified about what, exactly, the weapon was).

Groves had originally called the uranium bomb "Thin Man," after Roosevelt. When it was found necessary to shorten the bomb's gun barrel, Groves renamed it "Little Boy." The plutonium bomb, from its conception, was known as "Fat Man," after Churchill.

Work in Britain on the bomb was hidden under the guise of "The Directorate of Tube Alloys."

To keep track of who was who and what was what in the codified world of the Manhattan Project was hard even for the retentive memory Tibbets possessed.

But these instructions were clear enough. One of the B-29s at Wendover was to carry certain of the remaining bomb parts to Tinian; others would travel on board C-54 transport planes of the 509th.

Tibbets assigned crews for the flights and then prepared to travel to Alamogordo for the test-firing of the Fat Man.

Packed and just about to leave for New Mexico, he received an unexpected and urgent message from Tinian. It was signed by Ferebee, the one man above all others in the 509th whose judgment in all matters Tibbets trusted. The easygoing bombardier, who had just arrived on Tinian, was not a man to press the panic button. Yet there was no mistaking the gravity of Ferebee's words urging Tibbets to fly at once to Tinian to deal with a major crisis. It looked as if the 509th were going to be dumped from the atomic bomb ticket.

Pausing only to send a coded message to Groves that he would not be at Alamogordo, Tibbets set off on the fifty-five-hundred-mile flight to Tinian. He had not spent the past ten months working himself to the bone, sacrificing his family life, his leisure, and his friendships only to have someone snatch the atomic mission from him at the last moment.

• 8 •

Using for illumination the jagged shafts of lightning that intermittently broke through the pitch-blackness before dawn on this chilly July 16 morning, many of the 425 scientists and technicians gathered at the test site at Alamogordo, New Mexico, carefully rubbed sun lotion on their faces and hands. Though some of them were twenty miles away from its source, they feared the flash, when it came, might cause instant sunburn. But that could be the least harmful of its side effects. They all knew the radioactive fallout accompanying the flash could kill. If it reached them, no lotion or potion could prevent them from being contaminated.

And since nobody knew for certain what the outer limits of an uncontrolled nuclear chain reaction were, it was conceivable the destruction could spread beyond this semidesert area, which Groves and the scientists called Site S, and the natives called *Jornada del Muerto*, the "tract of death." Even those scientists who, along with Groves, believed that the world's first atomic explosion would not spread too far, shared a feeling of taking a huge leap into the unknown.

Nine miles from the base camp where Groves and Oppenheimer spent most of these early-morning hours, the plutonium bomb stood on a one-hundred-foot-high structural-steel scaffold. This point in the desert was code-named "Ground Zero."

In mid-May, when the tower was still under construction, the air force had bombed the site, mistakenly believing the area to be part of a practice target range. Two buildings had been hit and fires started, but, miraculously, there had been no casualties. Then, a few days ago, during a rehearsal using a conventional bomb, a bolt of forked lightning had struck the tower and detonated the explosive. Again, no one had been hurt.

Now, with the test scheduled for 2:00 A.M., everyone hoped there would be no further mishaps. But the weather was getting worse. Lightning was accompanied by showers. Sporadic rain could be a serious danger, causing shorts in the electrical circuits leading to the bomb; heavy rain could prevent the test-firing altogether.

It was one more worry for Groves, already concerned that Tibbets was not at Alamogordo. And because of the weather, the B-29 Tibbets had ordered to be in the air at the time of the explosion was grounded. Now there was no way of knowing what effect the bomb would have on the airplane that would drop it over Japan.

Groves was further distressed by the way some of the scientists were trying to pressure Oppenheimer to postpone the test. The brilliant physicist was now wound up "like the spring in a very expensive watch."

Groves decided to cast himself in the unusual role of the man who would dispel the tension. Clutching his scientific director firmly by the arm, the project chief marched him up and down around the base camp area, assuring him that the weather would improve. In Groves's opinion:

> All the personnel had been brought up to such a peak of tension and excitement that a postponement would be bound to result in a letdown which would affect their efficiency. . . . We simply could not adequately protect either our own people or the surrounding community or our security if a delayed firing did occur. . . . [Another] point of concern was the effect of a test delay on our schedule of bombing Japan. Our first combat bomb was to be a U-235 one, and while a successful test of the plutonium bomb without the complications of an air drop would not be a guarantee, it would be most reassuring. Moreover, it would give credence to our assurance to the President as to the probable effectiveness. A misfire might well have weighed heavily on the argument by some, particularly Admiral Leahy, that we were too optimistic and that we should wait for a successful test. After all, this was the first time in history since the Trojan Horse that a new weapon was to be used without prior testing.

The test was delayed while the harassed weathermen tried to predict conditions in the coming hours.

Finally, the firing was scheduled for approximately 5:30 A.M., Mountain War Time.

At 5:25 A.M., the observers who were out in the open took up their final positions, lying flat on the earth, faces down, feet toward the blast.

At 5:29 sharp, the last in a series of automatic timing devices took over. There were forty-five seconds to go.

Oppenheimer and his senior staff waited tensely in a concrete bunker. Groves was in a slit trench a short distance away from the scientific director, because "I wanted us to be separated in case of trouble."

5:29:35.

From another dugout, a man spoke into a microphone linked to the four lookout posts around the base camp. "Zero minus ten seconds."

A green flare flashed from the ground and burned against the low cloud base, briefly and eerily lighting up the darkness.

5:29:40.

"Zero minus five seconds."

A second flare cascaded.

5:29:43.

Silence and darkness reigned once more over the desert.

5:29:44.

At 5:29:45, everything happened at once. But it was too fast for the watchers to distinguish: no human eye can separate millionths of a second; no human brain can record such a fraction of time. No one, therefore, saw the actual first flash of cosmic fire. What they saw was its dazzling reflection on surrounding hills. It was, in the words of the observer from *The New York Times:*

> . . . a light not of this world, the light of many suns in one. It was a sunrise such as the world had never seen, a great green super-sun climbing in a fraction of a second to a height of more than

8,000 feet, rising ever higher until it touched the clouds, lighting up earth and sky all around with a dazzling luminosity. Up it went, a great ball of fire about a mile in diameter, changing colors as it kept shooting upward, from deep purple to orange, expanding, growing bigger, rising as it was expanding, an elemental force freed from its bonds after being chained for billions of years. For a fleeting instant the color was unearthly green, such as one only sees in the corona of the sun during a total eclipse. It was as though the earth had opened and the skies had split. One felt as though he had been privileged to witness the birth of the World—to be present at the moment of Creation when the Lord said: Let There Be Light.

Many of the observers were transfixed, rooted to the ground by a mixture of fear and awe at the immensity of the spectacle. Oppenheimer remembered a line from the *Bhagavad Gita,* the sacred epic of the Hindus. "I am become death, the destroyer of worlds."

The sinister cloud continued to billow upward, its internal pressures finding relief in one mushroom after another, finally disappearing into the dawning sky at well over forty thousand feet. At Ground Zero, the temperature at that moment of explosion had been 100 million degrees Fahrenheit, three times hotter than the interior of the sun and ten thousand times the heat on its surface.

Within a mile radius of Ground Zero, all life, plant and animal, had vanished; around what had been the base of the tower, the sand had been hammered into the desert to form a white-hot saucer five hundred yards in diameter. There had never before been sand like it on earth. When it cooled, it turned into a jade-green, glazed substance unknown to scientists.

The steel scaffold, impervious to any heat known in the preatomic age, had been transformed into gas and dispersed.

Groves was among the first to regain his composure. He turned to his deputy, Brigadier General Thomas Farrell, and uttered a prediction. "The war's over. One or two of these things and Japan will be finished."

• 9 •

Furman and Nolan, the two young Manhattan Project specialists who were escorting some of the vital bomb components to Tinian, watched the final sailing preparations of the *Indianapolis*.

Knowing as little about ships as they did about guns, Furman and Nolan were impressed by the *Indianapolis*'s towering super-structure and her eight-inch gun batteries. She was the flagship of Admiral Raymond A. Spruance, commander of the Fifth Fleet. He was now on Guam helping to plan the invasion of Japan. They were blissfully unaware that the admiral believed the ship's center of gravity was entirely too high, and, as a result, he had once remarked that if she ever took a clean torpedo hit, she could capsize and sink in short order.

The *Indianapolis*'s problem was age. Her keel had been laid in 1932, well before the advent of radar. To remain on active service, she had been fitted with lookout aids following Pearl Harbor; her superstructure, from the bridge aft, bristled with radar devices which were efficient but heavy. To those who knew her well, the venerable old warship seemed always to be in danger of toppling over. She was a curious choice to carry the crucial components of the world's most sophisticated weapon.

For Furman and Nolan, the journey to Tinian would have all the trappings of a luxury cruise. There would be nothing for them to do except take turns sitting in their spacious cabin watching over the lead bucket containing the uranium projectile. It had been welded to the cabin floor. The fifteen-foot-long crate carrying the cannon was lashed to the deck and guarded around the clock by marines. With an armed man at each corner, it resembled a bier.

Gossip spread to every corner of the ship. In wardrooms and mess halls, bets were laid that the mystery cargo was anything from a secret rocket to gold "to bribe the Japs to quit."

Even rosy-cheeked Captain Charles Butler McVay III, the ship's forty-six-year-old commander, knew little more than any enlisted man as to what his ship was carrying or why she was making this headlong dash to the Marianas.

Yesterday, Parsons had come from Los Alamos to brief McVay. The two men had met in Admiral William Purnell's office at the Embarcadero in San Francisco. Parsons had spelled out the mission in words McVay would always remember. "You will sail at high speed to Tinian where your cargo will be taken off by others. You will not be told what the cargo is, but it is to be guarded even after the life of your vessel. If she goes down, save the cargo at all costs, in a lifeboat if necessary. And every day you save on your voyage will cut the length of the war by just that much."

Mystified but having the good sense not to ask questions, McVay had returned to his ship still wondering what his cargo was and why his ship had been chosen.

Pure chance had decided on the *Indianapolis*. She was available, and, from the standpoint of speed and space, she was right. But nobody could be sure how well the cruiser had recovered from the mauling she had received at Okinawa, when a kamikaze plane had killed nine of her crew and blown two huge holes in her hull. Skilled artisans at Mare Island, the largest repair yard on the West Coast, had given her a new port quarter, radio and radar equipment, and fire-control mechanisms. She had also received a new "team." Captain McVay and some of his senior officers were still there, but over 30 officers, almost half the cruiser's complement, and 250 enlisted men had come aboard as replacements for the veterans of Okinawa. Most of the new officers were distinctly junior; 20 of them had come straight from midshipman's school or the Naval Academy, and many of the enlisted men from basic training.

McVay had planned to work them up in a series of training exercises off the California coast. Now, these plans were scrapped. With untried officers and crew, with a ship that had undergone the skimpiest of sea trials after major repairs, he was about to set off.

He sent for Nolan, who, as Parsons had suggested, told the captain he was not a gunnery officer but "a medical orderly," and that, as such, he could state "the cargo contained nothing dangerous to the ship or crew."

McVay looked at Nolan and said, "I didn't think we were going to use bacteriological weapons in this war."

Nolan did not reply. He rejoined Furman in their cabin keeping watch over the bucket, leaving McVay as baffled as ever.

At exactly 8:00 A.M., the *Indianapolis* weighed anchor. Thirty-six minutes later, she passed under the Golden Gate Bridge, outward bound.

• 10 •

Soon after his arrival in Potsdam on the morning of Monday, July 16, Churchill had paid a brief call on Truman. It was the first time the two men had met. Truman had taken an "instant liking" to Churchill, who had entered into "an amiable relationship" with Truman, showing "a marked disposition to agree with him as far as possible."

The two leaders had parted after discussing the news that Stalin was unwell and would be one day late for the conference. They had guessed, correctly, that the Soviet leader was recovering from a minor heart attack.

Truman had taken advantage of the delay to go

sightseeing in the ruins of Berlin. He had been much affected by what he saw, remarking that the destruction "is a demonstration of what can happen when a man [Hitler] overreaches himself."

Upon his return to Babelsberg, Truman had been given a message by Stimson which had just arrived from Washington. It made Truman the most powerful of the three leaders soon to meet over the negotiating table.

The message read:

OPERATED ON THIS MORNING. DIAGNOSIS NOT YET COMPLETE BUT RESULTS SEEM SATISFACTORY AND ALREADY EXCEED EXPECTATIONS. LOCAL PRESS RELEASE NECESSARY AS INTEREST EXTENDS GREAT DISTANCE. DR. GROVES PLEASED. HE RETURNS TOMORROW. I WILL KEEP YOU POSTED.

                                                    END

The message had let Truman know that the Alamogordo test had been a success, so much so that a fake, pre-prepared press release had been fed to the wire services claiming that an ammunition magazine had exploded, "producing a brilliant flash and blast" which had been observed over two hundred miles away.

As Truman had read the message, he realized "that the United States had in its possession an explosive force of unparalleled power." He had ordered Stimson to respond. From Potsdam had gone the message:

I SEND MY WARMEST CONGRATULATIONS TO THE DOCTOR AND HIS CONSULTANT.

Now, at noon on this Tuesday, as Stimson met with Churchill and told him the good news from Alamogordo, Stalin called on Truman.

Truman was impressed enough by the Soviet leader to feel that at this first meeting he could "talk to him straight from the shoulder. He looked me in the eye when he spoke and I felt hopeful that we could reach an agreement that would be satisfactory to the world and to ourselves."

But the president was not impressed enough by Stalin to confide in him what he had just learned about the atomic bomb. Nor did he do so later in the day when they met again at the opening session of the Potsdam Conference.

Not that it mattered much. The Russians already knew about the bomb—through the treachery of a few scientists in the Manhattan Project who were feeding information to the Soviet Union. Even now, Russian scientists were engaged in an attempt to catch up with the Americans.

That night, Truman discussed the Alamogordo results with Stimson, Secretary of State Byrnes, and Admiral Leahy, who had stubbornly refused to believe the bomb would work. Over dinner, the Joint Chiefs of Staff— General Marshall, General Arnold, and Admiral King —joined in the conversation.

Truman forbore asking Leahy if he wished to revise his estimate. Instead, in his later words:

We reviewed our military strategy in the light of this revolutionary development . . . we did not know as yet what effect the new weapon might have, physically or psychologically, when used against the enemy. For that reason the military advised that we go ahead with the existing military plans for the invasion of the Japanese home islands.

The die was cast. The bomb was ready. There would be no further tests to indicate what it might do in war. If the Japanese did not react positively to the final appeal for surrender Truman was planning, then he knew the responsibility was his to decide whether to use the new weapon.

• 11 •

Ferebee met Tibbets when his plane landed on July 18 after its three-day flight from Wendover. His first words were: "It's bad news, Paul, really bad news."

After listening to Ferebee, Tibbets knew he had been right to fly pell-mell to Tinian. The future of the 509th was endangered. In Ferebee's words, "They're trying to tear your outfit apart."

A determined effort was under way to break up the tightly knit 509th and reassign the flying and ground crews to other groups based on the island.

A number of reasons were advanced for this astonishing move: the 509th's fliers would benefit from working alongside combat veterans; they were needed to plug gaps in squadrons that had lost men over Japan; the ground crews were needed to help already harassed line chiefs keep the endless flow of bombers moving into the air.

Tibbets suspected these were mostly excuses. Like Ferebee, he now thought the trouble was caused mainly by others envious of the 509th's special situation.

Matters were not helped by a brush Ferebee had just had with LeMay on Guam. The two men knew each other from Europe; their mutual respect was strong. It was based partly on the fact that while there was a considerable gap in rank between Major Ferebee and General LeMay, they had always spoken frankly to each other.

LeMay had succeeded in angering Ferebee by casting doubt on Tibbets's ability to fly the atomic mission. Ferebee had exploded. "Look, General, if Colonel Tibbets is not qualified, then I'm not qualified, so neither one of us is qualified, so you don't have anybody qualified, and the navy doesn't have anybody qualified!"

LeMay had told Ferebee to cool down.

The advice had not been heeded. Today, the bombardier was as angry as ever, not only over LeMay's remarks but over an "attempt by the navy to have their own man fly the mission."

Tibbets knew the naval pilot—and disliked him. To Tibbets, the flier was "a prima donna, quite the wrong personality for the job."

Tibbets promised Ferebee that he would go to LeMay "tomorrow, and settle the whole shooting match once and for all."

The return of their commander acted as a tonic for the 509th. The sniping and sneering by other units had intensified: at night, some of the fliers lobbed stones onto the roofs of the group's Quonsets as they passed by on their way to North Field for another mission over Japan.

Tibbets's popular deputy, Lieutenant Colonel Tom Classen, had tried to ease the situation; Tibbets felt that Classen was finding the strain of a second tour overseas barely endurable.

The group's intelligence officer, the roly-poly Lieutenant Colonel Hazen Payette, had disappointed Tibbets. Payette was a trained lawyer and had always concerned himself with facts, not feelings; results, not excuses. On Tinian he had carried this to excess. "In trying to keep the men on their toes, he trod on too many feet," was how radio operator Dick Nelson saw Payette's behavior. Payette had also managed to ruffle Colonel E. E. Kirkpatrick, Groves's energetic engineering officer on Tinian, the man who had worked wonders to ready the island's facilities for the 509th before and since its arrival.

Unknown to Tibbets, Groves was receiving regular reports on the 509th from Kirkpatrick; it was a classic example of the way Groves worked: in his perfect world, everybody would watch everybody else.

To the 509th, Kirkpatrick was just one more outsider attached to their unit. Scientists from Los Alamos— men most of the 509th had never seen before—were now flying in and bedding down in the compound.

They created unexpected paperwork for Charles Perry. The mess officer had received written orders from the Air Force Quartermaster's Office that he must collect thirty-five cents for every meal the civilians ate, get receipts for the money, and send them in a special pouch by air to Washington.

Perry thought the idea "plain stupid." He did not suspect that behind it all was a continuing Manhattan Project concern about using civilian scientists alongside military personnel to make and maintain and eventually to help deliver a military weapon. At Los Alamos, some of the scientists refused to wear a uniform; here, on Tinian, they wore khakis without insignia or markings.

The charges for their meals kept a "distance" between them and the military.

Beser had no patience with such niceties. To him, it was "simply a matter of trying to play it both ways. The fact was, they were part of the American war effort like everybody else."

In the seven weeks he had been on Tinian, Beser had made only a few short flights to check out his equipment; the nearest he had come to seeing action was when a solitary flak battery on Rota opened up as the B-29 he was in cruised high overhead.

A few days ago, a friend in the 504th had invited Beser to fly with him as a passenger for a fire raid on Japan.

Classen and Sweeney, now the commanding officer of the 393rd Heavy Bombardment Squadron, refused Beser permission to go.

Beser saw Tibbets's arrival as fortunate: the raid was scheduled for this very night. He found Tibbets in his Quonset and repeated the request.

"I'm sorry, Jake, you can't go."

Beser looked miffed. "Colonel, it's just one raid—"

"No."

Tibbets settled back on his bunk, indicating that the interview was over.

Beser misunderstood the gesture. He thought Tibbets was merely tired after his trip from Wendover, and with a little more persuasion would let him go. "Paul, all I want to do is just this one mission to see what it's like."

Tibbets leaped from his bed. "Godammit, Lieutenant Beser, I've said no, and I mean no! Now get the hell out of here and go about your business. And the next time you come with a request, it's Colonel Tibbets. Understand?"

A chastened Beser backed out of the hut. He spread the word that "the Old Man's on a rampage."

Tibbets's long absences had convinced Lewis that when it came to the mission that really mattered, his commanding officer would not be on board; it would be Lewis himself who would fly the strike. Lewis's reasons for coming to this conclusion were based on a number of premises.

He believed that his own record and his crew's fitted them for the mission. Further, he assumed that Tibbets saw his own role as a "chairborne commander, planning the operation, leaving its execution to men who regularly flew B-29s."

Lewis also believed that Tibbets "didn't have an airplane." Technically, that was true. The 509th's commander had not assigned himself the aircraft; instead, he had chosen almost always to fly with Lewis. In Tibbets's view, this made it clear to everyone with "a couple of dimes' worth of sense that Lewis and his boys were actually my crew. When I went aboard, Lewis was copilot and I drove the plane."

Lewis interpreted the position "somewhat differently. First of all, Tibbets had never been inside my airplane since I collected it from the factory; secondly, he had not flown on Tinian with us; thirdly, I could do the job as well as he could—as well as anybody could."

Nobody doubted Lewis's flying ability. But the first atomic strike called for more than professional flying expertise. It called for decision making of the highest order. And indeed, it was Tibbets's duty to command the mission. But Lewis believed he should do the job.

Only Eatherly matched Lewis in eagerness to fly the mission. He had even named his B-29 *Straight Flush,* partly because of his obsession with gambling and partly because he believed his crew was the best in the group.

Whatever flying standards the officers of the *Straight Flush* had achieved, nobody could match them for the comfortable life they lived on the ground. Through Eatherly's good offices, they had inherited a group of five nurses on Tinian. On an island filled with men starved for female companionship, this was the most desirable gift Eatherly could bestow. The officers, equipped with perfume and silk stockings that they had brought from America, in the words of flight engineer Eugene Grennan, "came, saw, and conquered."

From then on, they had lived "in the laps of goddesses who waited on us hand and foot."

For other officers, the Tinian evenings were long; some, like navigator Russell Gackenbach, relieved their boredom by playing endless practical jokes. His specialty was to creep through the Stygian darkness tossing rescue flares into the campfires which at night flickered all over the compound. The flares created considerable panic—and provided much amusement for Gackenbach.

Caron devised a different way to spend his nights. When he wasn't at the movies, he was stealthily removing, plank by plank, parts of the officers' club, and using the wood to build himself a porch at the back of his Quonset hut. The job was coming along nicely; he hoped he could finish it before the mission took place. If he was selected for that, he planned to wear the new Brooklyn Dodgers baseball cap that the team had just sent him.

Flight engineer Duzenbury had found potentially the most dangerous way of all to spend his free time. Despite having heard that the Japanese on Tinian had recently killed two GIs, at night he and a handful of friends, armed with carbines, went out into the jungle "in search of souvenirs—Japanese guns and bayonets." So far, during his scrambling down into caves, Duzenbury had discovered three bottles of sake; he didn't much like the taste.

Late in the evening of July 18, Tibbets received a coded message. It was from Groves. It told him the Alamogordo test had been a total success. Tibbets went to sleep knowing the "next atomic bang would be the real thing."

• 12 •

The July 19 confrontation between Tibbets and Le-May was brief and direct. Tibbets explained that it was necessary for the 509th to be left alone and intact, that he hoped there would be no more "meddling," and that *he* intended to fly the first atomic mission.

LeMay had crossed swords with Groves a month earlier over the question of who would be in charge once the weapon was ready for combat use. LeMay believed that "it was my baby once it came to my area." Groves thought otherwise.

LeMay still could not understand why Groves and the others in Washington wanted to entrust the bomb to a unit that had not been fully tested in combat over Japan. But he could see that "to turn it over now to someone else was a little more than they could swallow."

He decided to agree to Tibbets's request, with one proviso. LeMay would send his operations officer, Colonel William "Butch" Blanchard, up on a training ride with Tibbets and his crew later that day, "just to satisfy the requirement that you guys know what you're doing."

Tibbets took his time over the preflight checks. Just behind him, seated on a pile of cushions, Blanchard was listening to each instruction, watching every response of the crew.

Lewis was strapped in the copilot's seat. Van Kirk was at the navigator's table, Ferebee in the bombardier's position. Duzenbury was at the engineer's panel, Nelson at the radio, Shumard and Stiborik in the blister turrets, and Caron in the rear turret.

In the bomb bay was a single blockbuster filled with high explosive; the fuel tanks carried enough for the round trip from Tinian to Rota.

Tibbets taxied to the end of the airstrip and, having received clearance for takeoff, sent the B-29 thundering down the central runway on North Field. Just as the wheels were about to leave the ground, he feathered an engine. Many of the Tinian crashes on takeoff happened because an engine failed at this critical moment. Tibbets fought the bomber's yawing movement, brought it back on course, and deftly coaxed it into the air.

Then he ordered a second engine to be cut. On the same side.

"Yes, sir!" replied Duzenbury.

Pulled by only two engines, both on one wing, the huge plane, carrying its five-ton bomb, very slowly began to climb.

Banking the B-29, dipping the wing with the silent engines toward Tinian, Tibbets offered Blanchard an excellent view of what was now the world's largest operational airfield.

Blanchard was not interested in sightseeing; his eyes were on the two propellers gently windmilling in the air.

Tibbets winked at Lewis—and increased the aircraft's bank until the bomber seemed to be standing on one wing.

Blanchard called Tibbets on the intercom. "Okay, I'm satisfied with engine performance. Let's head for Rota."

Tibbets leveled off, and at full power, the B-29 roared toward the island. It arrived over the initial point at exactly the time van Kirk had predicted. Tibbets called Blanchard. "Guess we can agree navigational error was nil."

"Agreed."

"Now it's Ferebee's turn."

The bombardier was in the nose, head glued to the bombsight.

From thirty thousand feet, the blockbuster plummeted down. Blanchard watched it fall and hit. "It came so close to the target that there was no use even talking about it," Tibbets later said.

Then, without warning his passenger, Tibbets put the B-29 into the usual 155-degree turn.

A strangled cry came from Blanchard. "What—what's happening?"

"The damn tail is stalling on me!"

"What'ya mean?"

Blanchard, pinned to the cushions by centrifugal force, felt the plane shudder as if it were going to pieces.

Tibbets shouted to him. "This is the only way I can make a tight turn. I've got to keep the tail stalling, and then I know I'm doing it right. Now, you wouldn't want me to do it any other way, would you?"

"Okay, that's enough. I'm satisfied!"

"Oh, no, we're not through yet!"

Coming out of the turn, Tibbets yanked back the control column, sending the huge bomber up into a sickening stall. It hovered momentarily on its tail, then slid back, turned, and spun toward the ground.

Blanchard turned white. "For Chrissake, you're going to kill us!"

Judging the moment perfectly, Tibbets brought the B-29 under control and headed back for Tinian. He touched down within fifteen seconds of van Kirk's estimate.

Blanchard did not speak until his feet were firmly on the ground. "Okay. You've proved your point."

Tibbets laughed, now certain Blanchard would pose no further challenge to his authority.

Tibbets chose ten crews to fly the first 509th missions over Japan on July 20. Each flew separately, against a preselected target. The purpose was to accustom the fliers to combat, and the Japanese to seeing single high-flying aircraft that dropped only one bomb.

The crews had orders that if their given targets were weatherbound, they must "under no circumstances" drop their blockbusters on Hiroshima, Kyoto, Kokura, or Niigata. Otherwise, their choice of alternative targets was unrestricted.

The first of the B-29s took off from Tinian at 2:00 A.M. On the way to Japan, one of them had engine trouble and had to jettison its bomb in the sea; five managed to drop their blockbusters in or around their target areas; four, including the plane piloted by Claude Eatherly, found the weather so bad that they were forced to seek alternative targets.

Eatherly chose Tokyo—and the emperor's palace. He was completely oblivious of the fact that his plan was not only against the official policy of the United States but could also affect the Potsdam Conference and, perhaps more important, strengthen the will to resist of every person in Japan.

Only one thought concerned Eatherly. If he succeeded, he would be guaranteed a place in history. He believed he might even end the war.

Eatherly circled at thirty thousand feet just south of Tokyo while his navigator plotted a course that would allow the *Straight Flush* to drop its ten-thousand-pound high-explosive bomb directly on the emperor's palace.

The navigator, Francis Thornhill, was having trouble. Tokyo, like the original target they had been assigned, was socked in with cloud.

Bombardier Ken Wey said he could see no gaps in the overcast.

"Then drop it by radar!" Eatherly commanded.

"Right," replied the bombardier.

Wey lined up the *Straight Flush* for a radar drop and released the bomb. Eatherly, whooping with excitement, immediately threw the B-29 into a 155-degree turn.

They left the Tokyo area without being able to see where the bomb had fallen.

• 13 •

Kizo Imai, the Japanese naval warrant officer in hiding on Tinian, waited until images flickered on the outdoor movie screen. Then, moving swiftly and surely, he left the jungle and wriggled toward the high wire fence.

He ran his fingers along the barbed strands. The gap was still there. Imai eased himself through, moving slowly now, careful not to snag his clothes. He would leave no clue for the guards who patrolled the 509th's compound.

Imai squirmed on his belly to the nearest Quonset hut, then carefully checked himself and his surroundings. The mud he had smeared on his face and neck, buttons and belt buckle, was still there; so was the sacking he had wrapped around his boots to deaden his footsteps. Imai doubted whether in the darkness anybody could spot him from more than a few feet away. And then, if he was lucky, he could kill before the alarm was raised; he carried a small knife in his belt for just such a purpose.

Imai moved away from the hut, running in a half crouch, pausing from time to time to get his bearings. From behind him, the movie sound track carried clearly; the glow from the screen outlined nearby buildings.

Like a dog sniffing for a bone, Imai's nose directed him to Perry's kitchens. He found a door unlocked and sneaked inside.

On the table were rows of cooked chickens. He grabbed a couple, stuffed them in his tunic, and was reaching for another when he heard a sound. He darted outside as someone entered by another door.

Imai stealthily retraced his footsteps, stopping in the shadow of the hut near the hole in the fence to rummage through a garbage can. Tonight's haul yielded a chunk of smoked sausage, a half-full jar of jam, and some peanuts. Wrapping his find carefully in old newspapers, Imai stuffed the package inside his tunic and trousers and moved toward the wire.

A voice stopped him. The words were in English, but there was no mistaking the accent; it was a Japanese woman's.

Imai felt a sudden surge of excitement as from a nearby Quonset hut came the voice of Tokyo Rose, making her nightly broadcast from Japan.

His spirits raised, Imai fled into the jungle. He was eager to return to his cave to scan the American newspapers he had stolen for reports of a Japanese advance toward Tinian.

Grouped around the radio, Eatherly and his crew listened impatiently to Tokyo Rose's diatribe. Finally, she gave them the news they were all waiting to hear.

The tactics of the raiding enemy planes have become so complicated that they cannot be anticipated from experience or common sense. The single B-29 which passed over the capital this morning was apparently using a sneak tactic aimed at confusing the minds of the people.

No further reference was made to the raid. Clearly the bomb had not hit the palace.

Disappointed, Eatherly turned away from the radio, his hopes of worldwide fame temporarily quashed.

• 14 •

At 6:00 A.M. on July 21, as he did every morning, Field Marshal Shunroku Hata awoke, bathed, dressed in a kimono, and breakfasted with his wife.

Around 7:00, he padded in his slippers to the Shinto shrine that was an integral part of his home. His prayers said, he changed into his uniform and was ready to begin the next part of his daily ritual: tending the vegetables in the garden he had planted at the rear of his home. This outdoor manual work kept him lean and fit; his appearance belied his sixty-five years.

Near 8:00, Hata went into the house. Awaiting him was an overnight situation report, prepared with the help of Lieutenant Kakuzo Oya, presently acting as Hata's intelligence chief. This morning's summary offered no clue as to where or when the Americans intended to invade Japan, but the field marshal was ready for the assault. Hata's inland defenses stretched from the shores of Kyushu almost two hundred miles back as far as Hiroshima on the main island of Honshu. Designed to allow for an orderly falling back to prepared positions, the system utilized the natural terrain to the maximum: murderous arcs of cross fire, tank traps, and booby traps awaited the Americans at every turn.

Hata finished his tea. Then, at about 8:15 A.M., the most important soldier outside Tokyo left in his staff car for headquarters in Hiroshima.

Most of Hiroshima's officers rode on horseback to work, and their equestrian parade regularly earned admiration from the milling crowds on their way to or from Hiroshima's war factories.

The animals, like their owners, and in marked contrast to the civilians, were sleek and well-groomed.

Particular approbation was reserved for the Korean prince, Lieutenant Colonel RiGu, who was attached to Hata's staff. His was the most superb horse in Hiroshima, a huge stallion, snow white with black fetlocks.

Sitting bolt upright on his steed, ceremonial sword at his side, the handsome young prince was a reminder of past glories, when the Imperial Japanese Army's cavalry had swept all before them.

Mayor Awaya and his personal assistant, Kazumasa Maruyama, walked to work each morning. Today, their conversation turned to a recurring topic: what could be done for the children who still remained in Hiroshima? Many of them worked in the factories and were receiving only a token education. Teachers traveled from one war plant to another, holding short classes on the factory floors.

Awaya thought the situation appalling and wanted to enlarge the city's industrial college. Maruyama believed all children should be evacuated.

The two men entered the Town Hall and were immediately overwhelmed by complaints about food distribution; about the lack of fuel; about shops overcharging; about Kempei Tai brutality; about the need for more large air-raid shelters. The problems of caring for the children of Hiroshima was lost in the welter of demands.

Second Lieutenant Tatsuo Yokoyama received a letter this morning from his father in Tokyo. Carefully worded and showing signs of long deliberation, the message rejected Colonel Abe's marriage proposal.

Yokoyama's parents' investigation had shown that Abe's daughter "has an unhappy disposition. Her teachers indicate she is not obedient or good at her work. In spite of his high position, we do not see from our most patient inquiries that your colonel's antecedents are always what we would desire for uniting our two families."

As a dutiful son, the gunnery officer knew he must accept his parents' decision. But how would he break the news to Colonel Abe, who had been pressing for an answer for weeks? His commander, he knew, would regard the rejection of his offer as an unforgivable insult. Yokoyama might well find himself banished to a noncombat post.

Yokoyama's reverie was disturbed by excited shouts from his gunners. It was midday, and American bombers were back over Kure to bomb and machine-gun the port. They came regularly now at noon and at midnight. From his vantage point, just seven miles away, Yokoyama could clearly see the flashes from the ground batteries.

The feeling of hopelessness he had brought back from Tokyo lifted. The capital might, indeed, be in ruins. But here, in the west of Japan, the army was fighting back as hard as ever; he desperately wanted to be part of that fight.

Suddenly Yokoyama knew what he must do about the letter: he would pretend he had never received it. He would tell Abe that his parents were still considering the matter, that it might be some months before they were able to give a decision, as their life had been disrupted by the bombing.

· 15 ·

On July 20, Secretary of War Stimson was just finishing breakfast when OSS director Allen Dulles was shown into his Potsdam quarters. Dulles told Stimson of the Japanese offer relayed to him by Jacobsson five days earlier in Wiesbaden, and of his counterproposal: that America might allow Emperor Hirohito to retain his throne if he took a public stand now to end the war.

Stimson respected Dulles's judgment. But he believed it was unlikely that peripheral peace feelers stemming from Switzerland could represent official government thinking. In addition, although Stimson himself had come to Potsdam thinking that in the final appeal to Japan to surrender, some assurance might be given for the continuance of the imperial system, he knew that such a view was unpopular back home. To many Americans, the very idea of a ruling dynasty was repugnant. To some, Hirohito was not much different from Hitler.

Stimson thanked Dulles for coming, but made it clear he had no faith in the Jacobsson connection.

On Sunday morning, July 22, Stimson called on President Truman in Potsdam. Washington had cabled that the uranium bomb would be ready for use "the first favorable opportunity in August"; if the mission was to go ahead, its complicated preparations must be set in motion no later than July 25.

Following Groves's detailed report of the success at Alamogordo, which had arrived the previous day, the news seemed to please Truman immensely.

At 10:40 A.M., Stimson called on Churchill, who read Groves's report in full and commented, "Stimson, what was gunpowder? Trivial. What was electricity? Meaningless. The atomic bomb is the Second Coming in wrath."

Stimson made it clear the president intended to tell Stalin about the weapon, although he would "withhold all details," merely "divulging the simple fact that the United States and Britain had the bomb." The question of how much to tell the Russian leader was a controversial one.

The prime minister agreed; he believed the current situation should be used as "an argument in the negotiations" going on at Potsdam.

Back in his quarters, Stimson summoned General Arnold, chief of the air force, and brought him up to date.

The air chief suggested that in place of Kyoto, Nagasaki should be considered one of the potential targets— the first time the city had been earmarked for possible atomic destruction.

Arnold told Stimson that General Carl A. Spaatz, recently promoted commander of the Strategic Air Forces and about to travel to the Marianas, could make the final choice in consultation with LeMay.

While Stimson talked with Arnold, Truman met with Churchill.

To the prime minister, the weapon was "a miracle of deliverance." It might make invasion unnecessary. It could end the war in "one or two violent shocks." Its almost supernatural power would afford the Japanese an excuse that would save their honor and release them from the samurai obligation to fight to the death. Nor would there now be a need to beg favors of Stalin, to rely on Russian intervention to help bring Japan to her knees.

Churchill concluded that "while the final decision lay in the main" with Truman, there was no disagreement between them. As he later put it:

> The historic fact remains, and it must be judged in the after time, that the decision whether or not to use the atomic bomb to compel the surrender of Japan was never an issue. There was unanimous, automatic, unquestioned agreement around the table.

But before resorting to use of the atomic weapon, the Allies would offer Japan one last chance to surrender.

• 16 •

At the foot of Mount Lasso, hemmed in by the pitch-black night, Jacob Beser was taking part in what had become a favorite Tinian pastime.

Clutching a carbine he had traded for a quart of whiskey, the skinny young officer had persuaded a marine patrol to take him with them into the jungle in search of Japanese.

The marine officer had explained the hunt rules to Beser. "First we surround the area where we think the Nip is hidden. Then we work inward, pen him into a few square yards, and illuminate the area with flashlights. Then we try to talk him into surrendering."

"And if he doesn't?"

"Wait and see."

At nightfall, the marines, with Beser in their midst, had entered the jungle. Twice they had encircled suspicious patches but had drawn blanks. Now the patrol was moving into higher ground.

Suddenly the marines froze.

Beser could hear nothing.

The lead soldier turned and tapped his nose.

Beser sniffed. Faint but unmistakable, he detected a human odor.

The marine officer deployed his men swiftly, ordering Beser to remain stationary while the soldiers melted into the dark.

Alone, crouching with his carbine, Beser wondered what he would do if a Japanese soldier appeared before him. He had never killed a man; he prayed he would not have to do so now. He wished he had stayed in his Quonset hut playing poker.

For long minutes, nothing happened. Then Beser heard the sound of branches being moved. Beams of light probed the darkness, and an American voice called out in Japanese. "Surrender! You are surrounded. Come out with your hands up."

Beser started to rise to his feet. Another American voice stopped him. "Stay down—or you'll be shot!"

There was a grunt from the jungle, followed by a movement through the foliage.

The flashlights followed the sound.

"He's coming out!"

Out of the undergrowth in front of Beser, a figure emerged. The lights held the Japanese soldier, blinding him, forcing him to close his eyes.

Beser joined the marines milling around their prisoner. The flashlights were lowered. The captured soldier opened his eyes and spoke in passable English. "Please. Cigarette."

He was given one. Inhaling deeply, he stood still while a marine frisked him and fished out of a pocket a silver cigarette case. In halting English, the prisoner explained he had taken the case from a dead Australian soldier in New Guinea.

The marine officer looked at the captured man, shook his head in disgust, and turned away. Two marines fell in beside the prisoner, pinioning his arms. In silence, the patrol returned to base.

• 17 •

In his office at General Army Headquarters in Tokyo, Major General Arisue listened carefully as Lieutenant Colonel Oya described the network of defenses that radiated outward from Hiroshima.

Oya had traveled 550 miles by train to make a personal report to Arisue on Field Marshal Hata's plans for repelling the invaders.

Arisue wished the area around Tokyo were in the same high state of readiness. By July 27, the city and its environs were devastated, its industries either obliterated by bombs or paralyzed by lack of manpower and materials. The attacks had driven millions of workers from Tokyo, reducing its population from seven million to less than four million.

Arisue and Oya were interrupted by the arrival of a messenger from the radio monitoring unit of army intelligence. Arisue took the batch of papers and realized they contained the long-expected communiqué from Potsdam. Excitedly, he studied the hurriedly prepared Japanese script, the result of transcribing and translating at high speed the words of a monitored shortwave transmission from Washington.

The Potsdam Proclamation, perhaps the most important message the Japanese received from the Allies in the entire war, reminded Japan of "the futile and senseless German resistance to the might of the aroused free peoples of the world" and spelled out the terms for ending the war. Japan must reject its militaristic leaders, submit to Allied occupation, respect fundamental democratic rights, and establish a "peacefully inclined" government. Except for war criminals, the Japanese military forces would be allowed to return home. Industry would be maintained, and eventually Japan would participate in world trade.

The proclamation concluded:

We call upon the government of Japan to proclaim now the unconditional surrender of all Japanese armed forces, and to provide proper and adequate assurances of their good faith in such action. The alternative for Japan is prompt and utter destruction.

Stimson had agreed to leave out mention of the emperor on the understanding from Truman that if the Japanese, in their reply, raised the question, it would be treated sympathetically, if not at first publicly.

But to Arisue, as well as other Japanese, the Potsdam Proclamation was a "warning of annihilation unless we give up what we hold sacred."

Foreign Minister Shigenori Togo brought a copy of the communiqué to Emperor Hirohito in the audience hall of the imperial palace's Gobunko, or "Library Building."

The Gobunko, screened by trees near the north gate, was one of the few buildings within the palace grounds that was unscarred by war. On May 25, the emperor had suffered the agony of seeing many of the buildings and pavilions within the imperial compound burn to the ground. During the previous night there had been a firebomb raid; LeMay's bombers had concentrated on the two districts adjoining the palace. Though the Americans intentionally avoided dropping incendiaries within the imperial precincts, they had converted the surrounding areas into such tornadoes of flame that the conflagration jumped the moat around the palace and set fire to dry brushwood on the far side. In minutes the flames had spread and engulfed the old wooden imperial residence built by Hirohito's grandfather, the revered Emperor Meiji.

At dawn, Hirohito and his empress had emerged from their shelter and surveyed the destruction. The emperor had commented to a palace official, "Now the people will realize that I am sharing their ordeal with no special protection from the Gods."

As the emperor studied the Allies' proclamation, Togo sat bolt upright on a hard sofa. To Togo, steeped in the tradition of diplomatic exchanges, the manner in which the document had been sent to Japan—as the main story in a shortwave newscast emanating from Washington—was disheartening. Conveying such an important document by public broadcast "did not seem the way for government to speak to government."

Yet, under the emperor's questioning, Togo conceded that the communiqué did give detailed assurances of humane treatment, freedom of speech, religion, and thought. The occupation of strategic points of the home island would end once stability was restored. And the Japanese people were to be consulted on the form of government they wished after the surrender.

The emperor dissected the proclamation clause by clause, asking questions and making points. Finally, Hirohito asked his foreign minister whether he felt the terms "were the most reasonable to be expected in the circumstances."

Togo conceded this was the case.

"I agree. In principle they are acceptable."

Silence enveloped the audience chamber.

Then, abruptly, Togo rose to his feet and faced the emperor. It was the traditional gesture of the imperial court to signify that a visitor had no more to say.

The emperor also stood, and, in another ritual act, he turned and left the room.

Togo bowed from the waist to the retreating emperor.

Togo had not revealed to the emperor the hardening attitude of Japan's government and military leaders to the Potsdam Proclamation.

Prime Minister Suzuki and his colleagues were inclined to ignore the communiqué, partly on the grounds that officially they had not even received it. Further, the Cabinet still pinned its hopes on the Soviet Union's mediating for them a "reasonable surrender." There was total agreement that to "accept Potsdam would be to insult Russia."

Suzuki arranged a press conference with a reporter planted to ask the Cabinet's view of the proclamation.

Hands trembling, the prime minister read a prepared statement. He dismissed the proclamation, saying the government "does not regard it as a thing of great value. We have decided to *mokusatsu* the proclamation."

Within minutes, Suzuki's words were broadcast by the official Japanese news agency, Domei, which translated *mokusatsu* as "ignore."

• 18 •

On July 28, Beser discovered he was being watched by the 509th's flight surgeon for signs of psychological strain. Beser was delighted to discover the surveillance. "It meant we must be getting close to mission time."

On orders from Tibbets, Dr. Don Young was watching all the group's aircrews for such symptoms. He did his work so discreetly that few fliers suspected they were under observation.

Young himself still did not know exactly what the mission entailed. He had simply been told to report any flier showing "unusual behavior."

The doctor watched every crew going off on a flight; he carefully noted the way the men walked and carried their gear. He eavesdropped on their conversations, listening for complaints of lack of sleep or loss of appetite.

When the planes returned, he was waiting, a gentle, unobtrusive man with a sharp clinical mind. Young observed the fliers drinking their ration of bourbon issued at the end of each mission; he was looking for the crewman who gulped his whiskey too quickly or asked for a second shot.

He sat in on debriefings, assessing the fliers' choice of words for clues to their mental states.

Between missions, he dropped into the fliers' Quonsets, searching for the man who laughed too loudly, lost his temper too quickly, played too boisterously. In the officers' and enlisted men's clubs, he would move from one table to another, on the lookout for indications of tension.

On the sports fields, he watched the fliers at play, looking for signs of "undue aggression" or bad sportsmanship.

And, against all regulations, he read their mail after it had cleared the censor's office.

Then, late at night, the indefatigable Dr. Young would collate his findings into confidential reports for Tibbets.

He had tabbed Beser as one of the most normal men in the 509th: "balanced, filled with healthy aggression, calm under pressure."

In fact, Young told Tibbets, his crews were psychologically "probably among the most balanced in the air force."

Young spotted no signs of instability in Claude Eatherly. And Tibbets, well aware of Eatherly's quirks, still felt the pilot's skills outweighed all other considerations.

In the heavily guarded Tech Area where Beser worked, tension had increased markedly with the arrival from Los Alamos of Captain Parsons.

At Los Alamos, Beser had hardly known Parsons, whose punctuality, reserve, and exacting manner intimidated many of his fellow scientists. But here on Tinian, the midde-aged naval officer revealed himself to be a relaxed as well as dynamic leader; the faster the pace, the calmer he became. He impressed Beser as "a dignified officer and a fine gentleman."

Parsons had come to Tinian to supervise the final delivery and assembly of the atomic bomb.

Also now on Tinian were two Englishmen: Group Captain Leonard Cheshire, an RAF hero, and a fair-haired scientist, William Penney, whose brilliant mathematical calculations had played a part in developing the weapon.

The War Cabinet in London had insisted that Britain be represented when the bomb was dropped. President Truman had agreed "in principle" to this at Potsdam. As a result, Cheshire and Penney firmly believed they would be going on the flight that dropped the bomb and, afterward, would be reporting their observations to London.

Strangely, while everybody in the 509th was helpful "and very jolly," General LeMay had been evasive when the two Englishmen mentioned going on the mission.

Recently there had been a mysterious outbreak of diarrhea in the 509th. Dr. Young attributed it to "a generous quantity of soap" slipped into the cooking vats. Uanna, the group's security chief, suspected that "a mischievous Jap who had gotten into the compound was responsible." He was right; that was exactly what had happened. Security around the cookhouse was increased.

The hostility the group encountered outside the compound was an increasing concern for Tibbets. While every other flying unit on the island was putting in the maximum number of combat hours, the 509th was mainly occupied with practice missions around the Marianas. The group so far had been to Japan just three times—and on each of these occasions had used only ten bombers from its fleet of fifteen. At night, furious fliers from other groups hurled showers of rocks into the compound; it was a humiliating experience for the self-confident 509th.

Tibbets tried to dispel the frustration by holding regular pep talks. He encouraged Perry to excel himself in the kitchens. And he was pleased to see that Chaplain Downey was acting "like a cheerleader, always on hand to lend support."

Tibbets encouraged jokes about life in the compound; he reasoned that if the men could laugh at their troubles, they would not seem so bad. One of the most successful jests was a song, sung to the tune of "Rum and Coca-Cola."

> Have you ever been to Tinian?
> It's Heaven for the enlisted man.
> There's whisky, girls and other such,
> But all are labeled: "Mustn't touch."

> This tropic isle's a paradise,
> Of muddy roads and rainy skies.
> Outdoor latrines and fungus feet,
> And every day more goat to eat.

> Enlisted men are on the beam,
> Officers say, "We're one big team."
> But do they ever share the rum and Coke?
> Ha, ha, ha, that's one big joke.

As always, Tibbets was careful to hide the increasing strain he personally felt. His working day often stretched from 7:00 A.M. until midnight. His sleep was frequently disturbed by "eyes-only" messages from "Morose," the new code name Groves used for his Washington headquarters, or from "Misplay," Groves's new name for Los Alamos. Messages from Morose inevitably ended with a request for the latest readiness report for "Centerboard," the code name for the actual atomic strike.

• 19 •

At 12:50 P.M., July 28, the field telephone rang in Second Lieutenant Tatsuo Yokoyama's antiaircraft gun post on Mount Futaba. One of the controllers in Hiroshima Castle warned him of the possible approach of bombers from the south, the direction of Kure. Yokoyama already had his guns pointed that way, in case any of the American planes bombing the port were forced by the gun batteries there to flee toward Hiroshima.

Radio Hiroshima interrupted its program to announce an alert, and all over the city, people ran for shelter.

Dr. Kaoru Shima was performing an appendectomy when a nurse told him of the air-raid warning. He continued with the surgery. Outside the operating room, the staff hurried patients to the ground-floor shelter, carrying those unable to walk by themselves.

Mayor Senkichi Awaya and Kazumasa Maruyama were in the mayor's office when they heard the alert siren. Maruyama rushed to the window and stared into the sky but could see nothing. He and Awaya resumed their discussion.

Field Marshal Hata invited his officers to join him at the windows of the conference room to watch developments.

Yokoyama, peering through his binoculars, could see at least two B-24s coming toward him. They were climbing after their bomb run over Kure Naval Dockyard, now obscured by a towering pall of smoke.

With growing excitement, the gunnery officer estimated that if the oncoming aircraft maintained their present course, they would be well within range of his guns when they crossed Hiroshima.

The planes approaching Hiroshima were from the 866th Bombardment Squadron of the 494th Bombardment Group of the Seventh Bomber Command, based on Okinawa.

They were part of a force of thirty B-24s that had taken off earlier in the morning to attack the *Haruna,* one of the last Japanese battleships still afloat. Each bomber carried twenty-seven hundred gallons of fuel, three two-thousand-pound bombs, and propaganda leaflets giving the Potsdam Proclamation surrender terms.

The bombers had arrived over Kure at exactly 12:40. But even from the designated attack altitude of ten thousand feet, the *Haruna* proved a difficult target;

she was well camouflaged, and protected by shore batteries as well as her own guns.

By the time the B-24s from the 866th made their bomb run, some thirty misses had exploded at distances of between two hundred and six hundred yards from the *Haruna*. A number of other bombs had fallen on nearby dockyard buildings, and the immediate target area was shrouded in dense smoke.

Flying through heavy flak, the first bomber of the 866th, nicknamed *Taloa*, had dropped her three bombs into the smoke and broken away to the left, toward Hiroshima.

The eleven men aboard the *Taloa* were nervous. It was common knowledge that the Japanese often executed captured American fliers. Just over a month earlier, eight airmen had been publicly put to death—their bodies prodded into the ritual kneeling position and their heads chopped off by ceremonial swords.

The pilot of the *Taloa*, First Lieutenant Joseph Bubinsky, was too busy trying to gain height and chart a new course for home to dwell on such gruesome thoughts.

Bombardier Robert Johnston, also a first lieutenant, was still in the nose of the B-24, peering through the Plexiglas at the countryside below. His relief was considerable as the bomber cleared the concentration of gun batteries that made Kure one of the most heavily defended cities in Japan. Ahead, coming up fast, were the port facilities of Hiroshima and, just beyond, the welcome sight of wooded countryside.

The *Taloa* carried nine other frightened men: First Lieutenant Rudolph Flanagin, copilot; First Lieutenant Lawrence Falls, navigator; Technical Sergeant Walter Piskor, flight engineer; Technical Sergeant David Bushfield, radio operator; Staff Sergeant Charles Allison, upper turret gunner; Staff Sergeant Charles Baumgartner, ball turret gunner; Staff Sergeant Camillous Kirkpatrick, nose turret gunner; Staff Sergeant Julius Molnar, rear turret gunner; and a "passenger," Captain Donald Marvin, on board to gain combat experience.

Not far behind the *Taloa* flew the *Lonesome Lady,* with its crew of nine: Second Lieutenant Thomas Cartwright, pilot; Second Lieutenant Durden Looper, copilot; Second Lieutenant Roy Pedersen, navigator; Second Lieutenant James Mike Ryan, bombardier; Sergeant Hugh Atkinson, radio operator; Staff Sergeant William Abel, tail gunner; Staff Sergeant Ralph Neal, ball gunner; Corporal John Long, nose gunner; and Sergeant Buford Ellison, flight engineer.

The men aboard both B-24s knew of the standing orders that forbade their bombing Hiroshima; but as far as they knew, there was no restriction on simply flying over the city.

None of the fliers knew anything at all about the ground defenses of Hiroshima. When the city had been "reserved" for possible atomic attack, all information about it had been restricted.

As they approached the southern end of Hiroshima, a concentrated stream of shells was sent up by antiaircraft guns in batteries near the *gaisenkan,* the "hall of triumphant return," and in Eba Park, guarding the Mitsubishi factory.

The bombers continued their headlong dash over Hiroshima, toward Mount Futaba.

And then, with the time nearing 1:00 P.M., with two-thirds of the city behind them and the safety of open countryside ahead, the fate of the twenty men aboard the two bombers, although never publicly reported by the American government, was about to become inextricably linked with that of Hiroshima.

As soon as the B-24s were within range, Yokoyama ordered the battery to fire.

The first salvo bracketed the *Taloa*. Pretty puffs of smoke exploded above and below it. Yokoyama shouted an immediate correction.

The next salvo seemed to hit the *Taloa* squarely on the nose. A frenzied cheer came from the gunners. Yokoyama shouted at them to keep firing.

The sky around the striken bomber was now pockmarked with shrapnel bursts. Trailing smoke, the plane abruptly turned left, away from Mount Futaba.

Behind, the *Lonesome Lady* also seemed to have been hit.

From the conference room windows, Field Marshal Hata and his staff watched the tiny figures tumbling from the *Taloa*. Moments later, as the B-24 crossed western Hiroshima, their parachutes opened.

The bomber plunged into a hill between the two villages of Itsukaichi and Inokuchi. A great cloud of flame and oily smoke rose into the air. The sound of the crash brought people from nearby farms and hamlets out into the open. Some, workers from a local fish market, brandished knives and hatchets.

At least three men from the *Taloa* were now floating earthward. They were pilot Joseph Bubinsky, bombardier Robert Johnston, and tail gunner Julius Molnar.

All were deeply shocked and suffering superficial wounds, but instinctively they tried to juggle their parachute cords so they would drift away from the packs of civilians they could see converging below.

The *Lonesome Lady* was trailing smoke and coming under fire from a battery sited near Hiroshima Castle. The bomber banked sharply to the right, turning back in the direction of Kure. Yokoyama's gunners would forever believe it was they who delivered the coup de grâce to the stricken plane.

The *Lonesome Lady* lost altitude, passing over the Toyo factory and heading for the dense forest southeast of Hiroshima. Eight men managed to jump from the bomber. Only navigator Roy Pedersen was still on board as the *Lonesome Lady* crashed to the ground.

The excitement at the Mount Futaba gun post knew no bounds. For Tatsuo Yokoyama, "this was my most thrilling day in all the war." He promised his gunners the biggest celebration they could imagine. Then he turned his binoculars to the west, where those who had bailed out of the *Taloa* were about to touch down.

Squads of Kempei Tai military policemen were fanning out from Hiroshima in pursuit of the fliers.

One of those squads, led by Warrant Officer Hiroshi Yanagita, stopped to check its bearings with Imperial Army Corporal Kanai Hiroto, who lived locally and had been furiously peddling his bicycle in the direction of the crash.

Hiroto told Yanagita that he spoke English and would be happy to offer his services as an interpreter. He stepped onto the running board of the Kempei Tai car, and they sped toward Inokuchi.

Hiroto had attended a high school in Pasadena, near Los Angeles. He returned to Japan in 1934 and afterward was drafted. Following three years' fighting in Manchuria, he had experienced an uneventful war.

Yanagita was one of the most senior Kempei Tai leaders in Hiroshima. He was a tough, professional soldier.

When they reached the foot of the hill into which the *Taloa* had crashed, the Kempei Tai officer and his men raced toward the parachutes they could see caught in the trees.

Hiroto stopped by the still-smoldering bomber. It had split in two sections, lying some two hundred yards apart. He was about to go into the wreckage when Yanagita returned, saying one of the Americans had been caught and was being held a little way down the hill.

It was the tail gunner, Staff Sergeant Julius Molnar from Kalamazoo, Michigan.

Even before reaching him, Hiroto saw that Molnar was in grave danger. The slightly built sergeant was surrounded by civilians who "wanted to beat him to death. I forced my way in, took hold of him, and tried to ward off their blows."

Yanagita stepped forward, brandishing a pistol. He

threatened his men would shoot the next civilian who moved.

Sullenly, the crowd stood back.

Flanked by Hiroto and Yanagita, Molnar was escorted to the relative safety of a nearby farmstead. There, Molnar was surrounded by Kempei Tai policemen.

Hiroto could see that the young airman was making an effort to control his trembling. He spoke to the tail gunner for the first time, telling him in English that he had once lived in the United States. The terrified Molnar began to calm down.

Prompted by Yanagita, Hiroto questioned Molnar. He willingly gave his name, serial number 36453945, and rank. He said that he was twenty-one years old, had been trained in Texas, and that his plane had taken off from Okinawa to attack the port of Kure. He claimed he did not know the names of the other crew members of the *Taloa*.

Hiroto was then called to another part of the farmyard, where bombardier Robert Johnston was being held. The crowd of villagers menacing the officer were again warned back by the Kempei Tai.

Johnston concealed his fear better than Molnar, but Hiroto "could tell from his eyes that he was very frightened." Johnston also gave his name, serial number 0698565, and rank.

When Johnston refused to say more, the Kempei Tai leader told Hiroto his translation services were not needed further. Hiroto returned to the crash site, where he searched in the wreckage for food and radio components.

Yanagita and his men rounded up three other crew members from the *Taloa*, including its pilot, Joseph Bubinsky, and drove them to Kempei Tai headquarters at Hiroshima Castle, where specialist interrogators could question them more thoroughly.

By now the eight crewmen from the *Lonesome Lady* were also on their way to the castle.

Of the twenty original fliers in the two bombers,

thirteen had survived being shot down and captured. When they arrived in Hiroshima, there would be a total of twenty-three American prisoners of war being held in the city.

For them, the most terrible experience of all was yet to come.

• 20 •

In the early hours of July 29 on Tinian, eighty-one fliers assembled to be briefed for the fourth—and, as it turned out, last—practice mission the 509th would make over Japan. Lieutenant Colonel Hazen Payette, the group intelligence officer, confirmed the targets allocated at an earlier briefing to each of the nine crews.

Lewis was to bomb a factory complex at Koriyama; Captain Frederick Bock was to drop his ten-thousand-pound blockbuster on Osaka; Eatherly was to bomb the railway sidings at Maizuru; others were to attack targets at Kobe, Shimoda, Ube, Nagoya, Wakayama, and Hitachi. Ferebee, like Tibbets, had been forbidden to fly over Japan until the atomic mission.

For this mission, Lewis would be flying Sweeney's airplane, nicknamed the *Great Artiste,* while his usual B-29 was given a special inspection and servicing by group technicians. Van Kirk was taking the place of Lewis's regular navigator. The changes made Lewis uneasy.

The briefing was routine. Antiaircraft fire would probably be "moderate to light." Van Kirk spoke to the navigators about routes to the targets, where they planned to arrive, as usual, around nine in the morning. Then, trucks took the crews to their planes.

The *Straight Flush* was the first to take off. Eatherly was bent on making a record flight to Japan and back in order to resume an unfinished poker game.

Minutes later, *Bock's Car,* commanded by Captain Frederick Bock, trundled down the runway.

Next, it was the turn of Major James Hopkins in *Strange Cargo.* Lewis watched the four engines spin into life. Then *Strange Cargo* moved from its apron.

Suddenly, there was a rasping sound of metal grinding on metal. The bomb-bay doors of *Strange Cargo* were slowly forced open, their reinforced-steel hinges screeching under the pressure.

Hopkins brought the plane to a stop and, with a sickening thud, *Strange Cargo*'s blockbuster dropped onto the asphalt.

Lewis stared boggle-eyed at the huge bomb a few feet away. If it exploded, it would destroy everything within several hundred yards.

Quietly, Lewis warned his crew of what had happened. Over the radio he could hear Hopkins calling the control tower for help. In moments, the sound of crash trucks, ambulances, and MP jeeps filled the air.

The control officer told Lewis and Hopkins to keep their crews on board; the slightest jar might detonate the ten-thousand-pound blockbuster.

Portable searchlights were focused on the runway. Through binoculars, firemen and armorers studied the bright-orange bomb, its fins bent and twisted from its fall.

The firemen were the first to move in. They blanketed the blockbuster with foam, which they hoped would help deaden any explosion.

A volunteer gang of armorers pushed a dolly and winch crane under the gaping belly of the plane. Working in total silence, they gently placed shackles around the bomb and cranked it up, inch by inch. Then they slid the dolly under the bomb. A small tractor was backed into position, the dolly hooked up and towed away.

A relieved voice from the control tower told both crews they could relax.

Lewis bellowed a characteristic reply. "Like hell! We got a mission to fulfill!"

Within minutes, the engines of *Great Artiste* thundered into life. Without giving *Strange Cargo* a second look, Lewis and his crew took off on their night flight to Koriyama.

• 21 •

Six days previously, General Carl Spaatz had arrived in Washington, D.C., from Europe on his way to the Pacific to assume command of the Strategic Air Forces, newly created for the impending invasion of Japan. After Groves had briefed him on the atomic bomb, Spaatz, a graying, lean-faced Pennsylvania Dutchman, had faced General Thomas T. Handy, acting chief of staff while Marshall was in Potsdam, and stubbornly insisted that "if I'm going to kill 100,000 people I'm not going to do it on verbal orders. I want a piece of paper."

The document was drafted by Groves on July 23. It was then transmitted to the Little White House in Potsdam for approval—immediately granted. The document had been prepared by Handy and, on July 25, handed to Spaatz.

When Spaatz arrived on Guam, his new chief of staff, LeMay, suggested that he hold an immediate meeting with the key personnel involved in the atomic mission. Spaatz agreed, and assembled now, on July 29, in LeMay's office were LeMay, Tibbets, Parsons, Blanchard, and LeMay's senior meteorologist. The exact date of the first mission would depend on his forecast of "a good bombing day," when there would be a maximum of three-tenths cloud cover and favorable winds over Japan.

Spaatz read the order aloud.

To: General Carl Spaatz, CG, USASAF:

1. The 509 Composite Group, 20th Air Force

will deliver its first special bomb as soon as weather will permit visual bombing after about 3 August 1945 on one of the targets: Hiroshima, Kokura, Niigata and Nagasaki. To carry military and civilian scientific personnel from the War Department to observe and record the effects of the explosion of the bomb, additional aircraft will accompany the airplane carrying the bomb. The observing planes will stay several miles distant from the point of impact of the bomb.

2. Additional bombs will be delivered on the above targets as soon as made ready by the project staff. Further instructions will be issued concerning targets other than those listed above.

3. Dissemination of any and all information concerning the use of the weapon against Japan is reserved to the Secretary of War and the President of the United States. No communiqués on the subject of releases of information will be issued by commanders in the field without specific prior authority. Any news stories will be sent to the War Department for special clearance.

4. The foregoing directive is issued to you by direction and with the approval of the Secretary of War and of the Chief of Staff, USA. It is desired that you personally deliver one copy of this directive to General MacArthur and one copy to Admiral Nimitz for their information.

> Signed: Thos. T. Handy,
> General, G.S.C.
> Acting Chief of Staff

At last, America's senior soldier in the Pacific, MacArthur, was to be told about the revolutionary weapon.

Spaatz folded the document and placed it back in his briefcase. "Gentlemen," he asked, "are your preparations on schedule?"

The men around the table nodded. Parsons then read a memorandum he had just received from Oppenheimer in Los Alamos.

Following the Alamogordo test, Oppenheimer had calculated that the energy release from the bomb to be dropped on Japan would be in the region of twelve thousand to twenty thousand tons, and the blast should be equivalent to that from eight thousand to fifteen thousand tons of TNT.

It would take nearly two thousand B-29s, carrying full loads of conventional high-explosive bombs, to match one atomic bomb. Even now, after almost a year with the Manhattan Project, Tibbets found such a thought "just awesome."

Perhaps Oppenheimer felt the same when he wrote his memo to Parsons. In it, after mentioning the bomb would probably be fuzed to go off 1,850 feet above the target city, he stated:

It is not expected that radioactive contamination will reach the ground. The Ball of Fire should have a brilliance which should persist longer than at Trinity [Alamogordo] since no dust should be mixed with it. In general, the visible light emitted by the unit should be even more spectacular. Lethal radiation will, of course, reach the ground from the bomb itself.

Oppenheimer ended his memo: "Good luck."

The meeting in LeMay's office concluded with the introduction of two further code names. LeMay was to be known as "Cannon"; General Farrell, on route to Guam to function as the senior representative of the Manhattan Project in the Marianas, would be "Scale."

As he flew back to Tinian with Parsons, whose code name was "Judge," Tibbets mused that if he had a choice of pseudonym, he would like to be known as "Justice."

Soon after returning to Tinian, Tibbets was again out on the runway, waiting to greet his crews as they returned from their solo missions to Japan.

None had been hit by flak. The weather over the targets was reasonable, and each aircraft had been able to bomb visually.

When Lewis landed, Tibbets congratulated him and his men for not being unnerved by the experience with the errant bomb just before takeoff. Lewis took the opportunity to remind his commander, "My crew is the best you've got."

There then occurred a short conversation whose meaning Tibbets and Lewis would later dispute.

Although Lewis had expected to drop the first new weapon with "his crew" in "his plane," Tibbets had already told him that van Kirk and Ferebee would be going along. Lewis did not like the idea but had come to accept it, viewing van Kirk's flight with him today as confirmation of the plan.

Now, according to Lewis, Tibbets told him that he, Lewis, "would be flying the mission." Lewis took that to mean that he would be the aircraft commander.

Tibbets would not deny that he made the remark, but he would differ radically from Lewis in interpreting it: "Lewis would fly as copilot; van Kirk and Ferebee would replace his usual navigator and bombardier. It was clear to anybody that on such a mission I had to be in the driver's seat."

• 22 •

Aboard submarine *I.58,* shortly before midnight, the officer of the watch awakened Lieutenant Commander Mochitsura Hashimoto from his catnap and reported all was well. Hashimoto told him he thought "it was going to be a good night for hunting."

The previous day at 2:00 P.M., Hashimoto had sighted a tanker escorted by a destroyer. Judging it unwise to approach close enough to use conventional torpedoes, he had decided instead to launch two of his six *kaitens*. After quickly saying good-bye to Hashimoto, each suicide pilot had climbed through a hatch from *I.58* into his torpedo, lashed to the mother submarine's deck. When Hashimoto heard the young officers shout over the intercom, "Three cheers for the emperor," he knew they were ready to be launched. In poor visibility, the *kaitens* had steered toward the tanker. Hashimoto tracked them through his periscope until the rain blotted them out. He waited. Then, faint but unmistakable, came the sound of explosions. Hashimoto guessed the tanker had been hit, but not being absolutely sure, he had logged it as a "probable."

After leading the crew in prayers for the departed *kaiten* pilots, Hashimoto had set course for "the crossroads," the intersection of American shipping lanes connecting Guam with Leyte in the Philippine Islands, and Okinawa with Peleliu in the Palau Islands.

The crossroads was exactly six hundred miles from Guam. The *I.58* had reached there earlier this Sunday; the sea was calm, and the submarine had remained surfaced for most of the day. Toward evening, visibility had dropped as mist drifted over the area. Hashimoto had ordered the submarine to submerge until moonrise, at about 11:00 P.M.

Now, having completed his prayers at the ship's shrine, Hashimoto ordered night action stations. As the chief engineer increased speed to three knots, the crew moved to a state of alert.

Hashimoto ordered the submarine up to sixty feet and sent the night periscope hissing upward to break the Pacific surface. After adjusting the eyepiece, he swept the quarters of the compass. The moon was some twenty degrees high in the east, and there were a few scattered clouds.

He ordered the submarine brought to within ten feet of the surface. "Stand by type-thirteen radar."

The mechanism for detecting aircraft rose just above the swell. Its operator reported no sign of planes.

"Stand by type-twenty-two radar."

The surface radar, which indicated the presence of other vessels within a three-mile radius of *I.58,* rose out of the water. From past experience, Hashimoto knew that the device was capable of mistaking driftwood, shoals of fish, and outcrops of rock for ships.

Only when the operator was satisfied that the vicinity was empty did the captain give his next order. "Stand by to surface."

Hashimoto lowered the periscope handles. "Blow main ballast."

High-pressure air entered the main tanks, expelling the last of the water and sending the boat swiftly to the surface.

As soon as the deck was awash, Hashimoto ordered the conning-tower hatch opened. The signalman and navigator climbed up to the bridge with the watch officer, and each began looking through high-powered night binoculars.

Below, in the control room, Hashimoto kept watch through the night periscope; the operator of the surface radar continued monitoring.

The routine was broken by the navigator's shout from the bridge. "Bearing red-nine-zero degrees. Possible enemy ship!"

Hashimoto lowered the periscope. "Action stations!"

The alarm bells rang and the crew ran to their battle stations as Hashimoto bounded up the ladder to the bridge. Peering through his binoculars, he could see in the moonlight a black spot clearly visible on the horizon. He leaped for the ladder shouting, "Dive!"

The bridge watch shinnied down behind him; the hatch was slammed shut. The main vents were opened, and *I.58* crash-dived, with Hashimoto glued to the night periscope so as not to lose sight of the target.

It was the *Indianapolis*.

The aged cruiser had sailed from Tinian on Thursday, July 26, having safely delivered her mysterious cargo. After stopping at Guam, the *Indianapolis* had headed for Leyte in the Philippines; from there, it was likely she would be ordered back to San Francisco to collect more nuclear material.

This Sunday at sea had followed a familiar pattern: morning church service on the fantail, no smoking until after the service was over, and no work before the noonday meal was served.

By evening, the small chop of the sea had increased to a rough swell, but not enough to affect the standard zigzag course the ship was following. Its engines were phased to produce staggered turns on her four screws, ensuring an uneven pattern of sounds to hamper any enemy submarines listening to hydrophones.

At dusk, Captain McVay had told the watch officer that the ship need not zigzag after twilight.

At 10:30 P.M., with visibility still poor, McVay had signed the night orders; they contained no request to resume zigzagging if the weather improved. He had retired to sleep in his cabin close to the bridge.

At sixteen knots, the *Indianapolis* now steamed in a direct line toward submarine *I.58*. Less than ten miles of sea separated them.

Thirty feet below the surface, trimmed level, *I.58* swung slowly to face the approaching ship. Hashimoto remained bent to the periscope, pressing so hard on the rubber eyepiece that his eyes watered. He blinked the tears away and resumed watching. As the target came closer, the black spot changed into a distinct triangular shape. Hashimoto felt a sense of excitement: this was no mere merchantman, but a large warship.

"All tubes to the ready. *Kaitens* stand by!"

The gap between the submarine and the *Indianapolis* was now five miles.

His eyes still firmly pressed to the periscope, Hashimoto assessed the ship's masthead height as ninety feet. She was too big to be a destroyer; he guessed she was either a battleship or a large cruiser—a prime target indeed.

The hydrophone operators reported they could pick up engine noises. At three miles' separation, Hashimoto fixed a set of earphones over his head. The target, clearly outlined in the moonlight, was on a near-collision course with his submarine.

Hashimoto suspected a trap: was the approaching ship acting as a decoy, drawing his fire while destroyers waited to pounce? Nervously, he scanned the field of view. There was nothing else in sight.

At two miles, he realized that his luck would hold. Turning to the men grouped around him, Hashimoto allowed himself a prediction. "We've got her!"

Silence fell over the boat. The crew waited tensely for the order to fire.

Suddenly, the *kaiten* pilots began clamoring to go. Hashimoto curtly told them they would be used only if the ordinary torpedo attack failed.

The range was three thousand yards as Hashimoto began his final calculations.

Aboard the *Indianapolis,* the 12:00 to 4:00 A.M. watch arrived on the bridge. There were now thirteen officers and men there, monitoring course and speed.

Aboard the *I.58,* Hashimoto revised his original estimate that the *Indianapolis* was traveling at twenty knots. Based on what he could see through the periscope and hear through the hydrophones, he now estimated that her true speed was twelve knots. He decided to delay firing until the range had closed to under a mile.

The torpedoes were set to travel through the water at a depth of twelve feet and a speed of forty-eight knots. Wakeless, they would be invisible to the most vigilant watchkeeper on the *Indianapolis*.

With less than fifteen hundred yards separating the cruiser and the submarine, Hashimoto finally shouted the words. "Stand by. Fire!"

At two-second intervals, the torpedo-release switch tripped. After twelve seconds, the torpedo officer reported. "All tubes fired and correct."

Six torpedoes, launched to give them a spread of three degrees, were speeding fanwise toward the *Indianapolis*.

It was two minutes past midnight.

Aboard the *Indianapolis*, one of the officers on the bridge commented that the visibility was improving as the moon rose higher in front of the ship.

Below the bridge, several hundred men slept on mattresses and blankets on the open deck to escape the broiling heat below.

A party, far forward in a starboard cabin, was coming to an end. And in his emergency cabin behind the bridge, Captain McVay was in his berth, asleep, stark naked.

Hashimoto counted the seconds as the submarine turned parallel with the cruiser.

"Fifty-one, fifty-two, fifty-three—"

A huge column of water rose into the air, blocking out the forward turret of the *Indianapolis*. Another column spouted near the aft turret. Then, bright-red flames leaped from various parts of the ship's superstructure. As each of the torpedoes struck home, Hashimoto gave an exultant cry. "A hit! A hit!"

The crew of *I.58* danced with joy, shouting and stamping their feet until the submarine resembled some underwater madhouse.

There was no panic aboard the *Indianapolis*, only stunned disbelief that the ship had been hit. Swiftly the crew moved to deal with the emergency. The cruiser was straining and groaning and settling at the bows.

Captain McVay ordered the radio room to transmit a distress message. Moments later, with smoke and flames enveloping the foredeck, without lights or power—certain indication of mortal damage—McVay gave the order to abandon ship.

The *Indianapolis* rolled onto her starboard side. As the cruiser filled rapidly with water, her stern rose higher and higher into the air until a hundred feet and more of hull reared straight up out of the Pacific, towering over hundreds of men, living and dying and already dead, floating in the sea.

For a few moments, the glistening hull remained poised. Screams of panic filled the air. Then, swiftly and cleanly, barely disturbing the Pacific swell, the *Indianapolis* plunged out of sight—the last major vessel to be lost in World War II, and victim of the greatest disaster at sea in the history of the U.S. Navy.

It was 12:14 A.M., July 30, 1945.

After reloading his six torpedo tubes, Hashimoto brought *I.58* to the surface. There was nothing to be seen in the darkness. It was over an hour since the action began. Finding nothing, he set course for the northeast.

A full ninety-six hours would pass before the first rescue ship would begin to drag from the water the few remaining survivors from the *Indianapolis*. When the news of the loss of four-fifths of its crew reached Tinian, it would cause shock and horror, and, in the case of Jake Beser, a sense of personal grief; before the *Indianapolis* had left Tinian, he had dined with an old classmate aboard the ship. Now his friend was dead, one of the nearly nine hundred victims of Hashimoto's torpedoes.

In Washington, when Groves heard of the loss, he was relieved the ship had delivered her precious cargo of uranium before sinking. On the very day that the

Indianapolis was attacked, **Groves was writing** a memo to the chief of staff in which he presented his projected production schedule for atomic bombs after August.

In September, we should have three or four bombs . . . four or three in October. . . . In November at least five and the rate will rise to seven in December and increase decidedly in early 1946.

Clearly, the Manhattan Project chief would have to think carefully in the future whether delivery by ship, as with the *Indianapolis,* was the most sensible course.

• 23 •

The thirteen surviving crewmen from the two B-24s were all being held prisoner within Hiroshima Castle's grounds: some at Kempei Tai headquarters, others in the dungeon of the castle itself, and two at the Second Infantry's divisional headquarters.

The newly arrived airmen had no knowledge of the ten other prisoners of war who had already spent weeks in solitary confinement within the castle.

For all twenty-three Americans now in Hiroshima, life was a mixture of despair and fear. Their cells were bereft of furnishings except for a washbasin and one blanket. They had no clothes other than those they had been wearing when captured. Long hours of solitude were interspersed with bouts of hard questioning. The bowls of cornmeal mush or rice they received three times a day in their cells were barely enough to sustain them.

Regularly, squads of curious Japanese soldiers came to stare into the cells. Peering through the grilles, they heaped insults on the prisoners as they attempted to squat over the stinking toilet holes set into the floor.

Occasionally, the prisoners were taken to the special interrogation room used by the Kempei Tai. Some of the Americans invented stories, hoping to stay alive by saying what they imagined their captors wanted to hear.

Those held at the Second Infantry's headquarters were guarded by Private Second Class Masaru Matsuoka, who was not a member of the Kempei Tai. The soldier stood guard, rifle and fixed bayonet at the ready, for a shift of three hours on, three hours off.

Matsuoka never spoke to the airmen, but he and his fellow guards thought their dress looked so shabby that "America must be in bad shape—we can win the war yet."

Matsuoka pitied his prisoners. Could not understand why they had not killed themselves to avoid capture, as "we would have done." To him, the disgrace of being shot down would have been sufficient reason to die.

The belts and shoelaces of the prisoners had been taken away, and when they asked for a razor to shave, the request was refused. The Japanese feared the Americans might yet commit suicide.

• 24 •

In Washington, Groves studied a copy of an urgent cable from Spaatz on Guam.

REFERENCE CENTERBOARD OPERATION SCHEDULED AFTER AUGUST 3RD AGAINST NAGASAKI. REPORTS, PRISONER OF WAR SOURCES, NOT VERIFIED BY PHOTOS, GIVE LOCATION OF ALLIED PRISONER OF WAR CAMP ONE MILE NORTH OF CENTER OF CITY OF NAGASAKI. DOES THIS INFLUENCE THE CHOICE OF THIS TARGET FOR INITIAL CENTERBOARD OPERATION? REQUEST IMMEDIATE REPLY.

Groves knew that the prisoners in Nagasaki could, at the very minimum, be blinded by an atomic blast. More likely, they would die.

Unwilling for once to assume total responsibility for everything involving the Manhattan Project, he consulted General Handy. Handy thought the query should be brought to the attention of Stimson, who had just returned from the Big Three Conference.

Before going to see Stimson, Groves prepared a reply to Spaatz telling him there was to be no change in the targets because of the POW situation; Spaatz could, however, adjust the aiming points "in such a way as to decrease the possibility of hitting any POW camps."

Mindful of his confrontation with Stimson over the proposal to bomb Kyoto, Groves presented the secretary with the Spaatz cable and the proposed reply. Groves later recalled, "His only reaction was to thank me for showing him the cable before it was sent."

In the meantime, Spaatz had sent another top-secret message to Handy. It read:

HIROSHIMA ACCORDING TO PRISONER OF WAR REPORTS IS THE ONLY ONE OF FOUR TARGET CITIES FOR CENTERBOARD THAT DOES NOT HAVE ALLIED PRISONERS OF WAR CAMPS. ADVISE.

Handy spoke with Groves by telephone before replying. He then cabled Spaatz:

IF YOU CONSIDER YOUR INFORMATION RELIABLE, HIROSHIMA SHOULD BE GIVEN FIRST PRIORITY.

Hiroshima was put at the top of the target list.

• 25 •

The biggest-ever task force from the Marianas was scheduled to bomb Japan on July 31. Almost a thousand bombers would take off at midday to attack a dozen selected Japanese cities.

Shortly after noon, the first Wright turbo-supercharged engine banged into life. Then the next one started, and the next, until the sound of hundreds of engines echoed back from the jungle.

After moving from the apron to the taxiways, the bombers took off four at a time from the eighty-five-hundred-foot parallel runways of North Field. It took two hours for all the bombers to become airborne; by the time the last plane rose from North Field, the lead bomber was almost five hundred miles away.

Scores of ground crewmen had forsworn lunch to watch part of the armada take off. Beser was one of the few from the 509th who thought it worthwhile to miss Perry's chow to "see the show." Beser's craving for action had not been satisfied in spite of his having by now made a number of trips over Japan. Today, as usual, he wished he were flying.

Yet Beser knew the planes carried a combined payload that in explosive power was less than that expected of the first atomic bomb.

And the radar officer was one of the few men on Tinian who knew that the weapon had now been finally assembled. It was resting on a cradle in a workshop in the Tech Area, ready for delivery. To Beser, the bomb looked like "an elongated trash can with fins."

Tibbets, Ferebee, and van Kirk spent the morning on Iwo Jima checking on plans to use the island as an emergency "pit stop" for the atomic mission. Months before, it had been decided that if for any reason the atomic bomb–carrying plane developed a serious malfunction on the outward leg of its journey, it should land on Iwo; it was better to put at risk the few thousand U.S. servicemen stationed there than to endanger the more than twenty thousand on Tinian—not to mention Tinian's second priceless piece of ordnance, the plutonium bomb.

In the center of one fenced-off area at Iwo Jima was a large, deep, open pit whose dimensions were precisely the same as another pit in a similarly fenced-off area on North Field, Tinian. The atomic bomb would first be lowered into the Tinian pit, then the B-29 wheeled into position over the hole so that the bomb could be winched up into the bomb bay. The pit on Iwo Jima would permit the quick transfer of the bomb to a standby plane if the original aircraft had to force-land on the island. A specially prepared communications center would act as a relay station between the strike aircraft and Tinian.

Satisfied, Tibbets and his companions left Iwo Jima as mysteriously as they had arrived. Flying south again, they found the airspace on the six-hundred-mile journey back to Tinian "a logjam of bombers." Tibbets thought to himself that "soon all this will be obsolete—if the atomic bomb works."

On August 1, after one of Perry's magnificent breakfasts, Tibbets adjourned to his office in the 509th's headquarters, closed the door, sat at his desk, and wrote rapidly. It took him only minutes to draft the top-secret order for the first atomic attack in history.

He sealed the order in an envelope and sent it by special courier to LeMay's headquarters on Guam.

The order specified that a total of seven B-29s would be used for the historic mission. One would be needed at Iwo Jima to serve as the standby aircraft. Three would fly well ahead of the bomb-carrying plane, one to each of the potential target cities, to appraise the local weather and to relay the information back to the bomb carrier. This aircraft would be accompanied by two observer planes.

Tibbets now had to decide which of his crews would fly with him on the mission, and what role each would have.

He started by assigning Eatherly to fly the weather plane to Hiroshima.

At noon, Tibbets sent for his group intelligence officer, Lieutenant Colonel Hazen Payette, and the intelligence officer of the 393rd Squadron, Captain Joseph Buscher. It was Buscher who on that first day at Wendover, almost a year ago now, had urged the complaining fliers to "give the place a chance."

Tibbets told the two men about the impending mission and ordered them to be ready to brief the selected crews on what the target cities looked like from thirty thousand feet.

On Guam, Brigadier General Thomas Farrell, Groves's deputy, who had just arrived in the Marianas to act as the project's "eyes and ears," received his first cable from Morose, Groves's Washington headquarters. It read:

IS THERE ANYTHING LEFT UNDONE EITHER HERE OR THERE WHICH IS DELAYING INITIATION OF LITTLE BOY OPERATION?

Farrell, a man of commendably few words, cabled: NO.

After lunch, Tibbets sent, in rapid succession, for Perry, the mess officer; Sweeney, the commander of the 393rd; and Classen, the deputy commander of the 509th.

Among other instructions, he ordered Perry to make sure he had "a goodly supply of pineapple fritters ready from August 3 onward." The fritters were Tibbets's favorite meal; he liked several helpings before he flew.

Tibbets briefed Sweeney on the forthcoming mission. He told the Boston Irishman that his plane, the *Great*

Artiste, would be turned into a flying laboratory, carrying sensitive instruments that would measure the blast and other effects of the bomb. Sweeney and a B-29 carrying photographic equipment would accompany Tibbets's plane to the target.

Classen received a general briefing. Tibbets sensed his somewhat neglected deputy was glad to be filled in at last.

Tibbets did not send for Lewis to tell him that he would be flying as his copilot on the flight. He felt that was "so self-evident it didn't warrant stating."

In Washington, D.C., Groves received a further laconic cable from Farrell. "As of 1000 hours Eastern War Time," the atomic bomb was ready to drop over Japan. Truman had insisted on giving Japan's leaders several more days to reconsider their original reaction to the Potsdam Proclamation, but since then everything they had reportedly said seemed to confirm their initial rejection of its terms. For Groves, the operation was now put "fully into motion."

• 26 •

In the early afternoon of August 2, Tibbets and Ferebee arrived at LeMay's headquarters on Guam to complete the details Tibbets had been unable to incorporate in the draft mission order he had sent yesterday.

LeMay had just been promoted to chief of staff of the Strategic Air Forces. He was in a receptive mood.

The first thing the two fliers needed to know was which target city LeMay personally preferred. When Groves had originally recommended Kyoto, LeMay had disapproved. In LeMay's view, Kyoto "wasn't much of a military target; only a lot of shrines and things of that sort, and anyway, bombing people gets you nowhere—it's just not profitable." But LeMay was happy with Hiroshima. He knew it contained a large number of troops and war factories. He turned to Tibbets and said, almost casually, "Paul, the primary's Hiroshima."

Tibbets's response was immediate. "I've always preferred it as the target."

LeMay led his visitors over to a large map table, its surface covered with the latest reconnaissance photographs of Hiroshima. As Tibbets and Ferebee studied them, LeMay called in operations officer Blanchard. LeMay broke the silence. "Bombing from the height you intend, crosswinds can be a big problem."

Ferebee agreed, saying his bombsight "could handle twenty-five to thirty degrees of crosswind, but it sometimes gets to forty to fifty degrees up there."

Blanchard proposed a solution. "You should fly directly downwind. That would have the double advantage of increasing your speed, so you wouldn't be vulnerable over the target so long and you wouldn't have to worry so much about crosswinds."

Tibbets disagreed. He thought it better to head directly into the wind, which could eliminate crosswind effect and give Ferebee the best chance to bomb accurately.

LeMay pointed out that going against the wind would also reduce the aircraft speed, making the journey over the target more hazardous.

Ferebee looked at Tibbets and then spoke for them both. "Our primary purpose is to hit the target. We're going up there to bomb, not to play safe."

"Okay, the heading will be into the wind."

LeMay then asked Ferebee to select his aiming point.

The bombardier unhesitatingly placed his index finger on the T-shaped Aioi Bridge in the center of Hiroshima.

LeMay nodded.

Tibbets agreed. "It's the most perfect AP I've seen in this whole damn war."

FISSION

---

*AUGUST 3, 1945,
TO 8:16 A.M., AUGUST 6, 1945*

· 1 ·

Less than half a mile from the Aioi Bridge, a solitary blindfolded American stood motionless inside the keep of Hiroshima Castle. His guard, Private Matsuoka, grasped the airman's arms, lifted them up and down. Once the prisoner began doing the movement himself, Matsuoka took hold of his knees, forcing them to bend.

Each morning, in turn, the twenty-three American POWs in Hiroshima received such exercise.

Although it was now barely eight o'clock, the August sun beat down on the prisoner, and soon his soiled coveralls were soaked with perspiration. Afterward, still blindfolded, he was marched for fifteen minutes around Hiroshima Castle's courtyard.

Some fifty yards away, in his Town Hall office, Mayor Awaya listened to Maruyama counting off the latest statistics. As of this morning, August 3, about 30,000 adults and 11,000 students, between the ages of eleven and seventeen, had been drafted into labor battalions to work on the firebreaks. Over 70,000 dwellings had been demolished; some 60,000 of the city's peak wartime civilian population of 340,000 had already been evacuated; a sixth exodus was due within a few days as more people lost their homes to the firebreaks. This morning, Maruyama estimated, there were 280,000 civilians left in the city.

Both men knew that Hiroshima's dwindling number of stores could not supply the needs of so many people. Before the war, there had been nearly 2,000 food shops in the city; today, there were fewer than 150. Many of the larger ones were allowed to supply only the military.

265

And Awaya also knew it was the demands of the military that made it necessary for so many of the citizens to remain in the city. The Toyo factory, for instance, needed 10,000 employees to turn out its 6,000 rifles a week. The Mitsubishi company also required a huge labor force and, like Japan Steel's complex on the edge of Hiroshima, it was working seven days a week, twenty-four hours a day.

Awaya told his assistant he would seek an immediate interview with Field Marshal Hata and ask for the commander's help in "changing the situation and ending this madness."

Maruyama cautioned him that in formal situations Hata was reputed to be stiffly uncompromising. Far better to catch the field marshal in more relaxed surroundings, he suggested. And in two days' time there would be just such an opportunity: the mayor had been invited to a cocktail party in the officers' club on August 5.

Awaya said he would think over the idea.

In the Shima Surgical Hospital, Dr. Kaoru Shima smiled at his earnest visitor. The man, a farmer, had walked several miles to ask Dr. Shima to call on his wife. From his description, Dr. Shima guessed that the woman was pregnant. He promised to call at the farm the next time he was in the area.

• 2 •

On August 2, Tibbets had told van Kirk that he was going on the mission.

Briefing the 509th's group navigator on the strike, Tibbets had stressed the importance of accuracy. That did not worry the experienced van Kirk. But he was concerned by the fact that Tibbets, Ferebee, and he had never flown together from Tinian, and now there would be no chance for them to do so. Further, some of the men he would be flying with were virtual strangers to him.

Van Kirk did not share his worries with Tibbets. Yet, shortly after he had left Tibbets's office, a painful rash erupted on various parts of his body. He reported to flight surgeon Young, who hospitalized him and reported the incident to Tibbets.

Tibbets was even more alarmed than van Kirk about the strange outbreak. In Tibbets's view, there "just wasn't anybody in the same class as Dutch when it came to accurate navigation." He sent Ferebee to the hospital to find out how ill van Kirk was.

It was an inspired choice. Ferebee made light of van Kirk's complaint, "accusing me of lying in bed just to get attention from some of the prettiest nurses you ever did see."

After Ferebee left, Dr. Young visited the navigator. Seeking "a possible emotional basis" for the illness, Dr. Young asked van Kirk, "Are you worried about the mission?"

"No."

"Do you really want to go? You've got a wife and son now."

"I want to go."

"Then go."

Within a few hours, van Kirk's rash completely cleared, and on August 3 he left the hospital.

The same day, LeMay flew into Tinian with the order for Special Bombing Mission No. 13. It was essentially the same document Tibbets had drafted the morning of August 1, with a number of details added. The strike was set for August 6. The targets were:

Primary—Hiroshima urban industrial area.

Secondary—Kokura arsenal and city.

Tertiary—Nagasaki urban area.

The order confirmed that no friendly aircraft, "other than those listed herein, will be within a fifty-mile area of any of the targets for this strike during a period of four hours prior to and six subsequent to strike time."

Thirty-two copies of the order were distributed to commands on Guam, Iwo Jima, and Tinian. Tibbets locked his copy in the office safe and then departed with LeMay to inspect Little Boy, nestling on its cradle in the heavily guarded Tech Area.

Shortly after 2:00 P.M. on August 4, the 509th's briefing hut was sealed off by carbine-carrying MPs who barred its entrance and entirely ringed the long, narrow building. Inside, intelligence officers Hazen Payette and Joseph Buscher attached enlarged reconnaissance photographs of Hiroshima and the alternative targets to two blackboards, then draped both boards with large cloths. The walls were covered with maps of Japan and reminders that "careless talk costs lives."

At 2:30 P.M., Parsons arrived with a group of scientists. Among them was Second Lieutenant Morris Jeppson, who a few days before had won a coin toss with another electronics officer to decide which would assist Parsons on the mission. Parsons produced a can of film from his briefcase, and a technician laced it on a projector.

At 2:45, the British contingent arrived. Both Cheshire and Penney were grim-faced, having just been told by LeMay that they were to be excluded from flying on the first atomic mission. Hoping for a last-minute reversal of the order, they seated themselves behind the scientists.

Caron, Duzenbury, Shumard, Stiborik, and Nelson arrived wearing flight coveralls. They had just returned from a local test run in which van Kirk, fully recovered, had navigated to Rota. Tibbets had made a four-minute bomb run, then banked sharply after Ferebee released the practice pumpkin. All the bomber's equipment had functioned perfectly.

During the practice flight, Lewis, in the copilot's seat, had said little. Prior to flying, he had performed the painful task of telling his regular bombardier and navigator that "they were being superseded by rank" and would not be flying the atomic strike. Tibbets had at last made it clear to Lewis that his role would be that of copilot, with Tibbets in command, but Lewis still felt it was "basically my crew" that would make the run.

Caron arrived at the briefing wearing his Brooklyn Dodgers cap and determined that nothing but a direct order would make him remove it. The night before, in a drunken moment, Caron had succumbed to Shumard's prompting for a haircut. A tipsy GI barber and Duzenbury had trimmed Caron's head until he "resembled a cross between a Blackfoot Indian and a patch of sprouting prairie."

Lewis came in with Eatherly's crew, who were in boisterous spirits after a night's carousing. They seated themselves next to Sweeney's crew, who, taking a cue from their commander, were in a more thoughtful mood. Before coming to the briefing, Sweeney had gone down the flight line with three scientists who were installing a range of radio receivers and automatic film-recording devices aboard the *Great Artiste*. The scientists had explained to Sweeney that three parachutes, carrying cylinders similar in shape and weight to fire extinguishers, would be dropped from the plane near the target. Radio transmitters in the cylinders would send data back to the plane. Sweeney realized he would have to fly in perfect sync with Tibbets to make sure the instruments fell into the designated area.

Beser arrived with Tom Classen; they sat down at the rear of the room, near the projector. For Beser, the briefing was a welcome respite "from the murderous pace up at the Tech Area." Having worked on the uranium bomb, he was now assisting with the final assembly of the plutonium bomb; shortly before coming to the briefing, scientist Ed Doll told him to "stand by to go on a second mission as well." Beser had asked how many missions were planned, and Doll had replied, "Just as many as it takes to make them quit."

Ferebee and van Kirk entered soon afterward and took seats up front, near General Farrell.

At 3:00 precisely, Tibbets arrived in freshly pressed

khakis. Flanked by Payette and Buscher, he walked to the platform. The two intelligence officers positioned themselves by the blackboards. Parsons joined Tibbets on the dais.

Sergeant Spitzer was concentrating hard to remember his impressions for his diary. He saw that Parsons was "perspiring and kept clearing his throat and shuffling his papers."

Two months earlier, at a Los Alamos conference, one of Parsons's staff had proposed "arming" the bomb in flight. Groves and Oppenheimer had opposed the idea, believing it would be too easy for something to go wrong. Nevertheless, Parsons, increasingly troubled by the spate of crashes on Tinian, had decided to insert the conventional explosive and its detonator into the rear of the bomb after the plane was airborne. While this plan would somewhat reduce the risk, in the event the plane crashed the uranium "bullet" might still slip down the barrel, hit its "target," and cause a nuclear explosion.

Parsons had told nobody yet of his plan. He feared that if Groves heard about it, he would reach out nearly seven thousand miles and stop him.

The hushed murmuring in the room ceased as Tibbets spoke. "The moment has arrived. Very recently, the weapon we are about to deliver was successfully tested in the States. We have received orders to drop it on the enemy."

He nodded to Payette and Buscher, who removed the cloths from the blackboards.

Tibbets announced the targets in order of priority: Hiroshima, Kokura, Nagasaki. He next assigned three B-29s to serve as weather scouts. Eatherly's *Straight Flush* would go to Hiroshima; *Jabbit III*, commanded by Major John Wilson, would fly to Kokura; the *Full House*, piloted by Major Ralph Taylor, was given Nagasaki.

Sweeney's *Great Artiste*, and *No. 91*, commanded by Major George Marquardt and carrying photographic equipment, would accompany Tibbets to the actual target—whose final selection would still depend on the weather reports radioed back by the scouting B-29s. If all three cities were ruled out by weather conditions, the plane would return to Iwo Jima, after Parsons had "disarmed" the bomb in the air.

The seventh B-29, *Top Secret,* commanded by Captain Charles McKnight, was assigned to fly to Iwo Jima and park on the guarded apron by the specially constructed pit.

Tibbets then introduced Parsons, who came directly to the point. "The bomb you are going to drop is something new in the history of warfare. It is the most destructive weapon ever produced. We think it will knock out almost everything within a three-mile area."

A stunned gasp swept the room.

Parsons sketched in the background of the Manhattan Project. Spitzer later recorded his reaction to what he had heard. "It is like some weird dream conceived by one with too vivid an imagination."

Parsons signaled the technician to switch on the projector. Nothing happened. The operator fiddled with the mechanism. Suddenly, the celluloid became entangled in the sprockets, and the machine started to rip up the film.

Parsons told the operator to stop the projector, walked back to the platform, and addressed the room. "The film you are not about to see"—he paused, and laughter lifted the tension—"was made of the only test we have performed. This is what happened. The flash of the explosion was seen for more than ten miles. A soldier ten thousand feet away was knocked off his feet. Another soldier more than five miles away was temporarily blinded. A girl in a town many miles away who had been blind all her life saw a flash of light. The explosion was heard fifty miles away."

Every man in the room was transfixed. Even Tibbets, who knew what was coming, was "overwhelmed by the presentation."

Parsons continued. "No one knows exactly what will happen when the bomb is dropped from the air. That has never been done before. But we do expect a cloud this shape"—he drew a mushroom on the blackboard—"will rise to at least thirty thousand feet and maybe sixty thousand feet, preceded by a flash of light much brighter than the sun's."

Buscher brought forward a cardboard box and pulled out a pair of tinted goggles similar to those worn by welders. Parsons explained that these would be worn by every crew member of the planes that would be near the target at the time of the explosion. He slipped them over his eyes, indicated a knob on the nose bridge, and told his audience that turning it would change the amount of light admitted by the glass. Over the AP, he said, the knob must be turned to its lowest setting.

Payette and Buscher distributed the goggles while Tibbets issued a warning. "You're now the hottest crews in the air force. No talking—even among yourselves. No writing home. No mention of the slightest possibility of a mission."

He then gave details of the route to be taken to Japan, the altitude along various stages of the flight, the bombing height, and the likely takeoff time: the early hours of Monday, August 6.

The air-sea rescue officer took over, saying no mission at any time was ever so thoroughly supported. Flying off the Japanese coast would be Superdumbos— B-29s specially equipped to coordinate rescue operations and fight off any enemy opposition. Dumbos— navy flying boats—would be patrolling the flight path to and from Japan, ready to swoop down and rescue any crew that ditched. Supporting the aircraft would be cruisers, destroyers, and "lifeguards"—submarines prepared to "come almost onto the enemy beaches to pick you up."

Before the briefing, Ed Doll had told Jeppson that if he fell into enemy hands, Jeppson "should tell the Japs everything you know. Then we'll know what you've told them. They'd find out anyway in the end."

Doll was a civilian. Buscher was a military man and delivered the formal air force attitude: captured crews were to give only their name, rank, and serial number. He reminded them to search through their flying kit to make sure they had removed all personal belongings —items which could be useful to the enemy.

Tibbets concluded the formal briefing with a short homily. Later, he would not be able to recall his exact words; it would be left to Spitzer to produce the only record.

The colonel began by saying that whatever any of us, including himself, had done before was small potatoes compared to what we were going to do now. Then he said the usual things, but he said them well, as if he meant them, about how proud he was to have been associated with us, about how high our morale had been, and how difficult it was not knowing what we were doing, thinking maybe we were wasting our time and that the "gimmick" was just somebody's wild dream. He was personally honored and he was sure all of us were, to have been chosen to take part in this raid, which, he said—and all the other big-wigs nodded when he said it—would shorten the war by at least six months. And you got the feeling that he really thought this bomb would end the war, period.

On August 5, a duplicating machine turned out the single-page operations order, No. 35, which described the final preparations for the strike.

The order was primarily a timetable of the day's activities, from mealtimes for the various crews to the last moment they could rest in their Quonsets before takeoff. Down on the flight line, the order gave the mechanics all the details they needed about which planes were going, and when, and how much fuel and ammunition each would carry. The one bomb to be taken was described only as "special."

Crucial data on the weather expected over western Japan in the next twenty-four hours were radioed from northern China on the orders of Mao Tse-tung.

After attending morning Mass, Sweeney was to make the last preatomic flight of the 509th. He was ordered by Tibbets to take the *Great Artiste* to thirty thousand feet and release an inert, concrete-filled bomb over the ocean while the scientists on Tinian tracked its fall. The fuzing test was similar to the one Sweeney's crew had performed at Wendover, when the firing system had triggered prematurely.

At altitude, Sweeney radioed that he was ready.

Among the knot of scientists waiting to track the falling bomb was Luis Alvarez, the son of a well-known surgeon at the Mayo Clinic. While at the Massachusetts Institute of Technology, Alvarez had invented the ground-control approach system that would one day be used on almost every airfield in the world. He had later headed the Los Alamos team that built the complex release mechanism for the bomb. On Tinian he had developed a device that would be carried by Sweeney's plane and dropped over the target city to help measure the atomic bomb's shock wave.

Now, wearing earphones, Alvarez was waiting for the steady tone he was hearing to be broken, signifying that Sweeney's test bomb had left the plane. He knew exactly the sequence of events which, if everything worked properly, would follow. It was precisely the same as for the real atomic bomb to be dropped the following day.

When the bomb fell from the plane, wires attached to it would be pulled out, not only cutting a tone signal but also closing a switch within the bomb—the first of a number of switches that had to be closed in sequence before the electricity traveling from batteries within the bomb reached the end of the circuit, the electrical detonator. Once the electricity reached the detonator, it would ignite the explosive powder. If there were no hitches the next day, this would send the uranium "bullet" down the gun barrel, causing the atomic explosion.

Alvarez heard the signal stop. He knew the test bomb

was on its way. The first switch should have closed. Sweeney started his 155-degree turn. A timing device in the bomb now waited a preset number of seconds before closing the second switch in the electrical circuit. Once that switch was closed, the electricity continued a little farther along the line, stopped by another, still-open switch which was controlled by a height-detecting device that measured barometric pressure. That device was set to close its switch when the bomb was five thousand feet above the ground. Then the final and most sensitive instrument in the chain took over. This was a miniature radar set, also enclosed within the bomb. Its transmitter sent out radio waves which hit the ground, bounced back, and were received by the bomb's radar antennas, sticking out like strange feelers near the front of the weapon. If all went well, the radar was set to close the final switch in the chain when the bomb was still 1,850 feet up in the air.

For this test run, to signify that the fuzing system had worked properly, the bomb was to emit a slight puff of smoke at 1,850 feet. Through binoculars, Alvarez and the other scientists watched carefully for the smoke.

In vain.

The test bomb plunged, smokeless, past the planned height of detonation and into the ocean.

Alvarez turned to his colleagues. "Great, just great," he said. "Tomorrow we're going to drop one of these on Japan, and we still haven't got the thing right."

Sweeney wasn't surprised. He knew that, whereas Japanese bombs had a tendency to explode prematurely, among the conventional bombs produced by the United States there were a fair number of duds. With such a new, complex bomb, the chances of success must be less.

He predicted the bomb Tibbets would drop tomorrow would be a dud.

In the hot, glaring sun down on the flight line, a group of men led by scientist Bernard Waldman, a physics professor on loan from Notre Dame University, completed fitting out *No. 91* for its photographic role; a fast-acting camera was to replace the plane's Norden bombsight. Waldman himself would be acting as cameraman.

At 2:15 P.M., the telecon machine in the 509th's operations room clattered out confirmation from LeMay on Guam that the takeoff time for the atomic bomb—carrying plane was to be in just over twelve hours, making the time over target between 8:00 and 9:00 the following morning.

At 2:30 P.M., Ed Doll sent an encoded telegram to Los Alamos. It was based on an interview he had conducted with Beser, who reported that a rigorous search "had so far detected no Japanese using the frequency on which the bomb's radar set will be operating."

By 3:00 P.M., Morris Jeppson and three officers from the First Ordnance Squadron had completed installing a control panel just forward of the bomb bay and just aft of the engineer and pilot compartments of the bomber Tibbets would be flying. The console was thirty inches high and about twenty inches wide. It contained switches, meters, and small, colored indicator lights. Attached to its back were four thick cables, each containing twenty-four individual wires. These cables stretched like umbilical cords back to the bomb bay, where, once the bomb was in place, they would be plugged into the weapon. They would automatically disconnect from the bomb when it was dropped.

The console was designed to monitor the bomb's batteries; to check for any electrical shorts along its firing circuit; to look out for a premature closing of any switch; to spot a malfunction in the barometric-pressure device, the timing mechanism, or the radar set.

While Jeppson and his team toiled inside the bomber, a sign painter placed a ladder against its nose and grumpily climbed to the top, carrying a can of paint and a brush.

He had been dragged away from a softball game by

Tibbets, who had handed him a piece of paper and told him to "paint that on the strike ship, nice and big."

The paper contained two words: *Enola Gay*.

At 3:30 P.M., a group of scientists, MPs, and security agents assembled around the atomic bomb, now resting on a trolley.

On a signal from Major Uanna, after he had carefully draped the bomb with a tarpaulin, the trolley was hooked to a tractor, pulled slowly out of the hut, and escorted out of the Tech Area.

Looking to some observers like a military funeral cortege, the trolley and its guards traveled a half mile down the asphalt to the *Enola Gay*. The weapon was winched up into the plane's front bomb bay and clamped to its special hook. The fifteen-foot doors banged shut.

There were just over ten hours to takeoff.

At 4:15, Tibbets, Ferebee, and van Kirk posed with Lewis and the regular crew of the *Enola Gay* for an official air force group photograph outside the 509th's headquarters. The mood was relaxed; there was some joshing of Caron over his refusal to remove his baseball cap. Afterward, Lewis and the rest of the crew decided to drive down to inspect the bomber.

At the *Enola Gay,* their progress was barred by MPs. Disappointed but still mellow, Lewis walked around the B-29.

Suddenly, as Caron would recall, Lewis bellowed: "What the hell is *that* doing on *my* plane?

The crew joined the pilot, who was staring up at the words *Enola Gay*.

Lewis, on his own later admission, was "very angry, so I called the officer in charge of maintenance and said, 'Who put this name on here?' He refused to tell me. So then I said to him, 'All right, I want it taken off. Get your men and remove the name from the plane.' He said, 'I can't do that!' I said, 'What the hell you talking about? Who authorized you to put it on?' He says, 'Colonel Tibbets.' "

Lewis drove back to group headquarters and stormed into Tibbets's office.

What followed is a matter of dispute. In Lewis's version, "Tibbets knew what I was coming in there for. I said, 'Colonel, you authorized men to put a name on my airplane?' He said, 'I didn't think you'd mind, Bob.' I guess he was embarrassed."

Tibbets would maintain he was anything but embarrassed. He had, in fact, consulted Ferebee, van Kirk, and Duzenbury before naming the bomber after his mother; none of the three had raised any objection. Tibbets had not consulted Lewis, "because I wasn't concerned whether Bob cared or didn't care."

During the morning in the Tech Area, and later, into the early evening, Parsons practiced inserting the explosive charge and detonator into the weapon, a delicate maneuver made more difficult by the cramped conditions, poor light, and stifling heat of the *Enola Gay*'s bomb bay.

When he finally emerged from the bomber, General Farrell was waiting for him. Pointing at Parson's lacerated hands, Groves's deputy offered to lend him a pair of thin pigskin gloves.

Parsons shook his head. "I wouldn't dare. I've got to feel the touch."

At 7:17 P.M., Farrell sent a message to Groves letting him know that Parsons intended to arm the bomb after takeoff. By the time Groves received the message, it was too late for him to do anything about it.

At 7:30 P.M., Classen, the 509th's deputy commander, following instructions from Tibbets, briefed a dozen ground officers on their various duties between then and takeoff.

They were to escort scientists and key military personnel to "safe" areas well away from North Field; there was to be no chance of losing irreplaceable atomic experts in an unscheduled nuclear explosion. When the time came, many of the scientists refused to budge, pointing out that almost nowhere on Tinian would be safe if an accident occurred.

Fire trucks were to be stationed every fifty feet down the sides of runway A, the North Field airstrip selected for takeoff.

Flight surgeon Young was told that in the event of a crash, his rescue teams must not touch anything until a specially detailed squad from the First Ordnance Squadron had monitored the crash area for radioactive contamination. It was the first and only inkling Young would receive that the weapon was an atomic bomb.

By 8:00, mess officer Charles Perry's cooks had begun to prepare the meals he would be offering the combat crews just after midnight: they could select a fullscale breakfast, dinner, or supper from a choice of thirty dishes. Afterward, the crews could collect packed sandwiches for eating over Japan in the morning. Satisfied that the fliers were cared for, Perry began personally to prepare the pineapple fritters that Tibbets had requested.

All Perry had been told about the mission was that it "was the most important in the war." That was enough for him. He started to lay plans for "a full-scale culinary celebration," to take place after the airmen returned.

· 3 ·

On the same day, at 6:00 P.M., guests began arriving at the officers' club in Hiroshima for the reception in honor of Field Marshal Hata's new chief of staff. Among the civilians were the local governor, senior civil servants, and Mayor Awaya.

Hata and his chief moved from group to group, sipping sake and making polite conversation. Periodically, Awaya drifted to the door of the salon, where Maruyama waited with a sake container filled with cold tea.

Awaya was a teetotaler, and it was Maruyama's duty to replenish the mayor's cup so that Awaya would be spared the embarrassment of having to refuse sake.

As soon as Lieutenant Colonel Oya arrived at the reception, Hata sought him out, eager for a firsthand report on the situation in Tokyo. Oya, who had just returned from the capital, reported that morale in the city was still high. The two men discussed briefly the update of the military situation which Oya had spent the day preparing; it was to be discussed at a full-scale communications conference called by Hata for the following morning at 9:00 A.M.

In less than twelve hours, gathered together in Hiroshima would be many of the senior commanders crucial to the defense of western Japan.

When Mayor Awaya cornered Hata, the field marshal gave a vague promise to discuss civilian matters in a few days. The disappointed mayor decided to go home. His wife had just returned to Hiroshima with their three-year-old grandchild.

Maruyama accompanied the mayor home and said he would see him in the morning, as usual, soon after 8:00.

Shortly after they parted, at 9:22 P.M. Radio Hiroshima broadcast an air-raid standby alert. Eight minutes later came the all clear.

For Dr. Shima, traveling toward the outskirts of Hiroshima, the warning presaged another nervous night. He always worried about his patients when he was away. But it would have been unthinkable for him to refuse to make house calls around the countryside. He had a busy night's work ahead of him, moving from one farm to another. He did not expect to be back in Hiroshima much before 8:00 the following morning.

As the communications bureau of Second General Army Headquarters continued its surveillance of exchanges between American aircraft and control towers, it was clear that Japan was in for another brutal series of raids. In fact, 30 bombers were en route to Japan to drop mines in the Inland Sea; 65 bombers were coming to bomb Saga; 102 planes were about to launch an incendiary attack on Maebashi; 261 bombers were heading for the Nishinomiya-Mikage area; 111 bombers were bound for Ube; and 66 for Imabari.

At 12:25 A.M., Hiroshima's radio station advised the civilian population to evacuate to their designated "safe areas." They would wait in their shelters for two hours before the all clear sounded. The alert would do nothing to improve the temper of a weary populace so often called from their homes by false alarms.

· 4 ·

During the night of August 5 to 6, some of the crewmen on Tinian went to the mess hall to sample the dishes Perry's cooks had prepared. Tibbets, Ferebee, and van Kirk ate several plates of pineapple fritters. But for many the idea of food was not tempting. They lay on their bunks and thought of their loved ones, became a little maudlin, and drowned their homesickness with surreptitious shots of whiskey. A few slept.

At 11:30 P.M., the crews of the three weather planes went to their final briefing. By then, Ferebee was heavily involved in a poker game, one of many being held that night. Between bids, he told a favorite Tinian story about the day one of the 509th's officers and a nurse had gone swimming in the nude. The clothes they left on the beach were stolen, and the two were forced to walk, naked, almost two miles back to their Quonset huts.

Van Kirk occupied his time checking his flight bag, making sure all his navigational instruments were there and his pencils sharpened; Caron sat quietly and thought of his wife; Nelson read the latest copy of the *Reader's Digest;* Shumard tried to sleep; Stiborik went to the Catholic church to make a sacramental confession; Parsons and Jeppson ran over a checklist of what they would do once they were airborne; Lewis prowled outside the combat crew lounge, where the final briefing would be held at midnight.

Beser was busy with a task ideally suited to his temperament. Tibbets had assigned him to brief Bill Laurence, *The New York Times* reporter attached to the Manhattan Project. Beser's vivid descriptions helped Laurence later to collect a Pulitzer Prize for his work.

Beser was still talking when, shortly before midnight, he was called to the briefing.

Outside the crew lounge, scientist Ed Doll handed Beser a piece of rice paper with numbers on it specifying the radio frequency the bomb's radar would use to measure the distance from the ground as it fell. The numbers were written on rice paper, explained Doll, so that Beser could swallow the paper if he were in danger of being captured.

At midnight, Paul Tibbets walked to one end of the lounge and addressed the twenty-six airmen who would be flying with him to Japan.

Not once in the year he had commanded them had Tibbets mentioned to anyone in the 509th the words *atomic* or *nuclear*. Now, in this final briefing, he continued to preserve security by merely referring to the weapon as being "very powerful" and "having the potential to end the war."

He reminded the crews to wear their welders' goggles at the time of the explosion. Then, in a crisp few sentences, he spelled out the rules for a successful mission. "Do your jobs. Obey your orders. Don't cut corners or take chances."

The weather officer stepped forward and gave the forecast: the route to Japan would be almost cloud-free, with only moderate winds; clouds over the target cities were likely to clear at dawn. The communications officer read out the frequencies to be used on various stages of the mission and gave the positions of rescue ships and planes.

Tibbets had a few final words for each of the specialists on the mission. Navigators were reminded of the
rendezvous point above Iwo Jima where the three planes
were to meet; tail gunners should check that each aircraft had its thousand rounds of ammunition; engineers,
that they were carrying seventy-four hundred gallons
of fuel (except for the strike aircraft, *Enola Gay,* which
would have four hundred gallons less to make its takeoff easier); radiomen, that the new call sign was
"Dimples."

At 12:15 A.M., Tibbets beckoned to Chaplain
Downey, who invited the gathering to bow their heads.
Then, in a richly resonant voice, consulting the back of
an envelope, Downey read the prayer he had composed for this moment.

> Almighty Father, Who wilt hear the prayer of them
> that love Thee, we pray Thee to be with those who
> brave the heights of Thy heaven and who carry
> the battle to our enemies. Guard and protect them,
> we pray Thee, as they fly their appointed rounds.
> May they, as well as we, know Thy strength and
> power, and armed with Thy might may they bring
> this war to a rapid end. We pray Thee that the end
> of the war may come soon, and that once more we
> may know peace on earth. May the men who fly
> this night be kept safe in Thy care, and may they
> be returned safely to us. We shall go forward trust-
> ing in Thee, knowing that we are in Thy care now
> and forever. In the Name of Jesus Christ. Amen.

At 1:12 A.M., trucks picked up the crews of the two
B-29s assigned to fly alongside the *Enola Gay:* the
Great Artiste, piloted by Sweeney; and *No. 91,* com-
manded by Marquardt.

At 1:15 A.M., a truck picked up the crew of the
Enola Gay. Tibbets and Parsons sat up front with the
driver. Squeezed in the back were van Kirk, Ferebee,
Lewis, Beser, Jeppson, Caron, Shumard, Stiborik, and
Nelson. They all wore pale-green combat overalls; the

only identification they carried were dog tags around their necks. Beser's was stamped with an "H" for "Hebrew."

At 1:37 A.M., the three weather-scout planes took off simultaneously from separate runways on North Field. At 1:51 A.M., *Top Secret* took off for its standby role at Iwo Jima.

Duzenbury had spent every available minute since the final briefing with the *Enola Gay*. He always took at least two hours for his "preflight," for whatever Tibbets and Lewis might have thought, the flight engineer "*knew* she was *my* ship."

First, Duzenbury walked slowly around the bomber, checking it visually, "watching out for the slightest thing that didn't look normal," making sure even that every rivet was in place on all the control surfaces. Then, around 1:00, Duzenbury went aboard *Enola Gay* alone, checklist in hand.

Duzenbury went first to his own station, behind Lewis's seat. It took him little time to inspect his instrument panel; he prided himself that it was always in perfect working order. Then he stepped into the cockpit and examined the controls, switches, and dials. After he had verified that all was in order there, Duzenbury made his way back into the spacious area he shared with navigator van Kirk and radioman Nelson. Now it also contained Jeppson's console for monitoring the bomb.

Duzenbury opened a small, circular, airtight door situated just below the entrance to the long tunnel that led to the after end of the plane, swung himself feet first through the hatch, and found himself in back of the bomb.

Using a flashlight, he crawled to the right side of the weapon and onto the catwalk that ran along the length of the bay; from there, he had his first overall view of the world's most expensive bomb. To Duzenbury, who had worked as a tree surgeon before enlisting, it resembled a long, heavy tree trunk. The cables leading into it from Jeppson's monitoring panel, and its antennas, made it look like no bomb he'd ever seen before.

He continued along the catwalk, checking everything as he went, past the nose of the bomb and back along the other side. When he once again reached the fins, he noticed two unusual containers that, he thought, shouldn't be there. Almost unconsciously, he kicked them.

The flight engineer had not been told they contained the explosive powder and tools Parsons would use later to arm the bomb.

He was about to remove the containers when a bright shaft of light shone through the hatch into the bomb bay. Puzzled, Duzenbury climbed back through the hatch into van Kirk's compartment. The light filled the area. Duzenbury walked forward into the cockpit and stopped, openmouthed.

The *Enola Gay* was ringed by floodlights.

Interspersed between the klieg stands and mobile generators were close to a hundred people—photographers, film crews, officers, scientists, project security agents, and MPs. Dumbfounded and a little annoyed, Duzenbury turned back to his checklist.

The lights and camera crews had been ordered by General Groves, who wanted a pictorial record of the *Enola Gay*'s departure. Only space had prevented a movie crew from flying on the mission.

Now Tibbets stepped from the truck and found himself surrounded by a film crew. He had been warned in a message from Groves that there would be "a little publicity," but in his view, "this was full-scale Hollywood premiere treatment. I expected to see MGM's lion walk onto the field or Warner's logo to light up the sky. It was crazy."

With a touch worthy of an epic production, the "extras" on the asphalt formed an avenue for the "stars" in the crew.

The 509th's commander complied with shouted requests to turn first *this* way, then *that* way, to smile, look serious, "look busy."

Parsons, mystified by the carnival atmosphere, turned to anybody who would listen and said, "What's going on?" Not recognizing the naval captain, a brash photographer shoved Parsons against one of the *Enola Gay*'s wheels and said, "You're gonna be famous—so smile!"

Parsons glared at the cameraman, who shrugged and joined the group swarming around Beser, still briefing Bill Laurence of *The New York Times*.

Beser himself was carrying a portable recording machine on which he planned to capture the crew's reactions to the atomic explosion.

In an expansive mood, Beser told the photographers to take some shots of the rest of the crew. "These guys are every bit as important as the rest of us," he said.

Shumard and Stiborik bowed in mock obsequiousness. Radioman Dick Nelson, raised on Hollywood's doorstep, thought "some of the people were behaving as if they were in some low-budget production."

Reporter Laurence asked Lewis to keep a log of the *Enola Gay*'s flight, which *The New York Times* would later publish. No money was mentioned, but Lewis thought it might earn him "a few dollars."

Lewis addressed the crew. Nelson later recalled, "He gave us a good long stare and said, 'You guys, this bomb cost more than an aircraft carrier. We've got it made; we're gonna win the war; just don't screw it up. Let's do this really great!' He made it clear that as far as he was concerned, we were still his crew, and we were doing it for him."

Caron peered around owlishly in the bright lights, smiling enigmatically when somebody said he had never before known a tail gunner who wore glasses. He doggedly refused to take off his baseball cap. In common with many on the apron, Caron found the scene "a trifle bizarre. I had to put my guns in their mount, and all the time I was getting stopped to have my picture taken."

Caron had planned to take his camera on the mission,

but in all the excitement he had left it on his bunk. Yet in the end he would take the most historic pictures of all. An army captain thrust a plate camera at Caron and told him, "Shoot whatever you can over the target."

At 2:20 A.M., the final group photo was taken. Tibbets turned to the crew and said, "Okay, let's go to work." ·

A photographer grabbed Beser and asked for "one last good-bye look."

Beser bridled. "Good-bye, hell! We're coming back!" He climbed up the ladder and through the hatch behind the *Enola Gay*'s nose wheel, suddenly tired of the publicity.

Beser was followed by Ferebee and van Kirk, who, like Caron, were wearing baseball caps; Shumard and Nelson wore GI work caps; Stiborik a ski cap.

Finally, only Parsons and Tibbets remained below, talking to Farrell. Suddenly the general pointed to Parsons's coveralls. "Where's your gun?"

Parsons had forgotten to draw a weapon from supply. He motioned to a nearby MP, who unstrapped his gun belt and handed it over. Parsons buckled it around his waist and, after a quick thank-you, climbed clumsily up the nose ladder. Like all the others, Parsons wore beneath his coveralls a survival vest with fishhooks, a drinking-water kit, first-aid package, and emergency food rations. Over this came a parachute harness with clips for a chest chute and a one-man life raft. On top was an armorlike flak suit for protection against shell fragments.

Unknown to the others, Paul Tibbets also carried a small metal box in a pocket of his coveralls. Inside the box were twelve capsules, each containing a lethal dose of cyanide. At the first sign of trouble over Japan, Tibbets was to distribute the capsules to the men on the plane. He would then explain to them the alternatives they faced before capture: they could either blow out their brains or commit suicide by poisoning. Tibbets knew this procedure had been devised especially for the atomic mission because "if you were shot down, can you imagine the measures the Japanese would take to find out what you were doing? So if you don't want to go through the torture that they might submit you to, the best way out is either with the gun or with the capsules."

As he said farewell to Farrell, Tibbets had a more immediate concern—the possibility of crashing on takeoff, as he had seen so many planes do during the past weeks on Tinian. The *Enola Gay* was probably the most thoroughly checked aircraft in the world. But no check devised could ensure there would be no last-minute failure of some crucial component.

Smiling and looking relaxed for the clamoring photographers, Tibbets boarded the *Enola Gay*. When he reached his seat, he automatically felt his breast pocket to make sure his battered aluminum cigarette case was still there. He regarded the case as a lucky charm, and he never made a flight without it.

A cameraman climbed a stepladder and photographed Ferebee's bomb-aiming position in the nose. The bombardier was glad he had earlier ordered the ground crew to make a thorough search of the plane and to remove "any unauthorized items." Among those found were six packs of condoms and three pairs of silk panties. Ferebee thought "such things had no place on a bomber."

Caron strapped himself in by his twin rear guns; in the event of a crash on takeoff, he believed "there was a marginally better chance of survival in the tail." For luck, Caron carried a photograph of his wife and baby daughter stuck in his oxygen flow chart. Shumard, squatting in one of the waist blister turrets, had with him a tiny doll; across from him, at the other turret, were Beser and Stiborik. They did not believe in talismans, though Stiborik thought his ski cap was as good as any.

At his station by the entrance hatch to the bomb bay, Nelson fished out a half-finished paperback and placed it on the table beside him. A few feet away, van Kirk laid out his pencils and chart.

Forward of the navigator, Parsons and Jeppson sat

on cushions on the floor, listening patiently to the final preparations for takeoff going on around them. Finally, Tibbets called up Duzenbury. "All set, Dooz?"

"All set, Colonel."

Tibbets slid open a side window in the cockpit and leaned out.

A battery of cameramen converged to photograph his head over the gleaming new sign, *Enola Gay.*

"Okay, fellows, cut those lights. We've gotta be going."

• 5 •

Tibbets ordered Duzenbury to start No. 3 engine; when it was running smoothly, he ordered No. 4, then No. 1, and finally No. 2 engine to be fired.

Lewis added a note on the scratch pad he was keeping for *The New York Times.* "Started engines at 2:27 A.M."

The copilot looked across at Tibbets, who nodded. Lewis depressed the switch on his intercom. "This is Dimples Eight-two to North Tinian Tower. Ready for taxi out and takeoff instructions."

"Tower to Dimples Eight-two. Clear to taxi. Take off on runway A for Able."

At 2:35 A.M., the *Enola Gay* reached her takeoff position.

The jeep that had led the bomber there now drove down the runway, its headlights briefly illuminating the fire trucks and ambulances parked every fifty feet down each side of the airstrip.

At 2:42 A.M., the jeep flashed its lights from the far end of the runway, then drove to the side.

Tibbets told Lewis to call the tower.

Its response was immediate. "Tower to Dimples Eight-two. Clear for takeoff."

Tibbets made a final careful check of the instrument panel. The takeoff weight was 150,000 pounds; the

65-ton *Enola Gay*, with 7,000 gallons of fuel, a 5-ton bomb, and 12 men on board, would have to build up enough engine thrust to lift an overload of 15,000 pounds into the air. Tibbets made a decision: he would hold the bomber on the ground until the last moment to build up every possible knot of speed before lifting it into the air.

He did not tell Lewis of his intention.

The copilot was feeling apprehensive; he, too, knew that the *Enola Gay* was well overweight, and he sensed that the next few seconds "could be traumatic."

Ferebee, on the other hand, felt completely relaxed and confident that Tibbets "had worked everything out."

Van Kirk watched the second hand of his watch reach 2:44 A.M. Until the bomber was actually airborne, there was nothing for him to do.

At 2:45 A.M., Tibbets said to Lewis, "Let's go," and thrust all throttles forward. The *Enola Gay* began to roll down the runway.

Tibbets kept his eye on the RPM counter and the manifold-pressure gauge. With two-thirds of the runway behind them, the counter was still below the 2,550 RPM Tibbets calculated he needed for takeoff; the manifold-pressure gauge registered only 40 inches—not enough.

In the waist blister turrets, Shumard and Stiborik exchanged nervous glances. Beser smiled back at them, oblivious of any danger. Far forward, at his panel, Duzenbury stirred uneasily. He knew what Tibbets was trying to do, but found himself wondering whether Tibbets "was *ever* going to take her up!"

Lewis stared anxiously at the instruments before him, a duplicate set of those in front of Tibbets. Outside, the ambulances and fire trucks flashed by.

"She's too heavy!" Lewis shouted. "Pull her off—now!"

Tibbets ignored Lewis, holding the bomber on the runway. Instinctively, Lewis's hands reached for his control column.

"No! Leave it!" Tibbets commanded.

Lewis's hand froze on the wheel.

Beser suddenly sensed the fear Stiborik and Shumard felt. He shouted, "Hey, aren't we going to run out of runway soon?"

Lewis glanced at Tibbets, who was staring ahead at the break in the darkness where the runway ended at the cliff's edge.

Lewis could wait no longer. But even as his hands tightened around the control column, Tibbets eased his wheel back. The *Enola Gay*'s nose lifted, and the bomber was airborne at what seemed to Lewis the very moment that the ground disappeared beneath them and was replaced by the blackness of the sea.

Watching the takeoff from his hiding place near the peak of Mount Lasso was Warrant Officer Kizo Imai. For the past ninety minutes he had observed the lights, the flashbulbs, the cameras, and the people. He could not imagine what it all meant.

When the bomber that was the center of all the attention had taken off, it left from the very runway that Imai had originally helped to build.

Two minutes after the *Enola Gay*, the *Great Artiste* took off, followed at 2:49 A.M. by *No. 91*. Now the three weather-scout planes and three combat planes of Special Bombing Mission No. 13 were airborne and heading, on course and on time, for Japan.

At 2:55:30 A.M., ten minutes after takeoff, van Kirk made his first entry in the navigator's log.

Position: N. Tip Saipan.   Air Speed: 213.   True course: 336.   True head: 338.   Temperature: $+ 22C$.   Distance to Iwo Jima RV: 622 miles. Height: 4700.

To make such calculations throughout the flight, van Kirk worked closely with radarman Stiborik. Between them, the two men would continually check bearings.

The *Enola Gay* was on the north-by-northwest course it would maintain for the three-hour leg to Iwo Jima. As the plane burrowed through the Pacific night, ten of the twelve men on board busied themselves.

Ferebee had nothing to do, and sat relaxed in his seat. There would be another six hours before his specialist skills as bombardier would be called into use. To tire himself now in pointless activity could have a detrimental effect on the role he would play later.

Beser, exhausted from over forty hours without sleep, was slumped on the floor at the back end of the tunnel, quietly snoring. He would be needed to man his electronic surveillance equipment only after the *Enola Gay* passed over Iwo Jima.

Apart from routine orders, Tibbets had not yet exchanged a word with Lewis. Both men were aware that Lewis had tried to take over at the crucial moment of takeoff. Lewis had acted instinctively; he had in no way intended to criticize Tibbets's flying ability. But he could not bring himself to say so. In turn, Tibbets recognized that his copilot's reaction had been perfectly understandable. "It was the response of a man used to sitting in the driver's seat." But Tibbets, too, could find no way of expressing himself. And so they sat in uncomfortable silence, Tibbets flying the plane, Lewis watching the instruments and adding a few lines to the log he was keeping. "Everything went well on take-off, nothing unusual was encountered."

Caron called Tibbets on the intercom and received permission to test his guns. He had a thousand rounds to defend the *Enola Gay* against attack, and now expended fifty of them. The sound rattled through the fuselage. In Caron's tail turret there was a smell of cordite and burned oil. Behind him, in the darkness, he watched tracers falling toward the sea.

Satisfied, and for the moment free of responsibility, Caron crawled into the rear compartment of the bomber. There, Stiborik was studying photographs of Hiroshima as the city would later appear on his radar screen. The unreal-looking pictures meant almost nothing to the tail gunner.

Close to 3:00 A.M., Parsons tapped Tibbets on the shoulder. "We're starting."

Tibbets nodded, switched on the low-frequency radio in the cockpit, and called Tinian Tower. "Judge going to work."

As arranged, there was no acknowledgment. But in the control tower on North Field, a small group of scientists studied a copy of a checklist that, on board the *Enola Gay,* Parsons had taken from a coverall pocket. It read:

Check List for loading charge in plane with special breech plug. (after all 0-3 tests are complete)
1: Check that green plugs are installed.
2: Remove rear plate.
3: Remove armor plate.
4: Insert breech wrench in breech plug.
5: Unscrew breech plug, place on rubber pad.
6: Insert charge, 4 sections, red ends to breech.
7: Insert breech plug and tighten home.
8: Connect firing line.
9: Install armor plate.
10: Install rear plate.
11: Remove and secure catwalk and tools.

This bald recital gave no clue as to the delicate nature of the task Parsons was to perform.

The naval officer lowered himself down through the hatch into the bomb bay. Jeppson followed him, carrying a flashlight.

The two men squatted, just inside the bay, their backs almost touching the open hatch, and faced the tail end of the bomb. Parsons took his tools out of the box that Duzenbury had kicked during his preflight check.

Ferebee left his bombardier's seat and came back to watch this critical stage of the mission.

To Ferebee, the two men crouching in the bomb

bay resembled car mechanics, with Jeppson handing tools to Parsons whenever he was asked.

As each stage on the checklist was reached, Parsons used the intercom to inform Tibbets, who radioed the news to Tinian.

But by stage 6—the actual insertion of the gunpowder and electrical detonator—Tinian was out of radio range of Tibbets's set. For security reasons, he had decided against using Nelson's more powerful transmitter: Tibbets feared that his messages would be picked up by Japanese monitors.

At 3:10 A.M., Parsons began inserting the gunpowder and detonator. He worked slowly and in total silence, his eyes and hands concentrating on the task. Gently, he placed the powder, in four sections, into position. Then he connected the detonator. Afterward, with sixteen measured turns, he tightened the breech plate, then the armor and rear plates.

The weapon was now "final" except for the last, crucial operation, which Jeppson would perform when he returned to the bomb bay and exchanged three green "safety" plugs for red ones. Until then, the weapon could not be detonated electrically—"unless, of course, the plane ran into an electrical storm."

At 3:20 A.M., the two men climbed out of the bomb bay.

Parsons went forward and informed Tibbets they had finished. Then he sat on the floor beside Jeppson, who was checking the bomb's circuits on his monitoring console.

· 6 ·

Five minutes after Parsons and Jeppson completed arming the bomb, in Hiroshima, where the time was 2:25 A.M., the all clear sounded. People emerged from the air-raid shelters.

On Mount Futaba, Second Lieutenant Tatsuo Yokoyama staggered sleepily back to his quarters. This was turning out to be a bad night: three alerts and not a sign of a bomber. He dismissed the gun crews and asked his orderly to bring him a pot of tea.

• 7 •

Tibbets stared into the night. The stars were out, pricking the inky blackness of the sky; below them, looking very white, were the clouds. Inside the *Enola Gay,* it was comfortably warm.

Tibbets finally broke the silence in the cockpit by asking his copilot what he was writing. Lewis replied he was "keeping a record." Tibbets did not pursue the matter, and the two men continued to sit, not speaking, peering into the darkness.

Nelson completed his check of the loran equipment. Loran was a long-range navigational device designed to determine a plane's position by the time it took to receive radio signals from two or more transmitters whose positions were known. Nelson had tuned to transmitters on Iwo Jima and Okinawa.

Duzenbury and Shumard were paralleling generators to ensure that the four motors remained smoothly synchronized.

At 4:01, Tibbets spoke first to Sweeney and then to Marquardt, both of whom were following some three miles behind. The *Great Artiste* and *No. 91* reported "conditions normal."

At 4:20, van Kirk called Lewis on the intercom to give the estimated time of arrival over Iwo Jima as 5:52 A.M.

Lewis noted this in his log, and then added, "we'll just check" to see whether the navigator's estimate turned out to be correct.

By now, Lewis was expanding his log from its original stark timetable to contain such observations as: "The Colonel, better known as the 'old bull,' shows signs of a tough day; with all he had to do to help get this mission off, he is deserving a few winks."

Tibbets, in fact, had never felt more relaxed or less tired. The trip, so far, was "a joyride."

At 4:25 A.M., he handed over the controls to Lewis, unstrapped himself, and climbed out of his seat to spend a little time with each man on the plane.

Parsons and Jeppson confirmed that the final adjustments to the bomb would be made in the last hour before the target was reached.

As he reached Duzenbury's position, Tibbets felt Lewis trim the controls so that the *Enola Gay* was flying on "George," the automatic pilot; the elevators gave a distinct kick as "George" engaged.

Tibbets chatted with Duzenbury for a few minutes and then moved on to Nelson. The young radioman hurriedly put down the paperback he was reading and reported, "Everything okay, Colonel." Tibbets smiled and said, "I know you'll do a good job, Dick." Nelson had never felt so proud.

Tibbets next watched van Kirk make a navigational check. Ferebee joined them, and the three men speculated as to whether conditions would allow them to bomb the "primary." Tibbets said that whatever Eatherly reported the weather over Hiroshima was, he would still go there first "to judge for myself."

Tibbets then crawled down the thirty-foot padded tunnel that ran over the two bomb bays to connect the forward and aft compartments of the *Enola Gay*.

In the rear compartment were Caron, Stiborik, Shumard, and a still-sleeping Beser.

Tibbets turned to the tail gunner. "Bob, have you figured out what we are doing this morning?"

"Colonel, I don't want to get put up against a wall and shot."

Tibbets smiled, recalling that day last September in Wendover when Caron had fervently promised to keep his mouth shut. Since then, the tail gunner had been an example to everybody when it came to security.

"Bob, we're on our way now. You can talk."

Caron had already guessed the *Enola Gay* was carrying a new superexplosive. "Are we carrying a chemist's nightmare?" he asked.

"No, not exactly."

"How about a physicist's nightmare?"

"Yes."

Tibbets turned to crawl back up the tunnel. Caron reached in and tugged at his leg.

Tibbets looked back. "What's the problem?"

"No problem, Colonel. Just a question. Are we splitting atoms?"

Tibbets stared at the tail gunner, then continued crawling up the tunnel.

Caron had recalled the phrase about splitting atoms from a popular science journal he had once read. He had no idea what it meant.

Back in the cockpit, Tibbets disengaged "George" and began the climb to nine thousand feet for the rendezvous at Iwo Jima.

Jeppson went into the navigator's dome; to the east he could see a waning moon, flashing in and out of the cloud banks. Ahead, apart from a high, thin cirrus, the sky was cerulean. All his life Jeppson would remember the grandeur of this night as it began to fade into dawn. By the time the *Enola Gay* arrived over Iwo Jima, the whole sky was a pale, incandescent pink.

Exactly on time, the *Enola Gay* reached the rendezvous point. Circling above Iwo Jima, Tibbets waited for the other two bombers.

At 4:55 A.M., Japanese time, Sweeney's *Great Artiste* and Marquardt's *No. 91* joined the orbit, swimming up to nine thousand feet.

At 5:05:30 (6:05:30 on van Kirk's chart, as the navigator would keep his entries on Tinian time), with daybreak in full flood, the three bombers formed a loose "V." Tibbets in the lead, they headed toward Shikoku, the large island off the southeast coast of Japan.

Crossing the pork-chop-shaped Iwo Jima for the last time, Tibbets used his cockpit radio to call Major Bud

Uanna in the communications center set up on the island especially for the mission. "Bud, we are proceeding as planned."

Through the early-morning static came Uanna's brief response. "Good luck."

• 8 •

On Iwo Jima, McKnight and the crew of *Top Secret* relaxed. Their standby bomber was unlikely to be needed now.

At a comfortable 205 miles an hour, the *Enola Gay*, the *Great Artiste*, and *No. 91* headed northward. Aboard all three bombers there was a constant routine of checking wind velocity and calculating drift.

Lewis, with little to do except fill in his log, found his entries becoming cryptic. Finally, when the bomber reached 9,200 feet, he simply wrote: "We'll stay here until we are about one hour away from the Empire."

Beser's sleep was disturbed when an orange rolled down the tunnel from the forward compartment and dropped on his head. He opened his eyes to see Shumard and Stiborik grinning at him. Caron thrust a cup of coffee into his hands. Gulping it down, Beser checked his equipment. He had arranged all the dials he needed to see at eye level when he sat on the floor; instruments he would only listen to were up in the racks that reached to the bomber's roof. Several shelves of receivers, direction finders, spectrum analyzers, and decoders allowed Beser to monitor enemy fighter-control frequencies and ground defenses, as well as radar signals that could prematurely detonate the bomb. His special headset allowed him to listen to a different frequency in each ear.

Beser fiddled with the sets, tuning dials and throwing switches. Into one of his ears came the sounds of a ground controller on Okinawa talking down a fleet of bombers returning from a mission; in his other ear were brief air-to-air exchanges between Superdumbos circling off the coast of Japan. Beser was relieved to hear the rescue craft were on station for the atomic strike.

Suddenly Beser saw the Japanese early-warning signal sweep by. "It made a second sweep, and then locked onto us. I could hear the constant pulse as they continued to track us," he said later.

The element of surprise, which had been counted the *Enola Gay*'s greatest protection, was gone.

The radarman decided to keep the knowledge to himself. "It wasn't Tibbets's worry at this stage. And it would be upsetting for the rest of the crew to have somebody say, 'Hey, they're watching us.' So I just used my discretion."

Sometime after 6:30 A.M., Japanese time, Jeppson climbed into the bomb bay carrying the three red plugs, and edged along the catwalk toward the middle of the bomb. The bay was unheated, and its temperature was about the same as that outside the plane, 18° C. Carefully he unscrewed the green plugs and inserted the red ones in their place, making the bomb a viable weapon. As he gave the last plug a final turn, even the ice-cool Jeppson had to reflect that "this was a *moment*."

Jeppson climbed out of the bay and reported to Parsons what he had done. Parsons went forward and informed Tibbets, who switched on the intercom and addressed the crew. "We are carrying the world's first atomic bomb."

An audible gasp came from several of his listeners. Lewis gave a long, low whistle; *now* it all made sense.

Tibbets continued. "When the bomb is dropped, Lieutenant Beser will record our reactions to what we see. This recording is being made for history. Watch your language and don't clutter up the intercom."

He had a final word for Caron. "Bob, you were right. We *are* splitting atoms. Now get back in your turret. We're going to start climbing."

• 9 •

In Hiroshima, Lieutenant Colonel Kakuzo Oya arrived at 7:00 A.M. at Second General Army Headquarters to read over the intelligence report he intended to submit to Hata's communications meeting in two hours' time. While he checked the report, Colonel Kumao Imoto and other senior officers arrived. After Lieutenant Colonel RiGu and Colonel Katayama joined them, they would all go to the officers' club, where the meeting was to be held. Field Marshal Hata was still at home, praying at the family shrine.

Captain Mitsuo Fuchida, hero of Pearl Harbor and now the Imperial Japanese Navy's air operations officer, had been in Hiroshima for the past ten days, discussing defense plans for the expected American invasion. Fuchida would miss the gathering of dignitaries scheduled for that morning. The previous afternoon he had been summoned from the conference to deal with some technical snags at the navy's new headquarters in Nara, near Kyoto. At about the time that Oya was checking over his report, Fuchida was still grappling with the bugs in the Nara communications system.

In the countryside west of Hiroshima, Dr. Kaoru Shima's house calls demanded more time than he had anticipated. Revising his schedule once again, he hoped to be back in his Hiroshima clinic around noon.

At the Japanese fighter base at Shimonoseki, some one hundred miles southwest of Hiroshima, Second Lieutenant Matsuo Yasuzawa started the engine of his two-seater training plane.

Yasuzawa, the flying instructor Yokoyama had seen at Hiroshima Airport with the kamikaze student pilots, had repeatedly requested combat flying, and was turned down each time on the grounds he was too valuable an instructor to risk in battle.

Recently, sensing Yasuzawa's rebellious mood, his commander had promised that soon they would each climb into a training aircraft and attempt to ram an attacking B-29. For Yasuzawa this would be the *rippa na saigo,* the "splendid death" the kamikazes so often spoke to him about.

Today, however, he was flying a major to Field Marshal Hata's communications meeting in Hiroshima. He expected to arrive in the city just before 8:00.

Yasuzawa turned to check that his passenger was strapped in behind him, taxied to the runway, received clearance to take off, and commenced the forty-minute flight from Shimonoseki to Hiroshima. Yasuzawa's course was roughly at right angles to that of the *Enola Gay,* now approaching Japanese airspace.

At 7:09 A.M., Radio Hiroshima interrupted its program with another air-raid alert. Simultaneously, the siren wailed its warning across the city. Everybody tensed for the series of intermittent blasts that would indicate an imminent attack.

• 10 •

Although the Japanese could not know it, Claude Eatherly's *Straight Flush* did not itself warrant an alert.

As the Hiroshima siren sounded, the *Straight Flush* reached the designated initial point, just sixteen miles from the Aioi Bridge. At 235 miles an hour, at a height of 30,200 feet, the *Straight Flush* made a straight run toward the aiming point, following exactly the course Tibbets and Ferebee had selected for the *Enola Gay.*

Eatherly looked for a break in the clouds. At first, he could find none. Then, immediately ahead, he saw a large opening. Six miles directly below, the city was so clear that the crew of the *Straight Flush* could see patches of greenery.

Whooping with delight, Eatherly flew across Hiroshima. Above the city's outskirts, he turned and made another pass. The break in the cloud was still there, a huge hole ten miles across. Shafts of light shone through the gap, as if to spotlight the target for the fliers.

At about the same time, the planes checking the weather over Nagasaki and Kokura found conditions there nearly as good. All three cities were available for the *Enola Gay,* now at 26,000 feet and still climbing at a steady 194 miles an hour.

At 7:24 A.M., Nelson switched off the IFF. A minute later, on 7310 kilocycles, he received a coded message from the *Straight Flush.*

Cloud cover less than 3/10ths at all altitudes.
Advice: bomb primary.

After Tibbets read the message, he switched on the intercom and announced, "It's Hiroshima."

Minutes later, the *Full House* and *Jabbit III* reported in. Nelson took the transcribed messages to Tibbets, who shoved them into his coverall pocket. He told Nelson to send a one-word message to Uanna on Iwo Jima.

"Primary."

On board the *Straight Flush,* just about to leave Japanese airspace, a debate broke out.

Eatherly, like the other two weather-scout planes, was under strict instructions to return directly to Tinian.

Instead, according to his flight engineer, Eugene Grennan, Eatherly switched on the intercom and suggested they orbit until Tibbets passed them, "and then follow him back to see what happens when the bomb goes off."

Grennan suggested this "wouldn't be smart." According to him, somebody else argued that "if Tibbets and the others get knocked out of the sky by the shock wave, we should be there to report what happens." So it started: everybody arguing, should we, shouldn't we go? Then, Eatherly said, "Listen, fellas, if we don't get back to Tinian by two o'clock, we won't be able to get into the afternoon poker game."

In the end, the consensus was that staying to watch one bomb drop wouldn't be much of a thrill. "What would we see?" asked Eatherly.

The crew of the *Straight Flush* decided to give the atomic bomb a miss.

• 11 •

At 7:31 A.M., the all clear sounded in Hiroshima. People relaxed, lit kitchen stoves, prepared breakfast, read the *Chugoku Shimbun*.

Warrant officer Hiroshi Yanagita, the Kempei Tai leader who had rounded up some of the American POWs now in their cells at Hiroshima Castle, did not hear any of the night's air-raid alerts. He was in bed, sleeping off a heavy hangover. The sake he had drunk at Field Marshal Hata's party the previous night was taking its toll.

On Mount Futaba, Second Lieutenant Tatsuo Yokoyama kept his men at their antiaircraft gun post. He thought it strange that the lone plane had circled and made a second run high over the city.

He ordered breakfast of rice, soup, pickles, and stewed vegetables to be served to the gunners at their posts, and a similar meal brought to his quarters. As a sign of respect, his aide carried the breakfast tray high above his head—to ensure that his breath did not fall on the food.

Inside Hiroshima Castle, bowls of mush were left on the cell floors of the American prisoners.

At the Shima clinic, the staff changed shifts while the patients had breakfast. As was the custom in Japanese hospitals, the food was prepared and served by relatives. By 7:35 A.M., most of them were hurrying from the clinic to put in another long day for the war effort.

At 7:40, Second Lieutenant Matsuo Yasuzawa's twin-seater aircraft landed at the arport. It had been a short, undemanding flight. Yasuzawa now had to find out for his passenger where Hata's communications meeting was being held. Yasuzawa felt like an errand boy.

The Korean prince, Lieutenant Colonel RiGu, had waited until Yasuzawa's trainer passed overhead before mounting his handsome white stallion. The sound of engines made the horse nervous. Prince RiGu was in no hurry; there was still over an hour before Hata was scheduled to open the communications conference. At a gentle trot, RiGu's stallion took him toward the Aioi Bridge, and Second General Army Headquarters.

In the center of Hiroshima, at 8:00, hundreds of youths began work on the fire lane leading to the Aioi Bridge.

Close by, on the grounds of Hiroshima Castle, many of the city's forty thousand soldiers were doing their morning calisthenics. Not far from them, a solitary blindfolded American was also being exercised.

• 12 •

Fifty miles from the Aioi Bridge, the *Enola Gay* flew at 30,800 feet, followed by the two observer planes at a few miles' distance. Van Kirk called out tiny course corrections to Tibbets.

At 8:05 A.M., van Kirk announced, "Ten minutes to AP."

In his cramped tail turret, Bob Caron tried to put on his armored vest. Hemmed in by his guns, and holding the unwieldy camera he had been given just before takeoff, he gave up and put his only protection from flak on the floor.

Beser was monitoring the Japanese fighter control

frequency. There was no indication of activity. Stiborik was glued to his radar screen. Shumard was peering out of a waist blister turret, also on the lookout for fighter planes.

Ferebee settled himself comfortably on his seat and leaned forward against the special bombardier's headrest he and Tibbets had designed months ago at Wendover.

Parsons and Jeppson knelt at the bomb console. All the lights remained green. Parsons rose to his feet and walked stiffly toward the cockpit.

Left alone, Jeppson also stood up, and buckled on his parachute. He saw Nelson and van Kirk look at him curiously. Their parachutes remained stacked in a corner.

Van Kirk called out another course change, bringing the *Enola Gay* on a heading of 264 degrees, slightly south of due west. At 31,060 feet and an indicated airspeed of 200 miles an hour, the bomber roared on.

Van Kirk called Tibbets on the intercom. "IP."

Exactly on time, at the right height and predetermined speed, van Kirk had navigated the *Enola Gay* to the initial point.

It was 8:12 A.M.

At that moment at Saijo, nineteen miles east of Hiroshima, an observer spotted the *Enola Gay*, the *Great Artiste*, and *No. 91*. He immediately cranked the field telephone that linked him with the communications center in Hiroshima Castle, and reported what he had seen. The center was manned by schoolgirls drafted to work as telephone operators. Having written down the details, one of the girls telephoned the Hiroshima radio station. At dictation speed, the announcer wrote down the message. "Eight-thirteen, Chugoku Regional Army reports three large enemy planes spotted, heading west from Saijo. Top alert."

The announcer rushed to a nearby studio.

It was now 8:14 A.M.

Tibbets spoke into the intercom. "On glasses."

Nine of the twelve men slipped the Polaroid goggles over their eyes and found themselves in total darkness. Only Tibbets, Ferebee, and Beser kept their glasses up on their foreheads; otherwise, it would have been impossible for them to do their work.

Before covering his eyes, Lewis made a notation in his log. "There will be a short intermission while we bomb our target."

With thirty seconds to go, Ferebee shouted that Hiroshima was coming into his viewfinder. Beser informed Parsons that no Japanese radar was threatening the bomb's proximity fuze.

Tibbets spoke quickly into the intercom. "Stand by for the tone break—and the turn."

Ferebee watched the blacks and whites of the reconnaissance photographs transform themselves into greens, soft pastels, and the duller shades of buildings cramming the fingers of land that reached into the dark blue of Hiroshima Bay. The six tributaries of the Ota River were brown; the city's principal roads a flat, metallic gray. A gossamer haze shimmered over the city, but it did not obscure Ferebee's view of the aiming point, the T-shaped Aioi Bridge, about to coincide with the cross hairs of his bombsight.

"I've got it."

Ferebee made his final adjustments and turned on the tone signal, a continuous, low-pitched hum, which indicated he had started the automatic synchronization for the final fifteen seconds of the bomb run.

A mile behind, in the *Great Artiste,* bombardier Kermit Beahan prepared to switch open the bomb doors and drop the parachute-slung blast gauges earthward.

Two miles behind, Marquardt's *No. 91* made a 90-degree turn to be in position to take photographs.

The tone signal was picked up by the crews of the three weather planes, including Eatherly's, now about 225 miles from Hiroshima and heading back to base.

It was heard on Iwo Jima by McKnight, still sitting

in the pilot's seat of *Top Secret*. McKnight told Uanna, "It's about to drop."

Precisely at 8:15:17, *Enola Gay*'s bomb-bay doors snapped open, and the world's first atomic bomb dropped clear of its restraining hook.

The monitoring cables were pulled from the bomb, and the tone signal stopped.

The *Enola Gay*, suddenly over nine thousand pounds lighter, lurched upward ten feet.

Caron, in the tail, gripped the plate camera and, blinded by the welder's goggles, wondered which way to point it.

Tibbets swung the *Enola Gay* into a diving right-hand turn.

Ferebee shouted, "Bomb away," and turned from his sight to look down through the Plexiglas of the *Enola Gay*'s nose.

He saw the bomb drop cleanly out of the bay and the doors slam shut. For a fleeting eyeblink of time, the weapon appeared to be suspended by some invisible force beneath the bomber. Then Ferebee saw it fall away. "It wobbled a little until it picked up speed, and then it went right on down just like it was supposed to."

On the ground, Lieutenant Colonel Oya stood at a window of Second General Army Headquarters and peered up at the *Enola Gay* and the *Great Artiste*. The two bombers seemed to be diving toward the city.

Field Marshal Hata, having tended his garden and prayed at his shrine, was dressing for the communications meeting.

Kempei Tai officer Hiroshi Yanagita snored insensibly in his bed.

Tatsuo Yokoyama, stripped to the waist in the midsummer heat, was raising a bowl of rice to his mouth, chopsticks poised.

Tibbets continued to hold the *Enola Gay* in a steep power dive and right turn of 155 degrees. Sweeney's

Great Ariste was performing an identical maneuver to the left.

Inside the bomb, a timer tripped the first switch in the firing circuit, letting the electricity travel a measured distance toward the detonator.

Tibbets asked Caron if he could see anything. Spread-eagled in his turret, the gravitational force draining the blood from his head, the gunner could merely gasp, "Nothing."

Beser, also trapped by the violence of the maneuver, stared at his instruments. He could not lift his hand to activate the wire recorder.

There were now twenty seconds left.

On the ground, Prince RiGu was cantering his horse onto the Aioi Bridge.

The announcer at Radio Hiroshima reached the studio to broadcast the air-raid warning.

In the half-underground communications center at Hiroshima Airport, Yasuzawa asked where Hata's meeting was to be held.

On the fire lanes, supervisors blew their whistles, signaling thousands of workers, many of them school-boys and -girls, to run to their designated "safe" areas.

Aboard the *Enola Gay*, Tibbets pulled down his glasses. He could see nothing. He yanked them off. In the nose, Ferebee had not bothered to put his on.

The *Enola Gay* was coming to the end of its breath-taking turn and was now some five miles from Ferebee's AP, heading away from the city. Tibbets called Caron. Again, the tail gunner reported there was nothing to see.

Beser at last managed to switch on the wire recorder. Stiborik turned up the brightness on his radar screen so he could see it through his glasses. Duzenbury, his hand on the throttles, worried about what the blast would do to the *Enola Gay's* engines.

Jeppson counted. Five seconds to go.

the bomb, the barometric switch tripped at five

thousand feet above the ground. The shriek of the casing through the air had now increased to a shattering sonic roar, not yet detectable below.

On the ground, Kazumasa Maruyama was on his way to pick up Mayor Awaya, as he did every morning before work.

At Radio Hiroshima, the announcer pushed the button that sounded the air-raid siren and, out of breath, spoke into a microphone. "Eight-thirteen, Chugoku Regional Army reports three large enemy planes spotted, heading—"

The bomb's detonator activated 1,890 feet above the ground.

At exactly 8:16 A.M., forty-three seconds after falling from the *Enola Gay,* having traveled nearly six miles, the atomic bomb missed the Aioi Bridge by eight hundred feet and exploded directly over Dr. Shima's clinic.

SHOCK WAVE

8:16 A.M.
TO MIDNIGHT, AUGUST 6, 1945

• 1 •

In the first millisecond after 8:16 A.M., a pinprick of purplish-red light expanded to a glowing fireball hundreds of feet wide. The temperature at its core was 50 million degrees centigrade. At "ground zero," the Shima clinic, directly beneath the detonation, the temperature reached several thousand degrees centigrade.

The flash heat started fires a mile away, and burned skin two miles distant.

Of the estimated 320,000 civilians and soldiers in the city, some 80,000 were killed instantly or mortally wounded. About one-third of the casualties were soldiers. Most deaths occurred in the four square miles around the Aioi Bridge, containing the city's principal residential, commercial, and military quarters.

The stone columns flanking the entrance to the Shima clinic were rammed straight down into the ground. The entire building collapsed. The occupants were vaporized.

Sixty-two thousand other buildings—out of a total of 90,000—were destroyed. All utilities and transportation services were wrecked. Over 70,000 breaks occurred in the water mains. Only sixteen pieces of fire-fighting equipment survived to plug into the ruptured system.

One hundred eighty of the city's 200 doctors and 1,654 of its 1,780 nurses were dead or injured. Only 3 of the city's 55 hospitals and first-aid centers remained usable.

The largest single group of casualties occurred around Hiroshima Castle, about nine hundred yards from the epicenter, where, out in the open, several thousand soldiers and one American POW were directly exposed to the blast. They were incinerated, their charred bodies burned into the parade ground. A similar fate befell thousands of others laboring on the fire lanes.

Hiroshima Castle was totally destroyed. The mortality rate for its occupants was about 90 percent. Among the casualties were the schoolgirls on duty in the communications center, and most, although apparently not all, of the American POWs.

The extreme temperatures set alight Radio Hiroshima and burned out trolley cars, trucks, and railroad rolling stock. Stone walls, steel doors, and asphalt pavements glowed red-hot. The heat burned the black lettering from books and newspapers, and fused clothing to skin. More than a mile from the epicenter, men had their caps etched onto their scalps, women their kimono patterns imprinted on their bodies, children their socks burned onto their legs.

The blast clogged six of the city's sewer pumping stations and affected the water table beneath the ground. It sent a whirlwind of glass through the area of destruction.

Almost all this happened in the time it took Bob Caron's eyelids to blink shut behind his goggles—his first, uncontrollable response to the flash.

Every man in the *Enola Gay* saw the light and was overwhelmed by its intensity.

Nobody spoke.

Tibbets could taste the brilliance. "It tasted like lead."

An ethereal glow illuminated the instruments in the cockpit, on Duzenbury's panel, on Nelson's radio, on the racks of instruments before Beser.

By the time Caron opened his eyes, the flash had gone.

Taking its place was something equally stunning. It was, in Caron's words, "a peep into Hell."

In Hiroshima, a firestorm raged. From within an area now over a mile wide, a monstrous, seething mass of red and purple began to rise into the sky; the column was sucking into its base superheated air which set fire to everything combustible.

Lieutenant Colonel Oya recovered consciousness to

find himself lying face down on the floor in the devastated Second General Army Headquarters. Sand was raining down on him from ruptured sandbags above the broken ceiling. The blast had hurled Oya ten feet from the window, and the heat rays had severely burned the back of his head and neck. Blood oozed from his skin where it was punctured by slivers of glass. Other officers in the room were in a similar state.

On Mount Futaba, slightly farther away, Second Lieutenant Yokoyama had no recollection of the initial flash, the searing blast of heat. His first memory was of standing almost naked outside his quarters, brandishing his ceremonial sword and screaming for his gun crews to open fire. But there was nothing for them to shoot at. Yokoyama turned to look down on Hiroshima and became aware of "a strange dense fog enveloping the city."

In the center of that fog, his commanding officer, Colonel Abe, was dead, along with his daughter. There would be no need for Yokoyama to invent further excuses about not marrying her.

Kazumasa Maruyama, about one mile from ground zero, was felled by a stone pillar. When he regained consciousness, darkness was descending on Hiroshima as the great mushroom cloud blotted out daylight. Staggering to his feet, Maruyama stumbled back to his home. He would remember nothing of the journey.

Not far from where Maruyama lay was the man he had served so faithfully, Mayor Awaya. The mayor's house was wrecked and on fire. Mayor Awaya, his fourteen-year-old son, and his three-year-old granddaughter had been killed instantly. His wife and daughter would die later. The following day, Maruyama would go to the still-smoldering ruins of the house and dig out what remained of the mayor's body.

• 2 •

From his vantage point in the tail of the *Enola Gay*, Bob Caron was the first to see a frightening phenomenon developing. A great, circular mass of air was rising upward, traveling at the speed of sound, toward the *Enola Gay*. Stupefied, the tail gunner tried to shout a warning, but his words were unintelligible.

Caron was the first man ever to witness an atomic bomb's shock wave, created by air being so compressed that it seemed to take on a physical form. It looked to Caron as if "the ring around some distant planet had detached itself and was coming up toward us."

He yelled again. At the same time, the great circle of air smashed against the *Enola Gay*, bouncing the plane higher. Tibbets grabbed the controls. But it was the noise accompanying the shock wave that caused him the greatest concern. Remembering his bombing missions over Europe, he thought "an eighty-eight-millimeter shell had exploded right beside us." He immediately shouted, "Flak!"

Ferebee had the same reaction. "The sonsofbitches are shooting at us!"

The two battle-hardened veterans frantically searched the sky for smoke puffs. Pandemonium broke out in the bomber.

In less than four seconds, above the cacophony of voices on the intercom, Caron screamed, "There's another one coming!"

With a spine-jarring crash, the second wall of air hit the *Enola Gay*. Once more, the bomber was tossed upward, tipping Nelson half out of his seat and sending Beser tumbling.

As quickly as it had arrived, the shock wave passed. The *Enola Gay* was back in calm air.

Tibbets addressed the crew. "Okay. That was the reflected shock wave, bounced back from the ground.

There won't be any more. It wasn't flak. Stay calm. Now, let's get these recordings going. Beser, you set?"

"Yes, Colonel."

"I want you to go around to each of the crew and record their impressions. Keep it short, and keep it clean. Bob, start talking."

"Gee, Colonel. It's just spectacular."

"Just describe what you can see. Imagine you're doing a radio broadcast."

With the *Enola Gay* beginning to orbit at 29,200 feet, eleven miles from Hiroshima, the tail gunner produced a vivid eyewitness account. "A column of smoke rising fast. It has a fiery red core. A bubbling mass, purple-gray in color, with that red core. It's all turbulent. Fires are springing up everywhere, like flames shooting out of a huge bed of coals. I am starting to count the fires. One, two, three, four, five, six . . . fourteen, fifteen . . . it's impossible. There are too many to count. Here it comes, the mushroom shape that Captain Parsons spoke about. . . . It's like a mass of bubbling molasses. The mushroom is spreading out. It's maybe a mile or two wide and half a mile high. It's nearly level with us and climbing. It's very black, but there is a purplish tint to the cloud. The base of the mushroom looks like a heavy undercast that is shot through with flames. The city must be below that. The flames and smoke are billowing out, whirling out into the foothills. All I can see now of the city is the main dock and what looks like an airfield. There are planes down there."

In a wide orbit, Tibbets circled the cloud as it climbed toward sixty thousand feet.

Waiting to speak on Beser's recorder, Lewis was groping for words to write in his log. There were those on board the plane who would insist his initial reaction to the mushroom cloud was: "My God, look at that sonofabitch go!" But Lewis later decided to pen: "My God, what have we done?"

Tibbets was "surprised, even shocked. I had been expecting to see something big, but what is big? What I saw was of a magnitude and carried with it a connotation of destruction bigger than I had really imagined."

Beser confined himself to a few words for posterity. "It's pretty terrific. What a relief it worked."

Nelson, Shumard, and Duzenbury used such words as "just awesome," "unbelievable," "stunning," and "shattering" to try to convey what they saw. Stiborik thought, "This is the end of the war." Ferebee and Parsons were too busy preparing the strike report to record their impressions.

In the tail, Caron took photographs that would be used around the world.

The *Enola Gay* completed its first circle around the stricken city.

• 3 •

Second Lieutenant Matsuo Yasuzawa emerged from the communications center and saw the bombers as three specks in the smoke-filled sky. "Humiliated and furious" they had not yet been attacked by fighters or antiaircraft fire, he determined to go after them.

Weaving his way past burning fuel trucks and aircraft, he ran toward the "99 Superior Trainer" he had landed in Hiroshima less than one hour before. Every plane he passed was severely damaged.

The airfield was over two miles from the epicenter, and the force of the explosion was largely spent by the time it struck the base. Even so, hardly a window was left intact, and many of the buildings had suffered structural damage.

Yasuzawa reached his plane panting, out of breath, and shook his head in wonderment.

The plane was bent like a banana.

It had been broadside to the shock wave, which had blown out all the glass along one side of the cockpit and reshaped the fuselage into a shallow "C." The tail was swung ten degrees off true, and the nose was similarly bent.

Yasuzawa climbed into the cockpit and pressed the starter button. The engine kicked and, incredibly, sputtered into life.

Then, Yasuzawa saw a sight that made him shudder. Coming onto the airfield was the vanguard of a procession of "living corpses." Bleeding and blackened, their skin hanging in shreds, their hair scorched to the roots, the first survivors were seeking sanctuary. Many were totally naked, their clothes burned from their bodies. Some of the women carried babies.

Horrified, Yasuzawa looked away. There was now a new thought in his mind: he had to get out and report what had happened to Hiroshima.

He taxied his plane slowly to the runway, revved the engine, and released the brakes. When he pulled back the stick, the bent trainer sidled uncertainly into the air. Yasuzawa held it about three feet off the ground for a moment, then touched down again.

Now confident the plane would fly, he taxied back to the other end of the runway and prepared for take-off.

• 4 •

Aboard the *Enola Gay,* Nelson had already sent word that the mission was a success. Now Parsons handed him a second message that, when decoded, would tell General Farrell, waiting anxiously in the 509th's operations room on Tinian, the news he had been waiting hours to hear.

CLEAR CUT. SUCCESSFUL IN ALL RESPECTS. VISIBLE EFFECTS GREATER THAN ALAMOGORDO. CONDITIONS NORMAL IN AIRPLANE FOLLOWING DELIVERY. PROCEEDING TO BASE.

After a third and final circle around Hiroshima, Tibbets put the *Enola Gay* on course for Tinian. The *Great Artiste* and *No. 91* formed up behind, and the three bombers headed down the "Hirohito Highway" for home.

· 5 ·

Second Lieutenant Yasuzawa was about to take off when out of the murk stumbled the officer he had earlier flown to Hiroshima. When he saw that Yasuzawa intended to take off, he insisted on going as well. The pilot pointed to the precarious state of the plane, but the major would not be put off. He climbed into the seat behind Yasuzawa.

With both men leaning hard to the left, sheltering behind what little glass remained on that side of the cockpit, the misshapen trainer moved, crablike, down the runway. Almost at the end, Yasuzawa pulled back the stick, and the plane skewed into the air.

Over Hiroshima Harbor, he turned back toward the city and the smoke. He knew that if he made one false move on the controls, "the plane would flip over, and that would be the end."

As he climbed, the wind howled through the open cockpit. Yasuzawa, concentrating on keeping his distorted plane in the air, was conscious only of "a thick haze, dust and smoke and flames."

At two thousand feet, he leveled out to do what Tibbets had done fifteen times higher—circle the city to estimate the damage. But where the *Enola Gay* had remained well clear of the cloud, Yasuzawa was now flying in and out of the pall, unaware of the risk to which he was subjecting himself and his passenger.

After about five minutes' reconnaissance, the intrepid pilot put the crippled plane on course for his Kyushu air base, one hundred miles away.

There, after completing one of the most unusual

flights in the history of aviation, he would exchange his extraordinary-looking aircraft for a transport plane, and spend the rest of the day ferrying survivors out of Hiroshima.

· 6 ·

At 10:30 A.M., when mess officer Charles Perry heard that the strike was a success, he turned to his cooks and shouted, "The party's on!"

The 509th's kitchens became the center of activity as Perry masterminded a celebration to mark the victors' return.

His staff prepared hundreds of pies for a pie-eating contest, cooled scores of crates of beer and lemonade, made thousands of hot dogs, sliced beef and salami for open sandwiches, mixed potato and fruit salads.

Satisfied that the "biggest blowout" Tinian had ever known was safely under way, Perry sat down at a typewriter and prepared a program to mark the occasion. It read:

509TH
FREE BEER PARTY TODAY 2 P.M.
TODAY—TODAY—TODAY—TODAY—TODAY
PLACE—509TH BALL DIAMOND
FOR ALL MEN OF THE 509TH COMPOSITE GROUP
FOUR (4) BOTTLES OF BEER PER MAN—
NO RATION CARD NEEDED
LEMONADE FOR THOSE WHO DO NOT CARE FOR BEER
ALL-STAR SOFT BALL GAME 2 P.M.
JITTER BUG CONTEST
HOT MUSIC
NOVELTY ACTS
SURPRISE CONTEST—YOU'LL FIND OUT
Extra-ADDED ATTRACTION, BLONDE, VIVACIOUS,
CURVACIOUS, STARLET DIRECT FROM ???????
PRIZES—GOOD ONES TOO

And Ration Free Beer
FOOD GALORE BY PERRY & CO. CATERERS
SPECIAL MOVIE WILL FOLLOW AT 1930,
"IT'S A PLEASURE"
IN TECHNICOLOR WITH SONJA HENIE AND
MICHAEL O'SHEA

———————————

CHECK WITH YOUR ORDERLY ROOM FOR MORE DETAILS

———————————

Wear Old Clothes   Wear Old Clothes
Wear Old Clothes
6 AUGUST 1945
WELCOME PARTY FOR RETURN OF ENOLA GAY
FROM
HIROSHIMA MISSION

• 7 •

Captain Mitsuo Fuchida, leader of the attack on Pearl Harbor and now flying toward Hiroshima in his navy bomber, wondered what force had created the strange cloud hovering over the city.

He called the airport's control tower. There was no reply.

As he got closer, Fuchida saw that Hiroshima, the city he had left only the afternoon before, "was simply not there anymore. Huge fires rose up in all quarters. But most of these fires seemed not to be consuming buildings; they were consuming debris."

Fuchida would have no conscious recollection of landing his plane on the runway, the same one from which Yasuzawa had made his epic takeoff. His next memory would be walking toward the airport exit, immaculately dressed in his white uniform, shoes, and gloves, and coming face-to-face with "a procession of people who seemed to have come out of Hell."

Horrified, Fuchida walked into Hiroshima. The dead and the dying clogged the gutters, floated in the rivers, blocked the streets. Near the city's center, whole areas had simply disappeared; for at least a square mile, "nothing remained." Utterly depressed and exhausted by what he could see, Fuchida wandered aimlessly through the wasteland.

• 8 •

The *Enola Gay* was 363 miles from Hiroshima when Caron reported that the mushroom cloud was no longer visible. Only then did Tibbets catnap, leaving Lewis to fly the plane.

At 2:20 P.M., Tinian time, Tibbets was awakened by Farrell calling from North Field tower to offer his congratulations. Refreshed after a can of fruit juice, Tibbets took over flying the bomber. At 2:58 P.M., the *Enola Gay* touched down at North Field. She had been in the air for twelve hours and thirteen minutes.

Two hundred officers and men were crowded on the macadam to greet her. Several thousand more lined the taxiways.

They cheered when Tibbets led the crew down through the hatch behind the nose wheel. All were swamped by cameramen and well-wishers. A brigadier general ordered the crowds back. Into the space he had cleared stepped General Spaatz. He walked up to Tibbets and pinned the Distinguished Service Cross on the breast of his coveralls. The two men separated, still not having spoken, and saluted each other. Then Spaatz turned and led away a coterie of high-ranking officers. The others again swarmed around the fliers and plied them with questions.

An officer took Caron's camera. The photographs were processed and rushed to Washington for worldwide distribution.

Another officer took Beser's wire recorder. The recordings vanished.

The debriefing was a relaxed, informal affair, helped along by generous shots of bourbon and free cigarettes. By the time it was over, Perry's party was in full swing.

Somehow, it didn't seem to matter. All Paul Tibbets and the other men on the *Enola Gay* wanted to do was sleep.

AFTERMATH

AUGUST 7
TO MIDDAY, AUGUST 15, 1945

By the morning of August 7, news had trickled through to the Japanese leaders that Hiroshima had been hit by a new kind of bomb. They were told the destruction caused was very great but, in devastated Tokyo, the reports sounded distressingly familiar.

President Truman's statement describing the weapon in some detail, which had been released to an astounded world and a delirious American public the day before, was then broadcast to Japan. It was dismissed by many politicians as propaganda. The Japanese public was told nothing by its leaders.

Worldwide reaction was mixed.

The Vatican condemned the new bomb as a "catastrophic conclusion to the war's apocalyptic surprises." A spokesman compared the bomb's invention with that of the submarine by Leonardo da Vinci and expressed regret that the nuclear scientists did not, like da Vinci, "destroy their creation in the interest of humanity."

In Britain, the government welcomed the bomb as a means of speedily ending the war. H. G. Wells, who had forecast atomic bombs twelve years earlier in his book *The Shape of Things to Come,* remarked, "This can wipe out everything bad, or good, in this world. It is up to the people to decide which."

In a Luxembourg prison camp, top-ranking Nazi war criminals—among them Göring, von Ribbentrop, and Field Marshal Keitel—agreed that warfare had reached a turning point. Von Ribbentrop, the former foreign minister, said, "No one would be so stupid as to start a war now. It is the opportunity for mankind to end war forever."

In the Soviet Union, the media did not rate the atomic bomb worthy of headline news. While expressing "interest in the new weapon," radio and newspaper reports stressed that Russian scientists were also "well advanced in atomic research."

In Washington, D.C., senators called on the newly created United Nations to ensure that the "peace-loving nations share the benefits of the discovery that led to the bomb."

What most everyone agreed on was that the world would never be quite the same again.

When the Japanese Cabinet learned about the bomb, Major General Arisue was chosen to head a group of high-ranking officers and scientists to go to Hiroshima to investigate. Among the scientists was Professor Asada, the physicist who had worked on Japan's atomic bomb and who was still perfecting his death ray.

In Hiroshima, with the mayor dead, Field Marshal Hata took over administrative control of the city. He himself had been only superficially injured, although his wife was severely burned. Hata moved his headquarters to the underground bunker cut into the side of Mount Futaba.

Many of his senior officers were dead. Prince RiGu and his white stallion were gone; so, too, Colonel Katayama, whose horse had been found compressed to half its breadth in a crack in the ground. Hata's orders were relayed through Colonel Imoto, who, although badly injured, was the field marshal's highest-ranking surviving officer.

Relief workers were slow to arrive in Hiroshima. The first help came from the soldiers based at Ujina. The harbor was over two miles from the epicenter, and little damage was done to it. Marines collected the explosive-filled suicide boats, prepared for the American invasion, from the coves around Hiroshima Harbor. The small craft were emptied of their charges, lashed together, and covered with planks. Raftlike, they moved slowly up the rivers to Hiroshima's center, collecting wounded and taking them to the military hospital at Ujina. The boats' passage was hampered by the dead bodies in the rivers; the corpses floated in and out with the tide for days.

The fate of the American prisoners of war is not certain. Two were reported to have been escorted, wounded but able to walk, to Ujina. One was seen under a bridge, apparently dying, wearing only a pair of red-and-white underpants. Two were said to have been battered to death in the castle grounds by their captors.

Warrant Officer Hiroshi Yanagita, the Kempei Tai leader, was still suffering from a hangover when the bomb exploded. Less than half a mile from the epicenter, he was thrown naked from the bed in his second-floor room. The house was on fire. He went to the window and jumped—only to find the house had collapsed and his room was at street level. Dressed in a sheet, skirting the edge of the city, Yanagita made his way to Ujina. There he collected some clothes and ten soldiers, and went to the leveled site where Hiroshima Castle once stood. He saw no American POWs. But when he reached his divisional Kempei Tai headquarters in the west of the city, one of his men told him he had tried to bring two prisoners to the headquarters but, finding it impossible, had left them by the Aioi Bridge. There, one person reported seeing them, hands tied behind their backs, being stoned to death.

American records so far available show that at least pilot Thomas Cartwright and tail gunner William Abel survived the war. Both were awarded the Purple Heart. Cartwright's commission terminated in 1953. Abel retired from the American forces in 1968. It is possible that they, and indeed other POWs, had been moved from Hiroshima before the bomb fell.

On Tinian, the day after the atomic bomb was dropped on Hiroshima, some 509th crews, including the *Enola Gay*'s, with Lewis in command, took off for a follow-up attack on Japan using conventional bombs. In the meantime, Tibbets flew to Guam, where, on August 8, he held a short press conference in which he confined his comments to a straightforward recital of the facts of the mission.

President Truman had warned the Japanese leaders

that if they "did not now accept our terms, they may expect a rain of ruin from the air, the like of which has never been seen on this earth."

The Japanese had not accepted the terms.

American leaders, fearing that the Hiroshima bomb might have hardened Japan's will to resist and might also be regarded as an unrepeatable phenomenon, decided to use the second bomb, which was the only other one then ready. They hoped to convince Japan's leaders that America's nuclear capability was far greater than it was.

LeMay asked Tibbets, "Don't you think you should lead the second attack?"

Tibbets replied, "No. I'm getting enough publicity. The other guys have worked long and hard and can do the job as well as I can."

Sweeney was chosen to command the second strike. He told his crew he wanted "to do it just like Paul did." Among those on board would be Jacob Beser, the only man to accompany both atomic bombs to Japan. Cheshire and Penney, the British representatives, would ride in one of the two observer planes.

There were only two potential targets. Kokura was the primary, Nagasaki the alternate. Both cities were on the island of Kyushu, southwest of Hiroshima.

From the beginning, the mission was bedeviled. The predicted weather over the targets was not promising. Sweeney's plane, the *Great Artiste,* had been fitted with scientific equipment for the first atomic run and would again be so used on the second. To carry the bomb, Sweeney borrowed another B-29, *Bock's Car.* Just before takeoff, a fault was found in the plane: six hundred gallons of gas were trapped in one tank and would not be available for use during the flight. Sweeney decided to risk it.

When he reached the rendezvous point, where the other two planes were to join him, Sweeney could find only one. He waited forty minutes for the third bomber to appear, but then could wait no longer. He headed for Kokura.

Bock's Car made three runs over the target, but the aiming point, a munitions complex, remained obscured. Puffs of antiaircraft fire were exploding below. Beser noticed signs of activity on the Japanese fighter-control circuits he was monitoring. Interceptor planes were on the way.

Sweeney, his fuel running low, decided to "go for Nagasaki." There, again, he found heavy overcast. Then, suddenly, bombardier Kermit Beahan, like Ferebee a veteran of the war in Europe, shouted that he had spotted a break in the clouds. He told Sweeney, "I'll take it."

Beahan called minor course corrections and then dropped the plutonium bomb. It fell wide of the intended aiming point, exploding above the northwest section of the city. Although the plutonium bomb was more powerful than the uranium bomb used at Hiroshima, it did less damage and caused fewer casualties, mainly because of the difference in Nagasaki's terrain. Even so, its effect was devastating.

Following a harrowing landing at Okinawa, its fuel supply almost gone, *Bock's Car* returned belatedly to Tinian, after twenty hours.

Tibbets praised Sweeney and Beahan for their achievement. Privately, he decided that if another atomic attack proved necessary, he himself would lead it.

Meanwhile, in Moscow on August 8, Naotake Sato, the Japanese ambassador who had tried repeatedly to get his government to surrender before it was too late, was bluntly told by Foreign Minister Vyacheslav Molotov that as of midnight the Soviet Union would be at war with Japan.

Next morning, while the six members of Japan's Inner Cabinet met for the first time since the nuclear bomb had fallen on Hiroshima, they learned that Russian troops had marched into Manchuria, and that an atomic bomb had been dropped on Nagasaki.

But the members of the Inner Cabinet could not

bring themselves to surrender. They talked all morning, afternoon, and into the evening. Those in favor of continuing the war pointed out that millions of Japanese soldiers had hardly been tested. They were spoiling for a fight and would probably not surrender even if ordered to do so.

Premier Suzuki, desperate to break the deadlock, suggested that Emperor Hirohito might graciously agree to help them come to a conclusion.

At 2:00 A.M., August 10, Japan's divine ruler stated that he was in complete accord with his foreign minister. He then left the meeting.

The view of Foreign Minister Togo was that Japan should accept the terms of the Potsdam Proclamation, on the understanding that the Allied demands did not "prejudice the prerogatives of His Majesty as a Sovereign Ruler."

When Truman and his advisers learned of this qualification, they, too, found themselves divided. Eventually, Secretary of State Byrnes came up with an agreeable formula. While making clear the emperor's authority to rule would at first be subject to that of the Allied supreme commander in Japan, it reiterated that eventually the Japanese people would be free to choose whatever form of government they wished.

When the Japanese leaders received America's reply, they still could not agree to capitulate. They talked through August 12, 13, and into August 14. Then Emperor Hirohito acted again. He told the military and civilian leaders that they should "bear the unbearable and accept the Allied reply." He agreed personally to inform his people by radio of the decision the next day.

The Japanese surrender was made known to the American public late in the afternoon of August 14. Most had no doubt that the atomic bomb had ended the war.

The Russian public was told the Red Army had forced Japan to submit.

In truth, it was probably the fact of the bomb plus

fear of the Russians that caused—or made it possible for—Japan to give up.

On August 15, just before noon, people all over Japan waited to hear their emperor speak. They had been told in the past—and most still believed—they were winning the war. They had no understanding yet of what had happened to Hiroshima and Nagasaki.

In Hiroshima, a crowd gathered by a loudspeaker in the demolished railway station to hear the sacred words of their divine monarch.

Emperor Hirohito used such formal and oblique phrases—the word *surrender* was never uttered—that it was almost impossible for the average person to grasp what he meant.

But when he ended his address, a great number no longer thought they were winning the war. They believed they had *won*. For, as one of those in the crowd at the Hiroshima railway station remarked, "How else could the war end?"

Epilogue

• 1 •

Early in September 1945, Tibbets, Ferebee, and van Kirk flew to Japan to inspect Nagasaki. After touring the city—a journey which had little emotional impact on Tibbets—he wound up shopping. "I bought rice bowls and wooden carved hand trays," he recalled. "So did Ferebee, and we became typical American tourists."

In America, Tibbets found himself a controversial figure. Unlike some members of the crew, he hated the publicity. He was glad to be sent to the Air War College in Alabama, where he could study war tactics. He wrote a thesis on "the employment of atomic bombs," used by the Strategic Air Command, America's answer to the Soviet Union's takeover of Eastern Europe.

In the late 1950s, Tibbets served as a senior officer with NATO in France. He returned to the United States and the Strategic Air Command, once again in a flying job he liked.

He remarried. This time the marriage was successful.

In May 1965, at the age of fifty, a brigadier general, Tibbets was appointed deputy director of the U.S. Military Supply Mission to India. Almost twenty years had passed since he flew the *Enola Gay* over Hiroshima, but within a week of his arrival in New Delhi, Tibbets was greeted by virulent headlines in the pro-Communist press, labeling him "the world's greatest killer."

He was given a Gurkha bodyguard, but nobody could protect him from the continued newspaper harassment.

An embarrassed State Department recalled Tibbets and closed down the mission.

Back in Washington, Tibbets was given a desk job. He believed his career in the air force was over. After thirty years in the service, he retired, convinced he was an "expendable victim" of a changing public attitude toward what he had been ordered to do over Hiroshima.

Withdrawn, even within his family circle, he has stayed close to his first love—airplanes. He is president of an executive jet company in the Midwest and still regularly flies Lear jets and, when the rare occasion arises, a B-29. He has arranged that when he dies, his ashes will be scattered in the sky.

Claude Eatherly, the flamboyant Texan whose off-duty conduct would have cost him his place in the 509th had he not been such an accomplished pilot, never adjusted to civilian life. His path was strewn with worthless checks, a conviction for forgery, post-office burglaries—interspersed with stays in Veterans Administration mental hospitals. His wife left him, and, after years of patient loyalty, even his brother Joe refused to put up with his drunkenness and penchant for petty crime. How, then, did this ne'er-do-well become a martyr, the American Dreyfus, the Hiroshima pilot who went mad because of his guilt over the bombing?

A reporter for the *Fort Worth Star-Telegram*, on the hunt for a human interest story, came across Eatherly in a routine check of the jail. The headline on his front-page story on March 20, 1957, read: WORLD WAR II HERO IN TROUBLE. The first sentence read: "The Air Force pilot who led the world's first atomic bombing mission into Hiroshima was in Tarrant County Jail Wednesday—charged with a crime against his country." The story, further on, clarified Eatherly's role as the pilot of one of four *(sic)* reconnaissance planes, but the harm was done. Eatherly was a "hero," and he had "led" the bombing mission. The next day's page 1 headline read: HERO TO PLEAD INSANITY IN POST OFFICE BREAK-INS.

The April 1, 1957, issue of *Newsweek* picked up the story; its research staff had not checked the facts. The Eatherly myth went national and international. Several European writers seized on a new cause: Eatherly was being punished because he had proclaimed his guilt over Hiroshima. Quickly the Texan became a figurehead for "Ban the Bomb" groups. Eatherly loved the publicity. A hero at last, he found himself repeating the views attributed to him before he ever pronounced them.

In 1964, William Bradford Huie, a distinguished reporter, published a book, *The Hiroshima Pilot,* that documented the fabrication of the Eatherly myth in the greatest detail. But myths are not subject to clarification. People believe what they want to believe.

In 1974, a throat malignancy robbed Eatherly of his voice, but in 1976, at the age of fifty-seven, remarried, the father of two young daughters, he seemed to have found his idea of serenity. He lives on social security and a disability pension in a modest cottage near Houston, Texas, a graying man in a straw hat and cowboy boots. He likes to watch television, fish, and play pool.

The crew of the *Enola Gay* go their separate ways. Since 1945, they have continued to receive hate mail, which peaks every year on August 6. From time to time, the police are called in to investigate death threats. For the most part, the fliers have learned to live with the anonymous insults and recriminations.

Beser still regrets "that I didn't get to drop the bomb on Berlin because of what the Germans did to the Jews." He spends a good deal of his time organizing the 509th reunions, which are held every three years.

Lewis auctioned his log in 1971 for thirty-seven thousand dollars. The money helped him buy marble, from which he sculpts religious motifs. Thirty years after Hiroshima, in 1976, he still felt it was "my plane" and "my crew" that flew the mission.

Van Kirk returned to college and got a degree in

chemical engineering, with honors. In 1950, he joined DuPont and has been with the firm ever since.

Nelson lives in California. Caron collects memorabilia of the atomic missions, but has so far failed to make any real money from selling color prints of the *Enola Gay*.

Duzenbury and Stiborik live quietly and have long since put the mission behind them. Shumard died in April 1967.

Parsons became a rear admiral. He died on December 5, 1953. His assistant over Hiroshima, Morris Jeppson, is now a scientific consultant.

Ferebee remained in the air force and, after a stint in Vietnam, retired. He divides his time between selling real estate, cultivating his one-acre flower and vegetable garden, and occasionally camping out. Although he found his visit with Tibbets to Nagasaki "horrible," he also remembers the hundreds of kamikaze planes he saw hidden in camouflaged hangars. He looks back on his experience as the world's first A-bombardier without regret, believing it "was a job that had to be done."

After the war, Field Marshal Hata was tried as one of the twenty-five major Japanese war criminals. He was found guilty in 1948 and sentenced to imprisonment for life. He died in 1962.

Lieutenant Commander Hashimoto, too, found himself involved in a trial—the court-martial of the captain of the *Indianapolis,* Charles McVay. Hashimoto's impending arrival in the United States was announced by the navy on December 8, 1945, the day after the fourth anniversary of Pearl Harbor. The barrel-chested submarine commander received a cool reception. He understood a little English and did not like what he heard. During the trial, he often felt his evidence was being incorrectly translated.

McVay was found guilty of negligence and was demoted; his sentence was later remitted. Hashimoto became a merchant ship's captain, often calling at U.S.

and British ports. Now retired, he is head priest at a Shinto shrine in Kyoto.

Lieutenant Colonel Oya was interrogated by the Americans about the way he had treated prisoners of war. He tried to conceal the fact that ten POWs were murdered after the war's end at Fukuoka on Kyushu; he told his interrogators the prisoners had died in Hiroshima along with the others held there. When the questions became difficult, Oya simply pointed at his injured neck and said, "Ever since the bomb my memory has gone." In 1976, Oya was alive and well, a frequent visitor to the United States.

After the war, the hero of Pearl Harbor, Mitsuo Fuchida, was converted from Buddhism to Christianity. He toured the United States as a "flying missionary" and was not always welcomed by his audiences. He wrote a booklet entitled *No More Pearl Harbors*, and was annoyed by the military medals and citations he continued to receive. Fuchida died on May 30, 1976.

Flying instructor Matsuo Yasuzawa, who had flown his bent plane from Hiroshima, was barred by the occupying forces from flying again until 1952. By then, his eyesight had deteriorated and he was afflicted by a constant cough. He was unable to fulfill his lifelong dream of becoming a civilian airline pilot, and today lives frugally on a small disability pension.

Chief Warrant Officer Imai, having been in hiding on Tinian for well over a year, gave himself up in September 1945, the last man in his cave to do so. He is now president of a large builders' association in Tokyo.

Today, Tinian has Commonwealth status within the U.S.–administered Trust Territories of the Pacific. The jungle has obliterated almost all signs of its wartime role. Some seven hundred Tinianese live in tin shanties in San Jose, the island's only village. A white-robed and -hooded Capuchin priest takes care of their spiritual needs in an imposing pink Catholic church. Its tabernacle and baptismal font are U.S. Navy World War II thirty-gallon smoke tanks. The inside upper walls of the church are made of plasterboard taken from the 509th's Tech Area.

On September 14, 1970, General Curtis LeMay was given a citation from the grateful people of Tinian for the "outstanding service" he had rendered them, "working untiringly to improve the welfare and living standards."

Six years earlier, LeMay had been decorated by the Japanese government with the First Class Order of the Grand Cordon of the Rising Sun, for helping them build their postwar air-defense force. The award was criticized in the Diet, but Minoru Genda, who had masterminded the Pearl Harbor raid, defended the decision.

Genda himself received in 1962 the coveted U.S. Legion of Merit, conferred by President John F. Kennedy. In 1976 Genda was a senator in the Japanese Parliament.

Hiroshima today is a bustling hodgepodge of a city with a population near nine hundred thousand, almost three times what it was before the bomb. The citizens seldom talk of August 6, 1945. Those who still show signs of their injuries tend to keep to themselves, often suffering guilt that they lived while so many died. The A-bomb dome has been left standing as it was in all its gruesomeness as a terrible reminder. Seeing it, sightseers shudder, avert their eyes, and pass on.

In October 1976, Paul Tibbets again hit the international headlines when the highlight of an air show in Texas was a simulated atom bomb drop from the restored B-29 Tibbets was flying. U.S. Army engineers provided explosives to make a mushroom-shaped cloud.

Many people were appalled. The Japanese government protested, and the American government apologized.

Tibbets thinks the fuss was "ridiculous." He, along with the organizers of the display, maintains that "the demonstration was simply a reenactment of history, similar to many such events held regularly all over the world."

Some years ago, the Department of Defense deeded the *Enola Gay* to the Smithsonian Institution. In 1977, the *Enola Gay* lay scattered in several pieces over the floor of a hangar in Silver Spring, Maryland, waiting to be reassembled one day and exhibited in the new Aeronautics and Space Museum in Washington, D.C.

APPENDICES

Chapter Notes

Throughout the preparation of this book, we have striven to be objective, factual, and impartial, allowing only our conscience and the facts as we have discovered them to guide us.

The source material we have used consists principally of extensive interviews which we conducted personally in Japan and the United States in 1975 and 1976 with participants in the events described, and of documentary evidence from both countries, much of which was originally classified as top secret and has only recently been released. Apart from the intrinsic importance of each of these two prime sources, we have used them as a means of providing checks and balances, one against the other, so enabling us to present the story as authentically and as true to the historical record as possible.

When dealing with the Japanese language, we were very much aware that it seldom allows a literal translation into English; with the help of our interpreters, to whom we owe special thanks, we tried to take every care to preserve in the translation the meaning and tone of the original.

In the detailed source notes which follow, documents and reports to the best of our knowledge unpublished at the time of writing are so indicated; *private papers,* a third valuable source of research material, comprise personal diaries, aide-mémoires, letters, manuscripts; *correspondence* indicates the authors' letters to and from those involved; *transcripts* refers to interviews conducted by others or to documentary broadcasts; finally, a number of published books and magazine and newspaper articles proved useful and are acknowledged.

The form of identification used is:

AI = Authors' Interviews
B = Books
C = Correspondence
D = Documents and Reports
M = Magazines, Periodicals, and Booklets

N = Newspapers
PP = Private Papers
T = Transcripts

A combined list of all written material consulted may be found in the Bibliography; a list of interviewees is in the Special Thanks section.

PROLOGUE

B: *The Birth of the Bomb* (Clark); *No High Ground* (Knebel/Bailey); *Now It Can Be Told* (Groves); *The New World* (Hewlett/Anderson).

D: Letter, Einstein to Roosevelt, August 2, 1939; record of meeting September 23, 1942, in office of secretary of war (unpublished); letter, Groves to Dill, January 17, 1944 (unpublished).

T: "The Building of the Bomb" (BBC-TV).

ACTIVATION

1

AI: Tibbets.
C: Montgomery.
D: Memo, Derry to Groves, August 29, 1944 (unpublished).
N: *Chicago Tribune* interviews with Tibbets, March 10 to 22, 1968 (Thomis); *The Register,* Newport Beach, California, August 3, 1975.
PP: Tibbets (notes made subsequent to events described here).
T: Ashworth.

2

AI: Tibbets.
M: *Air Force Magazine,* August 1973: "Training the 509th for Hiroshima" (Tibbets).
PP: Tibbets.

3

AI: Tibbets, Beser, Jeppson, Brode.
D: Letter, undated, written in April 1943, from Condon to

Oppenheimer; White House Appointments Register, August 26, 1944; memo, Somervell to Chief of Engineers, USA, September 17, 1944; Harrison-Bundy Files.

M: *Bulletin of the Atomic Scientists*, June 1970, April 1975, May 1975.

T: Groves.

4

AI: Yokoyama, Kaizuka, Kosakai, Genda, Fuchida.

B: *Hiroshima in Memoriam and Today* (Takayama); *A History of Modern Japan* (Storry); *Hiroshima* (Hersey); *The Fall of Japan* (Craig); *Death in Life* (Lipton); *Japan Subdued* (Feis); *Hirohito* (Mosley); *The Glory and the Dream* (Manchester); *The Hiroshima Memoirs* (Hiroshima City).

D: U.S. Strategic Bombing Surveys (USSBS); Mission Accomplished.

PP: Notes made by Yokoyama in 1944–45.

5

AI: Tibbets, Ferebee, Beser, King, Slusky, Grennan, Gackenbach, Perry, Caron, Strudwick, Biel, Jernigan.

B: *The Hiroshima Pilot* (Huie).

D: Roster of Officers, 393rd Squadron (unpublished); 509th Pictorial Album; Short Narrative History, 509th Group (unpublished); historical report, medical activity 509th Group (unpublished); History 509th/Twentieth Air Force (unpublished).

PP: Beser, Tibbets, Perry, Gackenbach.

T: Interview with Tibbets, USAF 5-4410-90 (unpublished); interview with Tibbets, Air Historical Branch, USAF, September 1966 (unpublished).

6

AI: Hashimoto.

B: *Sunk* (Hashimoto); *Abandon Ship!* (Newcomb).

7

AI: Tibbets, Beser, Brode, Jeppson.

B: *Dawn Over Zero* (Laurence); *Brighter Than a Thou-*

sand Suns (Jungk); *Now It Can Be Told* (Groves); *Atomic Quest* (Compton); *A Peril and a Hope* (Smith); *The Great Decision* (Amrine).

D: United States Atomic Energy Commission, In the Matter of J. Robert Oppenheimer; United States Atomic Energy Commission, Historical Document No. 279; Harrison-Bundy Files.

M: *Bulletin of the Atomic Scientists*, October 1958; *Look*, August 13, 1963; *American Historical Review*, October 1973; *Journal of American History*, March 1974.

T: Ashworth, Birch, Burroughs, Groves, Hayward.

8

AI: Asada, Suzuki, Nizuma.

B: *Imperial Tragedy* (Coffey).

D: Asada manuscript on Japanese navy and atomic energy, May 12, 1965 (unpublished); Asada research document 19176-2-18 (unpublished).

PP: Asada (notes made subsequent to events described).

9

AI: Arisue, Oya.

D: Office of Strategic Services: reports and intelligence data (unpublished); U.S. Army, Supreme Commander of the Allied Powers, Counter Intelligence Section: reports and intelligence data.

PP: Oya (notes made subsequent to events described).

10

AI: Tibbets, Lewis, Beser, van Kirk, Duzenbury, Caron, Perry, King, Slusky, Jernigan, Biel, Grennan.

B: *No High Ground* (Knebel/Bailey); *The Hiroshima Pilot* (Huie); *Seven Hours to Zero* (Marx).

D: B-29 Familiarization File, marked "Enola Gay," serial No. 15 (unpublished); Short Narrative History, 509th Group (unpublished).

PP: Notes kept by Tibbets, Beser, Perry, van Kirk; letters written by Lewis.

11

AI: Arisue, Sakai.
B: *The Fall of Japan* (Craig); *Imperial Tragedy* (Coffey); *The Nobility of Failure* (Morris); *Samurai* (Sakai).
D: Intelligence Summary No. 17 (vol. 2) Headquarters, Seventh Air Force, Central Pacific Area; analysis of Japanese radio broadcasts; Twentieth Air Force intelligence report ACESEA-WIS, No. 87 (unpublished); Japanese Research Division (ATIS) monographs Nos. 45, 53, 83.
N: *Sunday Times,* London, November 23, 1975.

12

AI: Tibbets, Lewis, King, van Kirk, Ferebee, Olivi, Sweeney, Beser, Grennan, Jernigan, Perry.
B: *Seven Hours to Zero* (Marx); *The Hiroshima Pilot* (Huie).
D: Short Narrative History, 509th Group (unpublished).
PP: Tibbets, Beser, Lewis, van Kirk.

13

AI: Yokoyama, Maruyama, Kosakai.
B: *Imperial Tragedy* (Coffey); *The Fall of Japan* (Craig); *No High Ground* (Knebel/Bailey); *The Hiroshima Memoirs.*
D: USSBS.

14

AI: Arisue, Oya.
B: *The Fall of Japan* (Craig); "Hiroshima Decision" (Balwin) in "Hiroshima Plus 20" *(New York Times).*
D: Office of Strategic Services: reports and intelligence data (unpublished).

15

B: *The Glory and the Dream* (Manchester); *Now It Can Be Told* (Groves).

D: Sachs's memo to Roosevelt, December 8, 1944.
N: *New York Times, Washington Post, Los Angeles Times, San Francisco Chronicle, Denver Post, Chicago Tribune,* all of December 7, 1944.

16

AI: Tibbets, Sweeney, Beser, Lewis, Ferebee, van Kirk, Grennan, Caron, Duzenbury, Stiborik.
D: General Order No. 6 USAAF (unpublished).
PP: Beser, Lewis, Tibbets.

17

AI: Perry, Tibbets, Beser, Downey, van Kirk, Ferebee.
PP: Beser (letters); van Kirk (notes).

18

AI: Tibbets.
D: Memo written by Groves of meeting at White House between Stimson and Roosevelt (unpublished); memo, Groves to Marshall (unpublished); memo, Groves to file (unpublished), all of December 30, 1944.
T: Groves.

19

AI: Hashimoto.
B: *Sunk* (Hashimoto); *Abandon Ship!* (Newcomb).

20

AI: Tibbets, Lewis, Slusky, Grennan, Caron, Ferebee, van Kirk, Perry, Beser, Sweeney, LeMay.
PP: Perry; Lewis (letters).

21

AI: LeMay, Tibbets, Lewis, Sweeney.
B: *The Fall of Japan* (Craig); *Mission with LeMay* (LeMay).
D: USSBS.

22

D: Letter, King to Nimitz; memo, Derry to Groves, February 10, 1945 (unpublished).
T: Groves, Ashworth.

23

AI: Beser, Perry, Duzenbury, Tibbets, King, Lewis.
B: *Brighter Than a Thousand Suns* (Jungk).
D: Short Narrative History of 509th Group (unpublished); historical report, medical activity 509th Group (unpublished); 509th Pictorial Album; History 509th/Twentieth Air Force (unpublished).
M: *Bulletin of the Atomic Scientists*, June 1970, April 1975, May 1975.
PP: Beser, Perry.
T: Groves, Ashworth.

24

AI: Shima.
B: *The Hiroshima Memoirs*.
D: USSBS; Mission Accomplished.

25

B: *The Glory and the Dream* (Manchester); *Brighter Than a Thousand Suns* (Jungk); *On Active Service in Peace and War* (Stimson/Bundy); *Now It Can Be Told* (Groves); *The Great Decision* (Amrine); *Speaking Frankly* (Byrnes).
D: Memo from Patterson to Styer, February 15, 1945 (unpublished); memo from Byrnes to Roosevelt, March 3, 1945 (unpublished); memo from Groves to file, March 3, 1945 (unpublished); memo from Groves to Stimson, March 8, 1945 (unpublished).
M: *Harper's Magazine*, February 1947.
PP: Stimson.
T: Groves.

26

AI: Tibbets, Jeppson, Beser, van Kirk, Jernigan, Caron, Perry, Grennan, Lewis, Gackenbach.
D: Short Narrative History of 509th Group (unpublished); 509th Pictorial Album; History 509th/Twentieth Air Force (unpublished).
PP: Beser, Lewis.

27

AI: LeMay.
B: *The Army Air Forces in World War Two, Vol. V, The Pacific: Matterhorn to Nagasaki, June 1944 to August 1945* (Craven/Cate); *The Fall of Japan* (Craig).

28

AI: Arisue, Maruyama, Yokoyama, Kosakai.
B: *The Fall of Japan* (Craig); *Imperial Tragedy* (Coffey); *The Hiroshima Memoirs.*
D: Office of Strategic Services: reports and intelligence data; U.S. Department of Defense: military plans (1941–45) for the entry of the Soviet Union into the war against Japan; USSBS.

29

AI: Tibbets, Jeppson, Slusky, Brode, Ferebee, Lewis, Duzenbury.
C: Alvarez.

30

B: *The Glory and the Dream* (Manchester); *Japan's Decision to Surrender* (Butow); *I was Roosevelt's Shadow* (Reilly); *F.D.R., My Boss* (Tully); *Thank You, Mr. President* (Smith); *When F.D.R. Died* (Asbell); *FDR's Last Year* (Bishop); *The Great Decision* (Amrine); *Speaking Frankly* (Byrnes); *Year of Decisions* (Truman); *Plain Speaking* (Miller).
N: *New York Times*, April 13, 1945.
PP: Truman.

31

AI: Tibbets, Lewis, King, Strudwick, Biel, Beser, Gackenbach, Grennan, Perry, Caron, Sweeney, Spitzer, Olivi.
B: *We Dropped the A-Bomb* (Miller/Spitzer).
D: Letters, quoted by Huie from Bowen and Thornhill, in *The Hiroshima Pilot*.
PP: Spitzer's diary.

32

AI: Asada, Arisue, Oya, Yokoyama, Maruyama, Yasuzawa.
B: *The Fall of Japan* (Craig); *Hirohito* (Mosley); *Japan Subdued* (Feis).
D: USSBS.
N: *New York Times*, August 8, 1976.
PP: Asada.

33

B: *Now It Can Be Told* (Groves); *Brighter Than a Thousand Suns* (Jungk); *The Great Decision* (Amrine); *On Active Service in Peace and War* (Stimson/Bundy).
D: Memo, Groves to Stimson, April 23, 1945 (unpublished); memo, Groves to file, April 25, 1945 (unpublished); memo, Stimson to Truman, April 25, 1945 (unpublished); letter, Stimson to Truman, April 24, 1945.

34

AI: Hashimoto, Shima, Kosakai.
B: *Sunk* (Hashimoto); *The Hiroshima Memoirs*.
D: USSBS.

35

AI: Maruyama, Oya, Yanagita.
B: *The Fall of Japan* (Craig); *Hirohito* (Mosley); *Japan Subdued* (Feis); *Japan's Decision to Surrender* (Butow); *Year of Decisions* (Truman); *The Knights of Bushido* (Russell); *History of the U.N. War Crimes Commission* (H.M.S.O., 1948); *Imperial Tragedy* (Coffey).

D: Notes for the Interrogation of Prisoners of War, IJA, issued on August 6, 1943; reports from the International Military Tribunal for the Far East, May 1946 through November 1948; reports from the United Nations Commission for the Investigation of War Crimes, 1946; USSBS.

36

AI: Tibbets.
D: Report of Target Committee, May 12, 1945 (unpublished).
PP: Beser.

37

AI: Tibbets, Beser.
B: *On Active Service in Peace and War* (Stimson/Bundy); *The Great Decision* (Amrine); *The Fall of Japan* (Craig); *Atomic Quest* (Compton); *A History of the U.S. Atomic Energy Commission* (Hewlett/Anderson); *Speaking Frankly* (Byrnes); *Now It Can Be Told* (Groves); *A Peril and a Hope* (Smith) for full text of the Franck Report; *Command Decisions* (Morton).
D: Memo, Samford to Chief of Staff, Twentieth Air Force, May 5, 1945 (unpublished); Interim Committee Notes and Minutes, May 1, May 4, May 9, May 15, May 18, May 31, June 1, 1945 (all unpublished); "The Decision to Use the Atomic Bomb," extracted from *Command Decisions*, published by the Office of the Chief of Military History, Department of the Army, 1971; memo, Groves to Marshall, June 12 (unpublished); Harrison-Bundy Files; Memo, Groves to Secretary of War on Szilard, October 29, 1945 (unpublished); MED TS Files (unpublished).
M: *Harper's Magazine*, vol. 194 (no. 1161), February 1947; *U.S. News & World Report*, vol. 1 (no. 49), August 15, 1960; *Bulletin of the Atomic Scientists*, vol. 26, June 1970, and vol. 31, February 1975.
T: Groves.

38

AI: Lewis, Duzenbury, Stiborik, Nelson, Caron.

B: *No High Ground* (Knebel/Bailey); *The Great Decision* (Amrine); *The Fall of Japan* (Craig); *On Active Service in Peace and War* (Stimson/Bundy); *The Glory and the Dream* (Manchester); *The Challenge to American Foreign Policy* (McCloy).

D: Memo, Chief of Staff, of Olympic invasion plan for Japan (June 1945), and staff study, Coronet invasion plan of same month (both unpublished); Recommended Bombing Program Study, May 1945 (unpublished); "The Decision to Use the Atomic Bomb," extracted from *Command Decisions*.

PP: Lewis (documents and letters); Caron (notes).

T: Eric Sevareid in conversation with John J. McCloy ("CBS News Special," July 20, 1975).

39

AI: Yokoyama, Imoto, Oya, Endo, Kosakai, Genda, Miura.

B: *The Hiroshima Memoirs.*

D: Reports from the International Military Tribunal for the Far East, May 1946 through November 1948 in relation to Hata; USSBS.

40

AI: Tibbets, LeMay, Lewis, Caron, Nelson, Duzenbury, Stiborik.

B: *Now It Can Be Told* (Groves).

D: Preliminary report on operational procedures by D. M. Dennison, May 5, 1945 (unpublished); notes on initial meeting of Target Committee, April 27, 1945 (unpublished); Twentieth Air Force target reports and summaries (unpublished); USAAF target photographs (unpublished).

PP: Lewis (letters); Caron (notes).

ACCELERATION

1

AI: Imai, Saito.

B: *The U.S. Marines and Amphibious Warfare* (Isley);

History of the United States Naval Operations in World War Two (Morison); *The Two-Ocean War* (Morison).
M: *Saturday Evening Post,* December 23, 1944.

2

AI: Tibbets, LeMay.
D: Memos, June 10 and July 21, Kirkpatrick to Groves (both unpublished); CINCPAC analysis of air operations, July 1944 (unpublished); VII AAF Intelligence Summary, No. 43 (unpublished); USSBS interrogations of Fuchida; Report on N.A.B. Tinian (unpublished).

3

AI: Lewis, Stiborik, Caron, Nelson, Duzenbury, Beser, Gackenbach.
D: Map of Tinian, Sixth Naval Construction Brigade (unpublished); Short Narrative History of the 509th Group (unpublished); 509th Pictorial Album.
PP: Lewis (letters); Caron and Nelson (notes).

4

AI: Arisue, Oya.
B: *Japan's Decision to Surrender* (Butow); *The Fall of Japan* (Craig); *No High Ground* (Knebel/Bailey); *Imperial Tragedy* (Coffey); *Hirohito* (Mosley).

5

AI: Perry, Beser, Lewis, Jeppson, van Kirk, Duzenbury, Nelson.
D: Ballad, "Nobody Knows," Short Narrative History of the 509th Group (unpublished); 509th Pictorial Album.

6

AI: Arisue.
B: *No High Ground* (Knebel/Bailey); *Fall of Japan* (Craig).

7

AI: Tibbets, Ferebee.
B: *No High Ground* (Knebel/Bailey); *The Great Decision*

(Amrine); *Now It Can Be Told* (Groves); *Abandon Ship!* (Newcomb).

D: Memo, Parsons to Tibbets, July 15, 1945 (unpublished); memo, Parsons and Oppenheimer to Groves, June 29, 1945 (unpublished); memo, Parsons to Tibbets, June 30, 1945 (unpublished).

T: Ashworth.

8

AI: Tibbets.

B: *Dawn Over Zero* (Laurence); *The Glory and the Dream* (Manchester); *All in Our Time* (Wilson); *Now It Can Be Told* (Groves).

D: Report on Test II at Trinity, 16 July 1945, Warren to Groves (unpublished); memo, Groves to Chief of Staff, July 30, 1945 (unpublished).

M: *Bulletin of the Atomic Scientists:* vol. 31, April 1975, "Prelude to Trinity," vol. 31, May 1975, "A Foul and Awesome Display" (both by Bainbridge); vol. 26, June 1970, "Some Recollections of July 16, 1945" (Groves).

N: *New York Times*, articles in issues between September 9 and October 9, 1945, by William Laurence.

T: "The Day the Sun Blew Up" (BBC-TV); "The Building of the Bomb" (BBC-TV): Groves.

9

B: *Abandon Ship!* (Newcomb); *History of the United States Naval Operations in World War Two* (Morison); *Sunk* (Hashimoto); *No High Ground* (Knebel/Bailey).

T: Ashworth.

10

AI: Elsey.

B: *Between War and Peace* (Feis); *Japan Subdued* (Feis); *Year of Decisions* (Truman); *Triumph and Tragedy* (Churchill); *On Active Service in Peace and War* (Stimson/Bundy); *Japan's Decision to Surrender* (Butow).

D: Telegrams, Harrison to Stimson and Stimson to Harrison, July 16, 1945; Log of the President's Trip (unpublished).

N: *New York Times*, July 18, 1945; *Daily Mirror*, London, August 2, 1945.

PP: Diaries, Stimson, Truman.

11

AI: Tibbets, Ferebee, Lewis, Caron, Beser, Duzenbury, Nelson, van Kirk, Perry, LeMay, Spitzer, Grennan, Gackenbach, Jernigan, Sweeney.

D: Memos, Kirkpatrick to Groves, June 10 and July 21, 1945 (unpublished).

PP: Spitzer's diary.

12

AI: Tibbets, LeMay, Ferebee, van Kirk, Lewis, Caron, Beser, Duzenbury.

B: *The Hiroshima Pilot* (Huie); *No High Ground* (Knebel/Bailey); *Seven Hours to Zero* (Marx).

D: History of the 509th (unpublished); 509th Pictorial Album; report of Combined Intelligence Committee, July 1945.

13

AI: Imai, Grennan.

B: *The Hiroshima Pilot* (Huie); *No High Ground* (Knebel/Bailey); *Seven Hours to Zero* (Marx).

14

AI: Imoto, Endo, Oya, Maruyama, Yanagita, Kaizuka, Yokoyama.

D: USSBS Interrogations of Hata (unpublished); reports from the International Military Tribunal for the Far East, May 1946 through November 1948, in relation to Hata.

15

B: *On Active Service in Peace and War* (Stimson); *Japan Subdued* (Feis); *Between War and Peace* (Feis); *Japan's Decision to Surrender* (Butow); *Year of Decisions* (Truman); *Triumph and Tragedy* (Churchill).

D: Memo, Groves to Stimson, July 18, 1945; Log of the President's Trip (unpublished).

16

AI: Beser.

17

AI: Arisue, Oya.

B: *Hirohito* (Mosley); *The New World* (Hewlett/Anderson); *Ten Years in Japan* (Grew); *Imperial Tragedy* (Coffey); *The Fall of Japan* (Craig); *Japan Subdued* (Feis); *Japan's Decision to Surrender* (Butow); *On Active Service in Peace and War* (Stimson/Bundy).

N: *Nippon Times,* July 29, 30, and August 1, 1945; *Asahi Shimbun,* July 28, 1945.

18

AI: Tibbets, Beser, Lewis, Jernigan, Grennan, King, van Kirk, Downey, Duzenbury, Caron, Nelson, Jeppson, Stiborik, Biel, Cheshire, Imai.

B: *No High Ground* (Knebel/Bailey).

D: History of 509th Group (unpublished); 509th Pictorial Album.

19

AI: Yanagita, Shima, Maruyama, Matsuoka, Kosakai, Hiroto, Yokoyama, Imoto, Endo.

B: *The Hiroshima Memoirs; Hirohito* (Mosley); *The Fall of Japan* (Craig).

D: Crew's Records (unpublished); two Missing Air Crew reports, 866th Bombardment Squadron (H), 494th Bombardment Group (H), July 30, 1945 (unpublished); Reports, CINCAFPAC, September 23, October 9, 18, 1945 (unpublished); mission orders, VII Bomber Command, 494th Bomb Group, Field Order 45-92, July 27, 1945 (unpublished); mission report, 494th Bomb Group (unpublished).

PP: Yokoyama (notes), Hiroto, Matsuoka.

20

AI: Lewis.
D: History of the 509th Group (unpublished).

21

AI: Tibbets, Lewis, LeMay, Sweeney.
B: *Now It Can Be Told* (Groves); *No High Ground* (Knebel/Bailey); *The Hiroshima Pilot* (Huie).
D: Memo, Oppenheimer to Parsons, July 23, 1945 (unpublished); memo, Groves to Marshall, July 18, 1945 (unpublished).

22

AI: Hashimoto, Beser.
B: *Sunk* (Hashimoto); *Abandon Ship!* (Newcomb); *Now It Can Be Told* (Groves).
D: Memo, Groves to Chief of Staff, July 30, 1945 (unpublished).

23

AI: Matsuoka, Oya, Kosakai, Yanagita.
B: *The Hiroshima Memoirs*.

24

B: *Now It Can Be Told* (Groves).
D: Cable No. 1005, Spaatz to War Department, July 31, 1945 (unpublished); cable No. 10027, Spaatz to War Department, July 31, 1945 (unpublished); cable, Handy to Spaatz, No. 3542, July 31, 1945 (unpublished); memo, Groves to Chief of Staff, July 30, 1945 (unpublished).

25

AI: Beser, Cheshire, Ferebee, van Kirk, Tibbets, Perry, Sweeney, LeMay, Lewis.
B: *No High Ground* (Knebel/Bailey); *Now It Can Be Told* (Groves).

C: Lord.
D: Daily intelligence summaries, Twentieth Air Force, Guam, July 1945 (unpublished); Field Order No. 13, Twentieth Air Force (unpublished); Cables, Groves to Farrell and Farrell to Groves, July 30, 1945 (unpublished).

26

AI: LeMay, Ferebee, Tibbets.

FISSION

1

AI: Matsuoka, Maruyama, Kosakai, Kaizuka, Shima.
B: *The Hiroshima Memoirs.*
D: USSBS.

2

AI: Tibbets, Lewis, Beser, Jeppson, Jernigan, Caron, Duzenbury, Nelson, Stiborik, Slusky, Gackenbach, Grennan, Ferebee, van Kirk, King, Spitzer, Sweeney, Cheshire, LeMay, Brode, Strudwick, Perry, Downey.
B: *We Dropped the A-Bomb* (Miller/Spitzer); *Now It Can Be Told* (Groves).
C: Alvarez.
D: Operations Order No. 35, 509th Group (unpublished); telecom message, LeMay to 509th, August 5, 1945 (unpublished); telegram, Doll to Oppenheimer, August 5, 1945 (unpublished).
PP: Spitzer's diary.
T: Ashworth.

3

AI: Maruyama, Oya, Imoto, Shima, Matsuoka, Kosakai.
B: *The Hiroshima Memoirs.*
PP: Oya, Maruyama.

4

AI: Tibbets, Lewis, Jeppson, Duzenbury, Nelson, Stiborik,

Caron, Beser, Ferebee, van Kirk, Imai, Downey, Spitzer, Sweeney, Grennan, King, Jernigan.

B: *Now It Can Be Told* (Groves).

M: "Time Out" (Downey's prayer); *Yank,* September 7, 1945.

T: Ashworth.

5

AI: Tibbets, Lewis, Jeppson, Duzenbury, Nelson, Stiborik, Caron, Beser, Ferebee, van Kirk, Sweeney, Spitzer, Gackenbach, Grennan, King, Brode, Imai.

B: *We Dropped the A-Bomb* (Miller/Spitzer); *Seven Hours to Zero* (Marx).

C: Alvarez.

D: Mission reports, August 1945 (unpublished); Parsons's check list (unpublished); navigator's log prepared by van Kirk; Twentieth Air Force intelligence summary for August 6, 1945 (unpublished); B-29 crew instruction manual.

PP: Spitzer's diary, Lewis's log.

T: Ashworth, Groves.

6

AI: Yokoyama.

7

AI: Tibbets, Lewis, Jeppson, Duzenbury, Nelson, Stiborik, Caron, Beser, Ferebee, van Kirk.

D: Mission reports, August 1945 (unpublished); navigator's log prepared by van Kirk; Twentieth Air Force intelligence summary for August 6, 1945 (unpublished).

PP: Lewis's log.

8

AI: Tibbets, Lewis, Jeppson, Duzenbury, Nelson, Stiborik, Caron, Beser, Ferebee, van Kirk.

D: Mission reports, August 1945 (unpublished); navigator's log prepared by van Kirk; Twentieth Air Force intelligence summary for August 6, 1945 (unpublished).

PP: Lewis's log.

9

AI: Maruyama, Oya, Shima, Yasuzawa, Fuchida, Imoto, Endo, Kosakai, Kaizuka, Yanagita.
B: *The Hiroshima Memoirs.*
D: USSBS interrogations of Oya, Hata, Fuchida.
PP: Imoto, Oya, Endo (notes made subsequent to events described).

10

AI: Grennan.
B: *The Hiroshima Pilot* (Huie); *No High Ground* (Knebel/ Bailey).

11

AI: Maruyama, Oya, Imoto, Endo, Yanagita, Hiroto, Matsuoka, Shima, Kosakai, Yokoyama, Yasuzawa, Fuchida, Kaizuka.
B: *The Hiroshima Memoirs; Imperial Tragedy* (Coffey); *Hiroshima in Memoriam and Today* (Takayama).
M: Booklets: *A-Bomb, A City Tells Its Story* (compiled by Kosakai); *Hiroshima* (foreword by Araki).

12

AI: Tibbets, Ferebee, Lewis, van Kirk, Beser, Sweeney, Stiborik, Caron, Jeppson, Nelson, Duzenbury, Yasuzawa, Yokoyama, Kosakai, Shima, Maruyama, Oya, Hiroto, Matsuoka, Matsushige, Hatsuko.
B: *The Hiroshima Memoirs; Hiroshima in Memoriam and Today* (Takayama).
D: Report, Manhattan Engineering District, *The Atomic Bombing of Hiroshima and Nagasaki;* Final Report, Mission No. 13, HQ, 509th Composite Group, dated August 6, 1945, prepared by Stevenson (unpublished); report to COMGENUSTAF, Guam, on Mission No. 13 (unpublished); USSBS.
M: Booklets: *A-Bomb, A City Tells Its Story* (compiled by Kosakai); *Hiroshima* (foreword by Araki).
PP: Oya, Endo, Imoto, Perry, Matsuoka, Hiroto, Maruyama.
T: "Hot to Handle" (BBC-TV): Groves, Ashworth.

SHOCK WAVE

1

AI: Tibbets, Caron, Lewis, Duzenbury, Nelson, Stiborik, Jeppson, van Kirk, Ferebee, Beser, Yokoyama, Maruyama, Oya, Nizuma, Suzuki, Hatsuko, Endo, Imoto, Miura, Matsushige.
B: *Hiroshima, 1945* (Ichiro Osako); *The Hiroshima Memoirs.*
D: Report, Manhattan Engineering District, The Atomic Bombing of Hiroshima and Nagasaki; Final Report, Mission No. 13, HQ, 509th Composite Group, dated August 6, 1945, prepared by Stevenson (unpublished); report to COMGENUSTAF, Guam, on Mission No. 13 (unpublished); USSBS.

2

AI: Tibbets, Caron, Lewis, Duzenbury, Nelson, Stiborik, Jeppson, van Kirk, Ferebee, Beser.

3

AI: Yasuzawa.

4

AI: Tibbets, Nelson.

5

AI: Yasuzawa.

6

AI: Perry.

7

AI: Fuchida.
B: *Imperial Tragedy* (Coffey).

8

AI: Tibbets, Lewis, Nelson, Duzenbury, Beser, Ferebee, Jeppson, Stiborik, Caron.

AFTERMATH

1

AI: Miura, Endo, Imoto, Oya, Tibbets, Sweeney, Yanagita, Hatsuko, Arisue, Asada, Nizuma, Suzuki, Matsushige.
B: *The Fall of Japan* (Craig); *Japan Subdued* (Feis); *Hirohito* (Mosley); *Year of Decisions* (Truman); *Japan's Decision to Surrender* (Butow); *Hiroshima, 1945* (Ichiro Osako); *The Hiroshima Memoirs.*
D: USSBS; Reports: CINCAFPAC to COMGEN Sixth Army, September 23, 1945 (unpublished); CG Sixth Army to CINCAFPAC, October 9, 1945 (unpublished); crew's records (unpublished).
M: *Time,* August 9, 1971.
N: *Los Angeles Times,* August 8 and 9, 1945; *Oakland Tribune,* August 8, 1945.
PP: Asada, Hiroto, Oya, Imoto, Endo, Matsuoka.

EPILOGUE

1

AI: Tibbets, Beser, Ferebee, van Kirk, Beser, Jeppson, Stiborik, Nelson, Grennan, Caron, Duzenbury, Lewis, King, Hashimoto, Oya, Fuchida, Yasuzawa, Imai, LeMay, Genda.
B: *The Hiroshima Pilot* (Huie); *Burning Conscience* (Anders); *Abandon Ship!* (Newcomb).
D: Reports from the International Military Tribunal for the Far East, May 1946 through November 1948, in relation to Hata; news release, Confederate Air Force, October 1976.
N: *Los Angeles Times,* June 15, 1969; *Japan Times,* February 26, 1976; *Washington Post,* October 14, 1976; *New York Times,* May 17, 1965.
M: *People* magazine, August 11, 1975.

Special Thanks

AUTHORS' INTERVIEWS

Arisue, Seizo
Asada, Tsunesaburo

Beser, Jacob
Biel, Raymond
Bock, Frederick
Brode, Robert

Caron, George
Casey, John
Cheshire, Leonard
Cole, Leon
Costa, Thomas
Costello, Edward

Downey, William
Duzenbury, Wyatt

Elsey, George
Endo, Shin

Ferebee, Tom
Fuchida, Kitaoka

Gackenbach, Russell
Genda, Minoru
Grennan, Thomas
Gruning, Wayne

Hashimoto, Mochitsura
Hatanaka, Kuniso

Hatsuko, Tominaga
Hiroto, Kanai

Iki, Haruki
Imai, Kizo
Imoto, Kumao

Jeppson, Morris
Jernigan, Norris

Kaizuka, Yoshiro
King, John
Kosakai, Yoshiteru

LeMay, Curtis
Lewis, Robert

McKnight, Charles
Maruyama, Kazumasa
Matsuoka, Masaru
Matsushige, Yoshito
Matubara, Miyoko
Miura, Hiroshi
Moritaki, Ichiro

Nasu, Yoshio
Nelson, Richard
Nizuma, Seichi

Olivi, Frederick
Osako, Ichiro

Oya, Kakuzo

Perry, Charles

Saito, Masatoshi
Sakai, Saburo
Shima, Kaoru
Slusky, Joseph
Spitzer, Abe
Stiborik, Joseph
Strudwick, James
Suzuki, Tatsusaburo
Sweeney, Charles

Takahashi, Akahiro
Takai, Sadao
Tibbets, Paul

van Kirk, Theodore

Yanagita, Hiroshi
Yasuzawa, Matsuo
Yokoyama, Tatsuo

and in correspondence
Alvarez, Luis
Lord, Edmund
Montgomery, J. B.

TRANSLATORS

We owe a special debt to our translators.

In Japan, John Silver achieved the impossible, always finding an acceptable way of putting our questions, which were sometimes extremely delicate. He was simply invaluable.

Shizuko Pritchard, a native of Hiroshima, has been exceedingly helpful in maintaining through correspondence certain of our contacts there. She has also translated many documents for us.

OTHERS

In Tokyo, Sen Matsuda and Ko Shioya, editor-in-chief and deputy editor, respectively, at the *Reader's Digest,* provided expert help and advice whenever we asked; they never attempted to impress upon us their personal views on the war and the bomb. We also much appreciated the help of two of their staff, Miss Katsuko Konno and Mr. Sekiya Hashimoto.

In Hiroshima, reporters Kawamoto and Kaneguchi from the *Chugoku Shimbun* were particularly cooperative; Yoshiteru Kosakai, chief, Historical Division, Hiroshima Library, supplied a wealth of important background information; Hideo Sasaki, director, Hiroshima Peace Culture Center, generously provided us with one of the last remaining complete sets of *Hiroshima Genbaku Sensai Shi,* a five-volume reference work of fundamental importance.

In Washington, D.C., as with our previous books, we benefited from the specialist guidance and information received from

John Taylor at the National Archives; from Sheila McGough at the Carnegie Institution; from Dr. D. C. Allard at the Naval Historical Center; and from air force archivist Gail Guido.

In New York, Bill Maxwell gave us unquestioned help at times when it was most needed.

In Dublin, as in the past, Bill Moloney aided us on the technical aspects of bombing.

And in London, as always, Michael Weigall was there to give us his own special kind of assistance.

ACKNOWLEDGMENTS

A-Bomb Survivors' Relief Organization, Hiroshima (K. Shimuza).

Albert F. Simpson Historical Research Center, Maxwell, Alabama (Gloria Atkinson and Allen Striepe).

American Embassy, London.

American National Red Cross, Washington, D.C. (George Elsey, Mac Slee).

Atomic Bomb Hospital, Hiroshima (I. Sadama).

Atomic Energy Commission, Historical Office, Washington, D.C.

British Embassy, Washington, D.C. (Peter Bond).

British Library, Reference Division, London; Newspaper Library, Colindale.

Chugoku Shimbun, Hiroshima (Akira Matsuura).

Hiroshima Peace Culture Center (K. Kiyama).

Imperial Army Officers' Club, Tokyo (Mr. Senno).

Japanese Defense Agency, Historical Division, Tokyo.

National Archives, Washington, D.C.; Modern Military Section (John Taylor); Historical Office, State Department, Bureau of Public Affairs; General Archives Division (Janet Hargett).

National Personnel Records Center, St. Louis, Missouri.

Naval Historical Center, Washington, D.C. (D. C. Allard).

Naval Weapons Center, China Lake, California (A. B. Christman).

New York Public Library.

Franklin D. Roosevelt Library, Hyde Park, New York (W. R. Emerson).

Town Hall, Hiroshima (A. Takahashi).

Harry S Truman Library, Independence, Missouri (P. H. Lagerquist).

Bibliography

BOOKS

These books, like other published material related to the subject, should be consulted with caution; Hiroshima has proved fertile ground for propagandists.

For readers interested in the aftereffects of the bomb in human terms, we recommend the documentary novel *Black Rain* by Masuji Ibuse (San Francisco: Kodansha, 1969).

Alperovitz, Gar. *Atomic Diplomacy: Hiroshima and Potsdam.* New York: Simon & Schuster, 1965.

Amrine, Michael. *The Great Decision.* New York: G. P. Putnam's Sons, 1959.

Anders, Gunther, with Eatherly, Claude. *Burning Conscience.* New York: Monthly Review Press, 1962.

Arisue, Seizo. *Memoirs,* Tokyo: Fuyo Shobo, 1974.

Arnold, Henry H. *Global Mission.* 1949. Reprint. New York: Arno Press, 1972.

Asahi Shimbun. *A-Bomb.* Hiroshima Peace Culture Center, 1972.

———. Foreword to *The Pacific Rivals,* by E. O. Reischauer. New York: Weatherhill/Asahi, 1972.

Asbell, Bernard. *When F.D.R. Died.* New York: Holt, Rinehart & Winston, 1961.

Baldwin, Hanson W. *Great Mistakes of the War.* New York: Harper & Bros., 1950.

Batchelder, Robert C. *The Irreversible Decision.* Boston: Houghton Mifflin, 1961.

Bateson, Charles. *The War with Japan.* Sydney: Ure Smith, 1968.

Bishop, Jim. *FDR's Last Year.* New York: William Morrow, 1974; Pocket Books, 1975.

Blackett, P. M. S. *Fear, War and the Bomb.* Folcroft: Folcroft Library Editions, 1948.

367

Boyle, Andrew. *No Passing Glory.* London: Collins, 1955.

Braddon, Russell. *Cheshire V.C.* London: Evans Bros., 1965.

Bush, Vannevar. *Pieces of the Action.* New York: William Morrow, 1970.

Butow, Robert J. C. *Japan's Decision to Surrender.* Stanford: Stanford University Press, 1954.

————. *Tojo and the Coming of the War.* Princeton: Princeton University Press, 1961.

Byrnes, James F. *Speaking Frankly.* 1947. Reprint. New York: Greenwood Press, 1974.

Campbell, J. W. *The Atomic Story.* New York: Henry Holt, 1947.

Churchill, Winston S. *The Second World War.* (Esp. vol. 6.) New York: Time, 1959; Bantam Books, 1962.

Clark, R. W. *The Birth of the Bomb.* New York: Horizon Press, 1961.

Coffey, Thomas M. *Imperial Tragedy.* New York: World Publishing, 1970.

Compton, Arthur Holly. *Atomic Quest.* New York: Oxford University Press, 1956.

Craig, William. *The Fall of Japan.* New York: Dial Press, 1967.

Craigie, Sir Robert. *Behind the Japanese Mask.* London: Hutchinson, 1946.

Craven, W. F., and Cate, J. L., eds. *The Army Air Forces in World War Two.* (Esp. vol. 5.) Chicago: University of Chicago Press, 1953.

Crowl, Philip A. *U.S. Army in World War II, The War in the Pacific, Campaign in the Marianas.* Washington Department of the Army, 1960.

Feis, Herbert. *The Road to Pearl Harbor.* Princeton: Princeton University Press, 1950.

————. *Between War and Peace.* Princeton: Princeton University Press, 1960.

————. *Japan Subdued.* Princeton: Princeton University Press, 1961.

————. *The Atomic Bomb and the End of World War Two.* Princeton: Princeton University Press, 1966.

Fuchida, Mitsuo, and Okumiya, Masatake. *Midway, the Battle That Doomed Japan.* Annapolis: U.S. Naval Institute Press, 1955.

Gigon, Fernand. *Formula for Death.* Translated by Constantine FitzGibbon. New York: Roy Publishers, 1959.

Giovannitti, Len, and Freed, Fred. *The Decision to Drop the Bomb*. New York: Coward-McCann, 1965.

Gowing, Margaret. *Britain and Atomic Energy 1939-1945*. New York: St. Martin's Press, 1964.

Grew, Joseph C. *Ten Years in Japan*. 1944. Reprint. New York: Arno Press, 1972.

Groueff, Stephane. *Manhattan Project*. Boston: Little, Brown, 1967.

Groves, Leslie R. *Now It Can Be Told*. 1962. Reprint. New York: Da Capo Press, 1975.

Hachiya, Michihiko. *Hiroshima Diary*. Translated by W. Wells. 1955. Reprinted. Chapel Hill: University of North Carolina Press, 1969.

Hashimoto, Mochitsura. *Sunk*. Translated by E. H. M. Colgrave. New York: Henry Holt, 1954.

Hewlett, Richard G., and Anderson, Oscar E. *A History of the United States Atomic Energy Commission*. (Esp. vol. 1.) University Park: Pennsylvania State University Press, 1962.

Hillman, William. *Mr. President*. New York: Farrar, Straus & Young, 1952.

Hines, Neal O. *Proving Ground*. Seattle: University of Washington Press, 1962.

Hiroshima City Hall. *Hiroshima City*. 1971.

Hirschfeld, Burt. *A Cloud Over Hiroshima*. New York: Julian Messner, 1967.

History of the U.N. War Crimes Commission. London: H.M.S.O., 1948.

Huie, William Bradford. *The Hiroshima Pilot*. New York: G. P. Putnam's Sons, 1964.

Hull, Cordell. *Memoirs*. (Esp. vol. 2.) New York: Macmillan, 1948.

Inoguchi, Rikihei, et al. *The Divine Wind*. Annapolis: U.S. Naval Institute Press, 1958.

Irving, David. *German Atomic Bomb*. (Orig. title, *The Virus House*.) New York: Simon and Schuster, 1968.

Isely, J.A., and Crowl, P.A. *The U.S. Marines and Amphibious Warfare*. Princeton: Princeton University Press, 1951.

James, David H. *The Rise and Fall of the Japanese Empire*. New York: Macmillan, 1951.

Jungk, Robert. *Children of the Ashes*. New York: Harcourt, Brace & World, 1961.

——. *Brighter Than a Thousand Suns*. New York: Harcourt Brace Jovanovich, 1970.

Knebel, Fletcher, and Bailey, Charles W. *No High Ground.* New York: Harper & Bros., 1960.

Konoye, Fumimaro. *Memoirs.* Tokyo: Asahi Shimbun, 1946.

Lamont, Lansing. *Day of Trinity.* New York: Atheneum, 1965.

Lapp, Ralph E. *Kill and Overkill.* New York: Basic Books, 1962.

Laurence, William L. *Dawn Over Zero.* 1947. Reprint. Westport: Greenwood Press, 1972.

Leahy, William D. *I Was There.* New York: Whittlesey House, 1950.

LeMay, Curtis E., with Kantor, M. *Mission with LeMay.* New York: Doubleday, 1965.

Lipton, Robert Jay. *Death in Life.* New York: Random House, 1967.

Lord, Walter. *Day of Infamy.* New York: Holt, Rinehart & Winston, 1957.

MacArthur, Douglas. *Reminiscences.* New York: McGraw-Hill, 1964.

McCloy, John J. *The Challenge to American Foreign Policy.* Cambridge: Harvard University Press, 1953.

Major, John. *The Oppenheimer Hearing.* New York: Stein & Day, 1971.

Manchester, William. *The Glory and the Dream.* Boston: Little, Brown, 1974; New York: Bantam Books, 1975.

Marx, Joseph L. *Seven Hours to Zero.* New York: G. P. Putnam's Sons, 1967.

Miller, Merle. *Plain Speaking.* New York: G. P. Putnam's Sons, 1974; Berkeley, 1974.

Miller, Merle, and Spitzer, Abe. *We Dropped the A-Bomb.* New York: Thomas Y. Crowell, 1946.

Millis, Walter, *This is Pearl!* 1947. Reprint. Westport: Greenwood Press, 1971.

Minear, Richard H. *Victor's Justice.* Princeton: Princeton University Press, 1973.

Morison, Samuel Eliot. *History of the United States Naval Operations in World War Two.* (Esp. vols. 3, 8, and 14.) Boston: Little, Brown, 1948–60.

———. *The Two-Ocean War.* Boston: Little, Brown, 1963.

Morris, Ivan. *The Nobility of Failure.* New York: New American Library, 1976.

Morton, Louis. *Command Decisions.* Washington: Department of the Army, 1971.

Mosley, Leonard. *Hirohito.* London: Weidenfeld & Nicholson, 1966.

Moss, Norman. *Men Who Play God*. New York: Harper & Row, 1969.

Nakamoto, Hiroko, and Pace, M. M. *My Japan 1930–51*. New York: McGraw-Hill, 1970.

Newcomb, Richard F. *Abandon Ship!* 1958. Reprint. Bloomington: Indiana University Press, 1976.

New York Times. *Hiroshima Plus 20*. New York: Delacorte Press, 1965. (Baldwin, H. W., "Hiroshima Decision"; Lapp, R. E., "The Einstein Letter.")

Osada, A. *Children of the A-Bomb*. New York: G. P. Putnam's Sons, 1963.

Osaka, Ichiro. *Hiroshima, 1945*. Tokyo: Chuko Shinso, 1975.

Ota, Y. *Shikabane no Machi* (Town of Corpses). Tokyo: Kawade Shobo, 1955.

Oughterson, A. W., and Warren, S., eds. *Medical Effects of the Atomic Bomb in Japan*. New York: McGraw-Hill, 1956.

Reilly, Michael F. *I Was Roosevelt's Shadow*. London: W. Foulsham, 1946.

Russell of Liverpool. *The Knights of Bushido*. New York: E. P. Dutton, 1958.

Ryder, Sue. *And the Tomorrow Is Theirs*. Bristol: Burleigh Press, 1975.

Sakai, Saburo. *Samurai*. New York: E. P. Dutton, 1957.

Schoenberger, Walter S. *Decision of Destiny*. Athens: Ohio University Press, 1970.

Shigemitsu, Mamoru. *Japan and Her Destiny*. Translated by Oswald White. New York: E. P. Dutton, 1958.

Smith, Alice Kimball. *A Peril and a Hope*. Chicago: University of Chicago Press, 1965.

Smith, Merriman. *Thank You, Mr. President*. 1946. Reprint. New York: Da Capo Press, 1975.

Stimson, Henry L., and Bundy, McGeorge. *On Active Service in Peace and War*. 1948. Reprint. New York: Octagon Books, 1971.

Storry, Richard. *A History of Modern Japan*. New York: Penguin Books, 1960.

Takayama, Hitoshi, ed. *Hiroshima in Memoriam and Today*. Hiroshima Peace Culture Center, 1973.

Taylor, A. J. P. *The Origins of the Second World War*. New York: Atheneum, 1962.

Teller, Edward, and Brown, Allen. *The Legacy of Hiroshima*. 1962. Reprint. Westport: Greenwood Press, 1975.

Togo, Shigenori. *The Cause of Japan*. Translated and edited by Togo Fumihiko and Ben Bruce Blakeney. New York: Simon and Schuster, 1956.

Toland, John. *The Rising Sun*. New York: Random House, 1970; Bantam Books, 1971.

Truman, Harry S. *Year of Decisions*. New York: Doubleday, 1955.

————. *Mr. Citizen*. New York: Bernard Geis, 1960.

Trumbull, Robert. *Nine Who Survived Hiroshima and Nagasaki*. New York: E. P. Dutton, 1957.

Tully, Grace. *F.D.R., My Boss*. New York: Charles Scribner's Sons, 1949.

Wilson, Jane, ed. *All in Our Time*. Chicago: *Bulletin of the Atomic Scientists*, 1975.

Zacharias, Ellis M. *Secret Missions*. New York: G. P. Putnam's Sons, 1946.

DOCUMENTS/REPORTS

Individual items, too numerous to mention, many recently declassified, may be found at:

American National Red Cross, Washington: Tinian, medical and social.

Atomic Energy Commission, Historical Office, Washington: Oppenheimer, Research and Development, etc.

Historical Office, State Department, Bureau of Public Affairs, Washington: Interim Committee, etc.

Japanese Defense Agency, Historical Section, Tokyo: General and Specific Naval and Army Activities During World War II.

National Archives, Washington: Record Group No. 77: MED Top Secret Files, MED H&B Files, Top Secret Files of Special Interest to General Groves; Record Group No. 165: OPD Project Decimal Files, OPD Olympic; U.S. Strategic Bombing Surveys, etc.

Naval Historical Center, Washington: Tinian NAB, USS *Indianapolis*, Oral Interviews, etc.

Albert F. Simpson Historical Research Center, Maxwell AFB: Record Groups: GP-509-SU, HI, RE (Comp), HI (Comp), OP-5, Oral Interviews.

B-29 Flight Manual (Familiarization File, USAAF).

Dull, Paul S., and Umemura, Michael T. *The Tokyo Trials*. Ann Arbor: University of Michigan Press, 1957.

Franck, James. *Report of the Committee on Social and*

Political Implications. June 1945 ("The Franck Report"; complete text in *A Peril and a Hope*).

History of the 509th Composite Group, 313 Bombardment Wing, Twentieth Air Force—Activation to 15 August, 1945. Official Historian, Tinian, August 31, 1945.

International Military Tribunal for the Far East (National Archives, esp. vols. 60, 61, 64, 65, 74).

Log of the President's Trip to the Berlin Conference, July 6, 1945, to August 7, 1945. Written and compiled by William M. Rigdon, USN, 1946, with a foreword by Lieutenant George M. Elsey, USNR.

Manhattan Engineer District. *The Atomic Bombings of Hiroshima and Nagasaki*. Washington, 1957.

Ossip, Jerome J., ed. 509th Pictorial Album, Tinian, 1945.

Report of the British Mission to Japan. *The Effects of the Atomic Bombs at Hiroshima and Nagasaki*. London: H.M.S.O., 1946.

Short History of the 509th Group. Roswell, 1947.

Smyth, H. D. *A General Account of the Development of the Methods of Using Atomic Energy for Military Purposes under the Auspices of the United States Government, 1940–1945*. Washington: Government Printing Office, 1946.

U.S. Army Air Forces. *Mission Accomplished*. (Interrogation of Japanese Industrial, Military and Civil Leaders of WW II). Washington: Government Printing Office, 1955.

U.S. Strategic Bombing Surveys: Interrogations; The Effects of Strategic Bombing on Japan's War Economy; Japan's Struggle to End the War; The Effects of the Atomic Bombs on Hiroshima and Nagasaki; The Effects of Strategic Bombing on Japanese Morale; Effects of Air Attack on the City of Hiroshima; Effects of the Atomic Bomb on Hiroshima, Japan. All published by Government Printing Office, Washington, 1945–47.

MAGAZINES/PERIODICALS/BOOKLETS

Araki, Takeshi (Foreword). *Hiroshima*. Hiroshima Peace Culture Center, 1975.

Bainbridge, Kenneth T. "Prelude to Trinity." *Bulletin of the Atomic Scientists*, vol. 31. No. 4, April 1975; "A Foul and Awesome Display," vol. 31, No. 5, May 1975.

Batchelor, John, ed. *Battle of the Pacific*. London: Purnell, 1975.

Bishop, John. "The Trick That Was a Steppingstone to Japan." *Saturday Evening Post*, December 23, 1944.

Caron, George R. "Mission Destruction." *Veterans of Foreign Wars Magazine*, November 1959.

Compton, Karl T. "If the Atomic Bomb Had Not Been Used." *Atlantic Monthly*, December 1946.

"Fifteen Years Later—The Men Who Bombed Hiroshima." *Coronet*, vol. 48, No. 4, August 1960.

Frisch, David H. "Scientists and the Decision to Bomb Japan." *Bulletin of the Atomic Scientists*, vol. 26, June 1970.

Groves, Leslie R. "Some Recollections of July 16, 1945." *Bulletin of the Atomic Scientists*, vol. 26, 1970.

Hersey, John. "Hiroshima." *The New Yorker*, August 31, 1946.

Kosakai, Yoshiteru (compiler). *A-Bomb: A City Tells Its Story.* Hiroshima Peace Culture Center, 1972.

Laurence, William L. "The Story of the Atomic Bomb." *The New York Times,* 1946.

Leighton, Alexander H. "That Day at Hiroshima." *Atlantic Monthly*, October 1946.

Lewis, Robert A. "How We Dropped the Bomb." *Popular Science*, vol. 171, No. 2, August 1957.

Penney, William; Samuels, D. E. J.; and Scorgie, G. C. "The Nuclear Yields at Hiroshima and Nagasaki." *Philosophical Transactions of the Royal Society*, vol. 266, No. 1177, June 11, 1970.

"Memories of Hiroshima." *People*, vol. 4, No. 6, August 11, 1975.

Ransom, Jay Ellis. "Wendover, Home of the Atom Bomb." *Code 41*, November 1973.

Schwartz, Robert L. "Atomic Bomb Away." *Yank*, September 7, 1945; "The Week the War Ended." *Life*, July 17, 1950.

Siemes, P. T. "The Atomic Bomb on Hiroshima." *Irish Monthly*, March–April 1946.

Small, Collie. "The Biggest Blast." *Collier's*, August 13, 1949.

Smith, Alice Kimball. "Los Alamos: Focus of an Age." *Bulletin of the Atomic Scientists*, vol. 26, June 1970.

Steiner, Arthur. "Baptism of the Atomic Scientists." *Bulletin of the Atomic Scientists*, vol. 31, No. 2, February 1945.

Stimson, Henry L. "The Decision to Use the Atomic Bomb." *Harper's Magazine*, vol. 194, No. 1161, February 1947.

Tibbets, Paul W. "Ten P.M. August 5—and After." *Survey Graphic*, vol. 35, January 1946; "How to Drop an Atom Bomb." *Saturday Evening Post*, June 8, 1946 (with Wesley

Price); "Training the 509th for Hiroshima." *Air Force Magazine*, August 1973.

"The Unmentioned Victims." *Time*, August 9, 1971.

"Time Out. Prayer or Curse?" (Downey's prayer.) Luther League of America, Philadelphia, vol. 1, No. 4, April 1961.

"Was A-Bomb on Japan a Mistake?" *U.S. News & World Report*, vol. 49, August 15, 1960.

NEWSPAPERS

The following were most useful:

Asahi Shimbun, Chicago Tribune, Chugoku Shimbun, Los Angeles Times, Mainichi Shimbun, The New York Times, San Francisco Chronicle, The Times of London, *Washington Post, Japan Times and Advertiser*, and the July and August 1945 editions of the *Daily Mission*, published by the 313th Bombardment Wing Information Office, Tinian, Marianas.

PRIVATE PAPERS

Tsunesaburo Asada	Masaru Matsuoka
Jacob Beser	Richard Nelson
George Caron	Kakuzo Oya
Shin Endo	Charles Perry
Russell Gackenbach	Abe Spitzer
Leslie Groves	Henry L. Stimson
Kanai Hiroto	Paul Tibbets
Kumao Imoto	Harry S Truman
Robert Lewis	Theodore van Kirk
Kazumasa Maruyama	Tatsuo Yokoyama

TRANSCRIPTS

Official interviews conducted by A. B. Christman, NOTS, China Lake:

Vice Admiral F. L. Ashworth, April 1969.

Dr. A. Francis Birch, February 1971.

Mrs. Robert Burroughs (formerly Mrs. W. S. Parsons), April 1966.

Lieutenant General Leslie R. Groves, May 1967.

Vice Admiral John T. Hayward, May 1966.

Others:

Brigadier General Paul W. Tibbets, December 1960 (Kenneth Leish); September 1966 (Arthur Marmor).

General Nathan F. Twining, November 1965 (Arthur Marmor).

And television documentaries:.

"The Building of the Bomb." BBC-TV, March 1975.

"Hot to Handle." BBC-TV, September 1966.

Eric Sevareid in "Conversation with John J. McCloy." CBS News Special in two parts, July 1975.

"The Day the Sun Blew Up." BBC-TV, October 1976.

Index